Less Legible Meanings

Between Poetry and Philosophy
in the Work of Emerson

Less Legible Meanings

*Between Poetry and Philosophy
in the Work of Emerson*

Pamela Schirmeister

Stanford University Press
Stanford, California
1999

Stanford University Press
Stanford, California
© 1999 by the Board of Trustees of the
Leland Stanford Junior University
Printed in the United States of America
CIP data appear at the end of the book

For Everett Seymour and Sara

Acknowledgments

One of this book's main ideas is that community occurs at an interface we neither will nor choose. When we are most ourselves, we simply offer *ourselves* and take one another up in ways we can neither guarantee nor answer for. We are possibilities for each other, and in this potential exchange lies the essence of responsible community. Writing is a pursuit that at every step implies community in this sense.

What I have been unable to take up in this project will become clear in the following pages, and yet I have also benefited, sometimes in the least expected of ways and from the least expected of places, from the community formed by making this book. I cannot promise that I have taken up the possibilities offered in the ways intended, but as Emerson has it, "The benefit overran the merit the first day and has overran the merit ever since. The merit itself, so-called, I reckon part of the receiving."[1]

For me these benefits have been of many different sorts, and I am grateful for all of them. Jacques Derrida's seminars, across many years, taught me to ask the kinds of questions that ultimately shape the work here. I was particularly fortunate to have the opportunity to team teach with him in the fall of 1997 on the subject of hospitality; perhaps more than any other single factor, his remarks in that class made this book a different and far better one than it could otherwise have been. In a quite different way, Stanley Cavell's work sparked the thoughts that enabled me to start on this book, and his continuing influence will be evident on every page. I can only hope that neither will object to the ways in which they have been taken for what Cavell would call "incentives for thinking."

Many of my colleagues offered untiring intellectual and personal support as I wrote this book. I would like to thank Josephine Hendin, in particular, for providing both the time and the encouragement that writing required, and also Kenneth Silverman, Denis Donoghue, John Maynard, Larry Lockridge, and Una Chaudhuri. Carolyn Dever very generously read parts of the manuscript, as did Edgar Dryden, and I thank them for their thoughtful commentary and patience. I have also been fortunate to know some extraordinary graduate students who helped me to think through the ideas that eventually showed up here. Sheila Boland, Peter Chapin, Elizabeth Duquette, Tony McGowan, Anthony Reynolds, Shaindy Rudoff, and Deanna Turner all deserve thanks for the intellectual community they created and for the privilege they offered of seeing their own work unfold. Robert Gunn provided important bibliographical help. Helen Tartar, as always, has been the best editor anyone could hope for, and Kate Warne was of indispensable help as this book reached its final stages.

Because a large amount of the thinking that gives contour to this book is psychoanalytic in nature, I also owe much of what I have written to colleagues well outside of my field. I have had the benefit and pleasure of working with them at various conferences, in study groups, and on graduate courses. Many of them have also been good friends. I am very thankful to Dr. Leonard Barkin, with whom I have cochaired a faculty colloquium on psychoanalysis and the humanities for a number of years, for many productive conversations and for making it worthwhile to go on trying to create a forum for genuinely interdisciplinary work; to Dr. Harvey Bezahler, for his help with the graduate course we team taught on the subject of reading and transference; to Dr. Charles Goodstein, for giving me the opportunity to try out some of my ideas on his appropriately skeptical analysts-in-training; and to Dr. Adrienne Harris, with whom I team taught a course on identification and transference in literature and psychoanalysis, for all of the comments and ideas that helped me as I revised and expanded a first draft of this work. I am especially grateful for the help of Dr. Patricia Stevens without whom this book would have been neither started nor finished. Her continued kindness and insight got me from one chapter to another and taught me much more than shows up in these pages.

Some debts are harder to discharge than others. As always, my parents have believed in what I do and supported it in many different ways. To Everett Seymour and Sara go special thanks: to Everett, for patiently putting up with the worst of me so that the best of me could come out on these pages; and to Sara, for her remarkable sense of perspective, which has helped me to keep mine. No, Sara, you still cannot practice dancing on the computer keypad, but yes, the next book may well have pictures.

P. S.
Konstanz, Germany
December 1998

Contents

Introduction: The Quarrel Between Poetry and Philosophy *1*

Part One. *American Letters and Cultural Therapeutics*

1. We Scholars *25*
   The Question of Letters 25
   By Way of Jena and Carlyle 34
   Receptivity 41

Part Two. *The Emersonian Subject: Reading and Transference*

2. From Philosophy to Rhetoric *59*
   Letting Go 59
   Reading 68
   Alienated Majesties: Beyond Representation 76

3. Reading Transference   86
    From Repetition to Remembering   86
    From Remembering to Repetition:
    Transference as Performativity   98
    The Subject in the Real: "Whim"   109

Part Three. Transfers of Reading:
Toward an Emersonian Politics

4. Settling Accounts: "Experience"   119
    What Counts? And Who?   119
    The Atopical Place of Community   127
    "Where Do We Find Ourselves?"   141

5. From Exemplarity to Representativeness   147
    The Evasions of Representativeness   147
    Two Exemplary Detours:
    The Example, and the Scarlet Letter   156
    Un-writing the Community   161

6. Measures of Silence   165
    Emerson's "Fate" and the
    Construction of America   165
    The Operations of Ideology   172
    Rhetoric and Responsibility   180
    Notes   191
    Works Cited   212
    Index   219

*The less legible meanings of sound, the little reds
Not often realized, the lighter words
In the heavy drum of speech . . .*

*. . . These are the edgings and inchings of final form,
The swarming activities of the formulae
Of statement, directly and indirectly getting at,*

*Like an evening evoking the spectrum of violet,
A philosopher practicing scales on his piano,
A woman writing a note and tearing it up.*

Wallace Stevens, "An Ordinary Evening in New Haven"

Introduction · · ·

The Quarrel Between Poetry and Philosophy

In 1837, writing on the habits of the Americans, de Tocqueville remarked upon the penchant for general ideas:

> Having contracted the habit of generalizing his ideas in the study which engages him most and interests him most, he transfers the same habit to all his pursuits; and thus it is that the craving to discover general laws in everything, to include a great number of objects under the same formula, and to explain a mass of facts by a single cause becomes an ardent and sometimes undiscerning passion in the human mind.[1]

Following a tendency of his own nation to classify, de Tocqueville formed his opinions on the basis of detailed observation of life as lived in America in the early nineteenth century. But his comments might just as well be taken as a brief definition of Western philosophy, irrespective of time and place. From Plato to Kant, through Nietzsche, Derrida, and Rorty, philosophers have agreed that one aim of the traditional philosophical project is to discover general laws. It is this very aim that has privileged philosophy as the foundational discipline, at least through the nineteenth century. Emerson so places Plato, "the philosopher," at the opening of *Representative Men*, as prefiguration for all the other disciplines and their representatives. From philosophy come science, rhetoric, history, ethics, art, politics, indeed all knowledge. De Tocqueville's remarks about the American habit of generalizing might then suggest that America of 1837 was a nation of philosophers. Yet more accurate is the sentence with which he begins the second volume of his book: "I think that in no country in the civilized world is less attention paid to philosophy than in the United States. . . . The Americans have no philosophical school of their own, and they care but little for all the schools into which Europe is divided, the very names of which are scarcely known to them."[2] One might account for the dearth of interest in European philosophy by way of the cultural nationalism that pervaded America until the Civil War, except that this nationalism in no way hindered the development of literature, religion, or the visual arts, which were often based upon European models. Not only did America fail to produce anything resembling Continental or British philosophy but also, until the 1870s when Charles Sanders Peirce began publishing isolated pieces of what would later be called Pragmatism, America produced no philosophy at all. Or rather it produced nothing philosophers would call philosophy.

Pondering this absence, Stanley Cavell has asked why, when by the mid-nineteenth century Americans had produced literary works as diverse and powerful as *Moby Dick, Walden, Leaves of Grass,* Emerson's essays, and Hawthorne's major romances, the nation had not expressed itself philosophically.[3] America not only had neither an Epsom nor Ascot but also no Descartes, no Hume, no Kant, no Hegel! Perhaps this is simply to say that American literature assumed the task traditionally performed by philosophy. Melville is no Plato. Yet there are ways in which he uses *Moby Dick* to entertain and explore philosophical concerns that, say, Dickens or Walpole do not. The line between poetry and philosophy in American literature becomes even more blurred in the works of Emerson and Thoreau. One cannot call their work fictional in the usual sense of the word, but neither can one speak of an Emersonian or Thoreauvian philosophy in the same way in which one speaks even of Nietzsche's, let alone Kant's.

Thinking on these shadow images of literature and philosophy in nineteenth-century America, one might say that the ancient quarrel between poetry and philosophy, first mentioned in Book X of *The Republic*, had been decisively won in America by the poets, or else that the quarrel never occurred here at all.[4] American poetry was philosophy; its philosophy, poetry. Emerson expresses as much when, speaking of Plato, he writes, "Plato is philosophy, and philosophy Plato," but he goes on to say that Plato achieved this representative status because "A philosopher must be more than a philosopher. Plato is clothed with the powers of the poet, stands upon the highest place of the poet."[5] Emerson's equation of poetry and philosophy is itself representative of American and Romantic attitudes in the mid-nineteenth century. Whitman, for example, in his preface to the 1855 edition of *Leaves of Grass*, echoing Shelley's *Defence of Poetry*, claims that the poets shall replace not only the philosophers but also the priests and politicians. For Plato, the philosopher-kings were to rule the state, and indeed, a significant portion of *The Republic* aims to show why this should be so. By contrast, Whitman claims that for Americans, "their Presidents shall not be their common referee so much as their poets shall," adding that of all brains, the poet's is "the ultimate brain," and that "soon there will be no more priests . . . a superior breed [the poets] shall take their place."[6] Thoreau, too, in the chapter entitled "Reading" in *Walden*, suggests that we seek the counsel of Homer and Aeschylus, rather than of Plato or Aristotle, placing himself at something of a distance from the philosophers. Books II and III of *The Republic* are devoted almost entirely to what poets should be allowed to say (not much), and Book X questions their suitability at all as citizens of the polis. Thoreau, by contrast, finds poetic works "nearest to life itself" and sees poetry as equivalent to "the Scriptures of the nations."[7]

These several examples collapse the ancient distinction between poetry and philosophy in a way that cannot perhaps be taken seriously from our own historical vantage point. As Derrida keeps reminding us, and as we have known anyway since Nietzsche's "Truth and Falsity in an Ultra-Moral Sense," philosophical discourse is no more privileged, which is to say, any less rhetorical, than any other form of discourse.[8] Similarly, the philosophical dimension of "literary" texts is receiving increasing attention from scholars such as Martha Nussbaum, Stanley Cavell, and Nelson Goodman.[9] This blurring of the line traditionally separating poetry and philosophy has perhaps more to do with subtle restructurings within the academy than with any inherent properties of poetry or philosophy. At the same time, however, this blurring has a history that precedes Derrida, Nietzsche, and America itself, and which can perhaps help illuminate what is at stake in the American evasion of the quarrel between poetry and philosophy.

While America presents particular cultural reasons for this evasion, at the same time, as a general tendency, it is by no means a uniquely American enterprise. Rather, it underlies, in a schematic sense, the Renaissance topos of literature designed to delight and instruct, just as it guides Milton when he says in *The Areopagitica* that "our sage and serious poet Spenser," is "a better teacher than Scotus or Aquinas."[10] Not only the poets but sometimes also the philosophers themselves propound these antiphilosophical views. Kierkegaard, for example, remarks, "What the philosophers say about Reality is often as disappointing as a sign you see in a shop window, which reads, 'pressing done here.' If you brought your clothes in to be pressed, you would be fooled; for the sign only is for sale."[11] Kierkegaard's complaint is leveled against the referentiality of the philosopher's language. As a set of signs within a self-enclosed system, such language works perfectly well, but it cannot point beyond itself and especially not to the pressing issues it purports to address. It is telling as well that the example Kierkegaard chooses involves getting the wrinkles out of things.

Philosophical language, of course, pretends to do just that, to present the smooth, unruffled truth, but it can do so only within the folds of language. The hope is that this language will be believed—that is, bought—even though the language refers only to itself and cannot be taken, so to speak, out of the shop except as a sign that marks precisely what it cannot do. Perhaps this is the constitutive inability of any shoptalk, and in this particular instance, it makes of philosophical language a kind of fiction, something that the Jena

Romantics understood very well. Friedrich Schlegel puts this notion most economically: "A philosophy of poetry . . . would hover between the union and division of philosophy and poetry, and it would conclude in their complete union."[12] Phillippe Lacoue-Labarthe and Jean-Luc Nancy have recently shown how complex is the agenda behind the Jena Romantics' attempt to write philosophy as poetry and poetry as philosophy, as well as the vicissitudes of intellectual history that lead to this attempt. They remind us that literature is itself a term with philosophical roots, a concept that arises only in response to Kant's critical enterprise, that is, as a completion of philosophy.[13] This history bears particularly on the thought of Emerson and Thoreau, but it by no means ends with them. Wittgenstein, for example, from within a very different philosophical world, writes, "I think I summed up my attitude when I said: philosophy ought really to be written only as a poetic composition."[14] Whereas Kierkegaard sees philosophy as a kind of unwitting fable, Wittgenstein more directly suggests that philosophy should openly acknowledge its creative status. As his emphasis on writing and composition makes clear, philosophy does not find and describe the truth but creates and composes a world of truths with and in language.

What Kierkegaard and Wittgenstein in particular underscore is that the traditional dividing line between poetry and philosophy hinges on views of discourse and its relation to truth. The difference between poetry and philosophy has always depended on the simple idea that philosophy can and should express itself independently of style and rhetoric and focus instead on what it expresses, as if language were simply an inconvenient vehicle that might be bypassed altogether once the Truth has been reached. For the philosopher, language is a transparent medium aimed at discovering general, universalizable conditions. Its goal is to work ever toward more comprehensive views of such conditions, or, as Richard Rorty has put it, to achieve universality by the transcendence of contingency, including that of language.[15] When, in some fictional future, philosophy has finally converged upon this comprehensive, universal Truth, we will need no further language (and, it should be added, no further philosophy, either). By contrast, poetry invests itself always in the vicissitudes of language and thus works ever against the reduction of the particular to the universal; it has no trouble with language that fails to converge upon some final truth. As Emerson puts it, "Thought seeks to know unity in unity; poetry to show it by variety,"[16] which is to say that poetry at least tells a different kind of truth than philosophy does, and tells it in a different language.[17]

These views concerning language and truth, in fact, determine the quarrel between poetry and philosophy as it occurs in *The Republic*, but even there, it is not simply a matter of the relation between language and truth. As in the Renaissance topos of literature that delights and instructs, language not only presents and represents but it also does so for someone whom it will affect in a particular way. When discussing whether or not the poets should be admitted into the city, Glaucon and Socrates fear two things from them: that the poets lie and, perhaps more importantly, that they will be believed. No one fears an unpersuasive liar. So although the poets as imitators can only present the truth at "three removes," the "spell" of their words may nonetheless capture the minds of the citizens.[18] From a rhetorical perspective, it is not simply that the poets can only offer metaphors of the truth but also that their language is persuasive. As Bentham put it centuries later, "Between poetry and truth there is a natural opposition. [The] business [of the poets] consists in stimulating our passions, and exciting our prejudices."[19] If this is what the philosophers fear, then it is what the poets and rhetoricians dream of. Once, however, the opposition between poetry and philosophy collapses, so too does the distinction between the concept of truth as an independent entity waiting to be discovered and truth as a product of the rhetorical and affective circuit between a reader and writer.

My purpose here is to explore the ways in which this ancient quarrel plays out in the work of Emerson. Although this is very much a book about Emerson, it also takes Emerson as representative in two central senses. In the first place, although the discussion is confined to Emerson, it is implicit throughout my argument that despite local differences, the same questions might well be raised about many of his contemporaries, perhaps most obviously about

Poe and Thoreau. I stick to the Emersonian example because I find the relation between literature and philosophy both at its most complex and in its sharpest focus in his work. Emerson himself called his work—his writing—simply, "letters"; I tend to refer to it broadly as "rhetoric." The quarrel between poetry and philosophy is, finally, nothing other than a quarrel in and about rhetoric. This is not to suggest that this quarrel, as it emerges in Emerson's work, is nothing but words, words, words. To say, for example, that the quarrel between literature and philosophy hinges on language in its persuasive and figurative capacities does not mean that "letters" belong to a wholly theoretical domain, a matter I will return to later. Indeed, it is just because of the centrality of rhetoric to the Emersonian project that this quarrel takes on important implications for a wide range of issues extending well beyond a classical topos, any restricted rhetorics, or the turf wars of academic departments. Ultimately, the tendency of Emersonian letters is pragmatic; it erases the line between poetry and philosophy for the purpose of redrawing the lineaments of character and nation.

To illustrate more specifically both how and why Emerson takes up the relation between literature and philosophy as he does, let us turn to an actual example. The text is Emerson's essay "The Poet," which is preceded by the following epigraph:

>   A moody child and wildly wise
>   Pursued the game with joyful eyes,
>   Which chose, like meteors, their way,
>   And rived the dark with private ray:
>   They overleapt the horizon's edge,
>   Searched with Apollo's privilege;
>   Through man, and woman, and sea, and star,
>   Saw the dance of nature forward far;
>   Through worlds, and races, and terms, and times,
>   Saw musical order, and pairing rhymes.[20]

Probably like most readers, I tend to want to ignore Emerson's epigraph poems, but this one deserves special attention because of the topic of the essay it precedes. Theoretically, it should illustrate the poetics that "The Poet" treats in prose. "The Poet" may be entirely characteristic of Emerson's thought, but before even getting to the essay, the reader is stopped by what for Emerson is an unusual moment: one of the oppositions paired by the moody child-poet is that between man and woman, an opposition which for the most part seems not to occupy Emerson's thoughts at all, except perhaps in the sense of masculine and feminine rhyme schemes. This particular choice of pairs, however, begins to make a different kind of sense in light of the opening paragraph of the essay itself, when Emerson laments the arbitrary way in which we relate what he calls form and soul, or, more conventionally, matter and spirit:

> It is a proof of the shallowness of the doctrine of beauty, as it lies in the minds of our amateurs, that men seem to have lost the perception of the instant dependence of form upon soul. There is no doctrine of forms in our philosophy. We were put into our bodies, as fire is put into a pan, to be carried about; but there is no accurate adjustment between the spirit and the organ, much less is the latter the germination of the former. (447)

The tension between matter and spirit, of course, becomes important later in the essay in terms of poetic meter and argument, and I will look at that distinction in a minute. More immediately interesting about this passage from the opening paragraph is that it generates an implicit pun that relates the opposition between man and woman in the epigraph to that between Spirit, or father, and matter, or, and this would be the pun, *mater*. The reading of this opposition as such a pun seems justified in that the paragraph concludes with the idea that we are "children of fire," as if this thought were the offspring of spirit and matter. But Emerson actually makes this pun more explicitly in the essay "Poetry and Imagination" when he writes, "Poets are standing transporters, whose employment consists in speaking to the Father and to matter," in a passage dealing specifically with the mediating function of the poet.[21] The pun both exemplifies and characterizes such mediation and, more importantly, reminds the reader that poetry is for Emerson most particularly a troping or a turning, here instanced by the troping of man and woman in the epigraph to spirit and matter in the opening paragraph of the essay.

As the essay tropes, or comments upon, the poem, what emerges is not the separation of poetry and a more discursive language but rather an enacted relation between poetry and the essay, which in this case is a kind of philosophy of poetry. It is here that one finds Emerson attempting to write poetry as philosophy, and philosophy as poetry, to turn them into one another by an act of troping or turning. This attempt to collapse the distinction between poetry and philosophy occurs again in the essay when Emerson insists, "It is not meters, but a meter-making argument, that makes a poem."[22] Given Emerson's notoriety as a poor maker of arguments, at least in the philosophical sense, it seems odd that he wants poems to be like arguments at all. Of course part of what Emerson means by *argument* is something like *content*, or as he calls it in the course of the paragraph, *thought*. He may also mean something like fiction or story, say of the sort at the beginning of each book of *Paradise Lost*. But there is still the resonance of argument as contention and as a certain sort of philosophical discourse. By qualifying "argument" as "meter-making" however, Emerson states the relation between poetry and philosophy he has already enacted at the essay's opening. He does so again when discussing an appreciation of symbols still later in the essay, but this time, his method is allusive: "We are like persons who come out of a cave or cellar into the open air. This is the effect on us of tropes, fables, oracles, and all poetic forms" (461). Suddenly, the function reserved for the philosopher in Plato's *Republic* has been delegated to the symbol-making poet, but this does not mean that Emerson is simply stealing the ground out from under the philosophers. Instead, by alluding to a fable that is itself part of the history of philosophy, he seems to be suggesting a common ground for both of them, a new topos they inhabit together despite the usual differences between their forms of discourse.

Emerson perhaps best describes this topos or place in the later essay from *Representative Men* on Plato. Plato may be representative of the philosopher, but he nonetheless prompts Emerson to speak of what he calls "poetic creativeness," which is "not found in staying at home, nor yet in travelling, but in transitions from one to the other, which must therefore be adroitly managed to present as much transitional surface as possible."[23] This surface exists only in its representation, or else beyond representation, in no more than the transition from the epigraph of "The Poet" to its first paragraph. It is a transition that inheres neither in the poem nor the essay as such. Instead it is the product of the tension between traveling: in this case the emergent turnings of the poem and reflexivity, of staying at home or referring to where one is, here figured as the reworking that appears in the opening paragraph. Put another way, transitional surface, or poetic creativeness itself, is a product neither of poetry nor of critical or philosophical reflexivity, but rather of both.

The desire to collapse poetry and philosophy as Emerson does here is not peculiar to this essay; it is central to his whole project. One can infer from this single example, and from the stakes of the quarrel between poetry and philosophy more generally, a number of things about that project. Insofar as Emerson is representative of the way in which America inherits philosophy, his work suggests the American mind of the nineteenth century did not invest itself in the transparency of language attributed to philosophy by traditional philosophers. Indeed, it had little interest in claims for absolute knowledge. If Emerson's rhetoric at the beginning of "The Poet" is any indication, meaning is not a matter of discovering an immutable truth beyond language, but rather the ongoing result of a process of interpretive strategies and exchanges. These strategies should not be taken as incidental, for as the very terms of the quarrel between poetry and philosophy underscore, each form of discourse enables different goals and rests on different assumptions. From a Wittgensteinian perspective, from within a view of language as a tool that fashions something rather than as a medium which describes something, the question is no longer why Americans produced no philosophy. Instead, one is encouraged to explore what the particular forms of discourse used by American writers allowed them to do. What kind of assumptions shaped the fashioning of a particular American philosophical/literary language? Why does American "philosophy" look like an Emersonian essay, rather than, say, a Cartesian meditation or a Kantian critique? What kind of a world did American language make possible, and what conditions produced the need for that language?

"The Poet," even as it raises such questions, begins as well to sketch an answer. In the epigraph, the moody child's eyes search with "Apollo's privilege," which is of course as it should be given the nominal subject of the essay. Perhaps equally significant, however, is Apollo's secondary association with prophecy and with healing, so say with poetry as a prophetic and a healing art. Indeed, the entire essay occupies itself with questions of "repair," reminding us that the "pairing rhymes" of the epigraph may carry a Spenserian undertone of poetry as "re-pair." The essay points to many re-pairings meant to repair various sorts of losses. As Emerson notes in the middle of the essay, "Genius is the activity which repairs the decays of things."[24] Not least of all, in rhyming the twin concerns of poetry and philosophy, the genius of the essay is to prophesy an American mode of letters that will give birth to an increased creativity. This heightened creativity may itself explain why Emerson begins so uncharacteristically with men and women and sets off their pairing against the idea in the opening paragraph that we know no germination. It is as if Emerson were saying that the separation of poetry and philosophy could lead only to sterility.

It is wholly typical of Emerson to begin with a statement of what we lack or have lost, but this emphasis is more than a rhetorical tic learned during his days in the pulpit. Moreover, the creativity that is to be the offspring of the pairing of poetry and philosophy may refer to more than a nationalistic boast about the potential of American letters. One of the first statements that Emerson makes about his poet is this: "He stands among partial men for the complete man, and apprises us not of his wealth, but of the commonwealth" (448). This brief passage is particularly suggestive of both the aims of Emerson's own writing and of the pressures to which it responds. In the first place, the poet represents something that the rest of us lack, or think that we lack, such that the work of joining literature and philosophy becomes to repair this supposed loss: we are but partial, the poet is whole; above all, it is our reading of his words that will mediate that difference. Far then from being "merely" literary, Emerson's ambition for his own writing would seem primarily to be therapeutic. In speaking, however, of the commonwealth, Emerson further suggests that in this therapeutic function, the poet performs a public and perhaps political task as well. Thus what appears to be a private enterprise may also be read as the result of a larger ambition for an entirely new social function for the poet or writer, a function that will bridge the dual realms of culture and politics. Put another way, Emerson's project, at least from "The American Scholar" forward, is neither wholly literary nor political, but rather responds to a dual crisis of self-definition in the individual and in culture for which "letters" will become the privileged place of expression.

In the largest sense, then, the passage between literature and philosophy—what Emerson calls "letters"—subtends the passage between the private and public. More specifically, in the following pages I want to suggest that the quarrel between poetry and philosophy allows readers a vantage point from which to reformulate their understanding of what is usually called Emerson's "radical individualism," and its relation to a public context both ethical and political. In the first section, I examine the particular ways in which Emerson envisions the union of poetry and philosophy and how such writing bears on the emergence of a subjectivity that has very little to do with the individual per se. In other words, this section of the book deals with Emerson's therapeutic efforts as they are directed toward each particular reader of his text. The second section explores the passage from private to public, first by considering how the Emersonian subject may be public in character, and second by asking if the Emersonian subject makes possible a community and a politics. Here, the emphasis is on Emerson's implicit claim that his text is therapeutic precisely insofar as it moves the reader from a private to public realm. This passage does not occur simply, but the hope for such passage could not be clearer in Emerson.

It is the philosophical and cultural history behind what Emerson terms "letters" that I take up in the prefatory chapter on "The American Scholar." As is well known, "The American Scholar" is Emerson's call for cultural independence, and as such, it is considered America's primary document of literary nationalism. Useful in its way, this view has become such a critical truism that it tends to obscure exactly how Emerson elaborates his project for American culture and what it is meant to accomplish. What will make American "letters" unique for Emerson is that they must collapse the distinction between literature and philosophy in order to redress what Emerson perceives as a loss of the thinking subject. Emerson's understanding of this loss and his solution to it are both part of a larger philosophical history: although his terminology differs, Emerson's "letters" clearly address a crisis in subjectivity bequeathed to the Romantics by Kant. As Kant radically severs reflection from self-knowledge, he also undoes the power of philosophical and specifically critical reflection as the central means of self-knowledge. Emerson, however, takes this epistemological problem and reformulates it as one of representation. Philosophy no longer gives us an image of ourselves, a failure that Emerson registers when he chides us in "The American Scholar" for the insufficiency of our thinking insofar as we "think" within a tradition specifically linked to Kant. Emersonian "letters" are meant to address this insufficiency, and they do so as if with the pragmatic intent of curing us from an illness.

In a certain respect whether Emerson inherits his understanding of this turn in philosophy from his own reading in the German Romantics, or from their sources or from their influence on Coleridge, Carlyle, and early American writers such as Reed and Hedge, can hardly matter. Although Kant may provide the immediate philosophical history out of which a certain strain in Emerson's thought grows, that history may be merely analogical in relation to Emerson's concerns. I address it at length because I think it is the most illuminating context for Emerson's project. However, these letters too grow out of and respond to their American context. It is entirely possible, for example, that the impulse to philosophize was subsumed from the beginning in America by a host of religious writings, and here is a prefiguration of the more mature attempts of Emerson to collapse the distinction between literature and philosophy. Theology naturally tends toward the statement of absolutes, but it is equally true that the evangelical intent of much American religious writing pushes it away from last things and toward a persuasive rhetoric designed to influence the individual. This may be all the more so when the theological content of the writing privileges the relation of the individual to the divine as it did in America. In any case, the writings of Emerson as well as those of Thoreau, Hawthorne, Melville, and Stowe, may simply replace a religious rhetoric that had been in place from the start. Such a replacement is not without a cost and will bear within it the history of the losses suffered. The trajectory and effects of secularization have been expertly explored by a number of scholars, and I do not intend to repeat them.[25] It is perhaps sufficient to say that these effects, empowering though they may finally be, nonetheless leave the individual with one less means of understanding and representing him- or herself, be it as an individual or as part of a collectivity. Surely this threatened loss of self-representation lies partially behind Kant's famous observation that he had to abolish knowledge to make room for faith. This loss of faith, as much as any of the particular crises faced by the United States in the first half of the nineteenth century, calls for a cultural project that will repair a fractured identity.

If American letters respond in part to religious and philosophical histories, then they point equally to the unfolding context of democracy, itself a secular and political extension of Calvinist doctrine. Emerson after all does not call his essay simply "The Scholar," and whatever exceptionalist claims he may intend with his title, the American scholar means the scholar or thinker in a democracy. Democracy predisposes one to focus on the individual and his or her constitution of perfection; de Tocqueville devotes a good amount of time to showing how democracy makes the individual the center of all concerns and his view of the consequences is not sanguine. I would suggest that Emerson was well aware of this problem, but that nonetheless the ideology of liberal democracy is what most powerfully steers him away from traditional philosophical discourse and toward a more experientially oriented mode of reading. Each of the subsequent chapters details this assertion in one way or another, but even in a general sense, if the contingencies of rhetoric replace the Truth of philosophy, then it is at least partially because the Truth of philosophy leaves no room for the individual and his or her self-creation. Without that individual's participation in the political system, without each person's thinking through and living in the world that they make, democracy becomes no more than an abstraction. This is precisely where the unconditional absolutes of philosophy become useless, for as they anticipate and foreclose the possibility of further thought, process and change, they also undermine the life of democracy itself.

I am not sure I want to say that traditional philosophy *is* antithetical to democracy; perhaps I only mean to say that construed in certain ways, it can be. Nonetheless, democracy requires an experiential epistemology, and Emerson's cultural project responds directly to this exigency. As philosophy becomes a form of reading, it likewise becomes a particular form of experience. Emerson's focus is epistemological in the sense that he is concerned with how and what we know, but his methods of exploration and verification are experiential, because experience is shown to be the very condition of possibility of knowledge. As Emerson puts it in "History," "Every mind must know the whole lesson for itself,—must go over the whole ground. What it does not see, what it does not live, it will not know."[26] It is for this reason that Emerson, unlike many philosophers, does not seek to present a universal, immutable truth, but rather to lead the reader into a process of change that occurs only within the ongoing vicissitudes of reading and interpretation. The degree of Emerson's belief in these vicissitudes evidences itself in a style and rhetoric that underscore themselves as such. For Emerson, as later for Nietzsche, Heidegger, and Wittgenstein, the fact that the categories of understanding determine what we see and know issues in a rhetoric that mirrors this insight, making of philosophy a form of rhetorical style.

For this reason, Chapters 2 and 3 examine the specific ways in which Emersonian rhetoric works and the nature of the subjectivity it creates.[27] Chapter 2 takes up the way in which Emersonian "letters" complicate themselves at the particular juncture of rhetorical effect and the experience of reading. Experience may be the condition of possibility of knowledge, but it is not a programmatic condition and, therefore, not really a condition at all. It cannot be grasped or fixed in a twelve-category system, for example. Experience as the condition of possibility of knowledge means something more like knowledge without condition or foundation. In terms of the reading experience, the point would no longer be to cut through the words to some bedrock of truth in which one sees and represents oneself as "out there" beyond the vicissitudes of experience, but rather to be in the experience itself. This kind of reading is, in short, always performative and cannot be had apart from this performativity. This suggests that no reader can have another reader's experience, and in a sense, no reader can have even his or her own experience. In this respect, each reader is wholly singular—elsewhere and other even from him- or herself—so that properly speaking, one is no longer dealing with subjects at all, or at least not with subjects construed as individuals in the nineteenth-century sense of the term. As the analysis of the dynamic of "alienated majesty" in Chapter 2 demonstrates, reading may begin as an act of self-creation for the reader, but what emerges is no more than a relation, neither here nor there, and never wholly itself. Emersonian reading operates a passage between self and other, but this passage is with neither origin nor destination. It is what Emerson calls "receptivity," perhaps in distinction to the Kantian idea of thinking as an active conceptualization; such receptivity can neither be thematized nor domesticated in a representation of any kind, except after the fact. In this respect, Emerson moves the Kantian problem of self-reflection onto a new ground by making the problem the solution.

Emersonian reading cannot get distance on itself. It occurs precisely as a kind of auto-enactment of the subject, which both exceeds and precludes representation. For this very reason, it cannot be examined without a detour through another discourse external to it. In Chapter 3, I suggest that the closest analogue for Emersonian reading is something like the psychoanalytic transference, where it is the reader who makes a transference onto the text.[28] It is, in fact, the matter of transference that distinguishes psychoanalysis from traditional philosophy. As Paul Ricoeur has exhaustively and persuasively argued, phenomenology or the philosophy of mind differs from psychoanalysis, philosophically speaking, only in the concept of transference. Jonathan Lear has made a similar argument about the relation between Socratic dialectics and the psychoanalytic process.[29] The transference is also, as Freud consistently maintained, what distinguishes psychoanalysis from any other form of psychotherapy. And, like Emersonian reading itself, what psychoanalysis does that neither philosophy nor any other form of psychotherapy can is to insist upon the experiential dimension of knowledge. In psychoanalysis, this knowledge is achieved only in the transference. The patient, in the transference, must experience his or her primitive affective ties in order to undo them, that is, in order to change.

There is, however, a crucial distinction to be made between Freudian transference and Emersonian reading. Transference is seen by Freud as a stumbling block, a moment in which the subject fails to represent him- or herself and instead blindly repeats without realizing that this is what he or she is doing. For Freud, the task of the analysis is to reappropriate such repetition or enactment in the form of narrative remembering. By contrast, Emerson's rhetoric constantly exceeds the thematizations of narrative and returns the reader to that state Emerson designates as "whim," or to what Lacan might simply call "desire." In this state, the reader experiences a kind of self-presence that resembles transference in that the reader is no longer presenting herself to herself. She simply performs herself, without the distance of reflection or representation. In this respect, our transference to Emerson's text is not a problem to be overcome, but rather an achievement.

Insofar as reading initiates a self-presence that lies beyond representation it may also seem to mark the impossibility of a public or a political self. In the second half of the book, however, I argue that the self articulated in Emersonian reading is always public and always political, and beyond that, that the Emersonian subject takes shape in response to a democratic imperative. Indeed, it is no accident that Emerson designates this self beyond itself with the term "representative," for in a paradoxical way, it is the very absence of an individual subject that makes possible the democratic community. It may seem odd to insist that Emerson's writings not only develop out of but also respond to the exigencies of life in a democracy, for readers persist in believing that, as the quintessential writer of the American Renaissance, Emerson was not concerned with social reality. This because either, as Henry James observed, there was none, or, in the view of most contemporary critics, because Americans were too enmeshed in the ideology of individualism to bother with social constructions in any direct way.[30] But from "The American Scholar" forward, the so-called individualism that emerges in Emerson's work is rather different than we have thought, a difference that in turn bears on the relation between the private individual and a public context. Usually this relation is construed as synecdochic; a part stands for the whole and can do so because all of the parts are homogeneous. By contrast, the Emersonian subject as engendered by its transference or receptivity to the text is entirely singular, incommensurable with every other and with itself. It is this incommensurability that Emerson posits as the basis for a broader sense of community and a reformed politics.

I trace the outlines of such a community and a politics across several of Emerson's later essays, with different emphases. In a chapter on "Experience" I begin with the idea that mourning serves as a basis for community. Since the Emersonian subject always finds itself, and therefore others, as lost, precisely because of a radical and traumatic alterity within itself and others, Emersonian reading articulates a fragmentary self and a fragmentary text that issue in a perpetual mourning, at once personal and cultural. Freud, in the 1915 paper "On Mourning and Melancholia," provides the initiative here. In another context, I would want to read this paper as a metapsychological account not just of a particular psychological dynamic but also of the entire analytic process. In the course of development, the individual internalizes various figures, attitudes, and values that prevent the free use of energy in and for the present. The "cure" of analysis is precisely a cure of these internalizations, a decathexis of the past with a concomitant turn toward the present. In this sense, regardless of a particular symptomatology, the neurotic is always melancholic. The goal of analysis, then, is to teach him to mourn instead and thus open the future. This is the agenda of Emersonian reading, but with a twist: only through such mourning can one achieve genuine relation at all. The question posed at the opening of "Experience," "Where do we find ourselves?" is very much a question about where and how we might find a "we," that is, a community, and since mourning will prove its only ground, the "work" of mourning becomes an ethical demand. The remainder of the essay seeks to teach us to perform that work and so to create the futurity in which a place of community might occur.

In the chapters on *Representative Men* and "Fate," I look at the question as to whether the creation of a community comprised of Emersonian subjects can realize itself in the form of a politics. The discussion of *Representative Men* returns to a problem left hanging at the close of "Experience." Perhaps the most curious aspect of the ethic that emerges in the course of "Experience" is that we can do nothing to bring that ethic about. We are responsible for our community, and this responsibility goes forward all the time, but it is not something that we can will or choose. The best we can do is create the conditions that make responsibility possible in the first place. Acknowledging our distance from ourselves as we must in the act of reading would be the first step, but ultimately, this acknowledgment itself must be marked, written. The term *representative* provides a pivot here, and in the text that most fully deploys that term, one finds an expanded sense of its meaning, particularly insofar as it distinguishes itself from exemplarity in the usual sense. To be representative in the Emersonian sense is to mark one's responsibility. Representativeness would thus be the interface on which one singularity makes itself available for another.

Insofar as representativeness is just that fluid boundary between a private and a public self, it portends a politics, and yet, even as *Representative Men* perpetually underscores the political dimension of representativeness, it does so abstractly. In "Fate," however, Emerson provides a rhetorical demonstration of how such a politics of representativeness might work. In this chapter, I focus on what might be called the operations of Emersonian ideology, an operation that moves well beyond the way in which most contemporary ideological criticism conducts itself. Here the Emersonian subject comes full circle: the very unrepresentability of this subject, its absence from all naming, passes through politics and returns politics to itself. Far from a politics based on the individual, or even on the ideology of individualism, the Emersonian strategy in "Fate" is to show that politics itself must evade representation. In one sense this would be an evasion of philosophy, but more particularly of polemics and consensus, in favor of recognizing the way in which desire itself structures belief irreversibly and beyond all or any justification. For Emerson, I would suggest, it is only in this area beyond representation that a democracy worthy of the name can begin. This would be a democracy rooted in the operations of Emersonian ideology.

In conclusion, let me just say a few words about my own interpretive strategies as they take shape in the following pages. I like what Owen Barfield says in *Saving the Appearances* when he writes,

"There may be times when what is most needed is not so much a new discovery or a new idea as a different slant. I mean a comparatively slight readjustment in our way of looking at the things and ideas on which attention is already fixed."[31] I think of my work here as performing this sort of readjustment. In the first place, scholarly attention is surely already fixed on the relation between American individualism and its sociopolitical consequences. It is hardly a new idea, for example, that Emerson is obsessed with the psychology of the self and its construction, and that this obsession has vexed the American sense of social responsibility. But if it turns out that we have not yet learned how to see the contours of this self clearly, let alone know how to assess its consequences, we cannot properly judge or live the politics it has bequeathed us, or might yet.

The readjustment I am attempting here involves renegotiating the relation between self and world as it takes shape in Emerson's work, and this means also renegotiating the relation between text and world. If the hermeticism of both close reading and of certain forms of theory have left readers frustrated with a stunted relation between literature and life, then it is equally the case that ideological criticism has failed utterly to improve that relation. To the chagrin of many, literary and philosophical texts have not proven amenable instruments of social change in any direct way. We should not expect them to be. As Cavell has rather soberly said while meditating on "Fate," "Philosophy cannot abolish slavery, and it can only call for abolition to the extent, or in the way, that it can call for thinking."[32] For all of that, Emerson's text nonetheless remains committed to a vision of its own efficacy as an agent of change. It cannot tell us how to change, but it can offer itself up as the call to do so. In trying to articulate this call, my own readings necessarily remain provisional. By emphasizing how Emerson's text works actively to enlist our participation in its construction, and so in our own self-constructions, my readings will exemplify the process that they are meant to describe. They cannot be disentangled from the language they engage. Because of this, it will perhaps seem at times I am bringing more pressure to bear on the language of Emerson than it can sustain. But it is just my contention that Emerson is self-consciously manipulating the poetic potential of his language to invite a high degree of rhetorical analysis.

Nonetheless, to some of Emerson's readers, the type of rhetorical analysis I undertake here may seem less a product of his text than of theory. In a certain respect, they would be right, but it is an implicit part of my argument that Emerson is the ambivalent parent of both a deconstructive and a pragmatic child. His work pushes always against the boundaries of representation and discursivity for the purpose of instituting actual and experiential change. These apparently opposed tendencies, however, necessarily work together in a way that takes us back to the quarrel with which I started. If the discursivity of philosophy in some sense discourages thinking, then it is because it has done everything for us. Conversely, the more deconstructive and resistant to thematization a text is, the more it insists on the reader's active participation. In this sense, Emersonian reading is very much about the relation between theory and practice, or about the possibility and consequences of putting theory put into practice.

This relation between theory and practice informs my readings here. They are pragmatic, meant less as readings of Emerson than as explorations of what it might mean to read Emerson in a particular way. In the second section particularly, this book takes Emerson as a kind of contingency, not so much an authorizing foundation as a means with which to envision new ways of thinking and acting. If this is spinning history out of theory, then its possibility is also the single most coherent and pragmatic hope of Emerson's writing.

Part One

American Letters and Cultural Therapeutics

Chapter 1 · · ·

We Scholars

We all read hundreds of books, but the reading does not make us great writers, nor does it very often change our lives. When we have canvased Emerson's vast reading, it will by itself have told us little or nothing about the creative process or the growth of character . . . anyone can amass an impressive amount of reading. But the active filtration and the tight focus of constant intention which convert that reading into real life experience and then into adequate expression, these are the exclusive properties of the great writer.
—Robert Richardson Jr.,
Emerson: The Mind on Fire

A strange process too, this, by which experience is converted into thought, as a mulberry leaf is converted into satin. The manufacture goes forward at all hours.
—Emerson, "The American Scholar"

The Question of Letters

Emerson, remember, was a great reader. Not a bibliomaniac, to use his word, but a great reader nonetheless, and this remained true throughout his life. He was also, nearly from the start, a prodigious writer. In college, he had begun to rise at 3:30 in order to make notations in his journal, a journal that during his lifetime, expanded to many volumes, that he indexed assiduously, and from which every essay he wrote came.[1] Emerson read to write; he came to books as one "comes to," after a faint or an illness.

If we fail to remember this, then none of Emerson's work will make sense, least of all the inaugural piece of his genuine vocation as a cultural therapist. "The American Scholar" is most frequently read as one of the central documents of American literary nationalism, as a call for cultural independence. And so it is. Emerson opens the essay with a lament about "the sluggard intellect of this continent," berates the "bibliomaniacs of all degrees," and proclaims by the end that "we have listened too long to the courtly muses of Europe."[2] All students of American literature know these phrases and understand that on the literal occasion of the commencement at Harvard University, Emerson finds that America has not yet commenced as a culture. We have no American letters.[3] The essay is a clear rallying cry for this beginning, and as such, it epitomizes an already pervasive concern among American intellectuals in the first half of the nineteenth century and of American intellectual history in general. Yet the very exemplarity of the essay—the clarity of its literary nationalism—takes shape from within a common conceptual circle. We derive our sense of American literary nationalism in good part from "The American Scholar," and we then read the essay as an example of literary nationalism, the claims of which seem quite simple to understand. This circle encompasses all topoi and genres, but it has particularly constricted our understanding of Emerson's thought. With few exceptions, we have been unable to read "The American Scholar" as anything but a nationalistic call for original American letters.[4] But the apparent call for originality is in fact the least original of Emerson's points. As Emerson would have known, commencement speakers at Harvard had regularly been warning graduates of the dangers of American dependence on Europe for a quarter of a century before his own memorable address.[5] And perhaps because the claims of literary nationalism have become so familiar a feature in the terrain of American intellectual history, they conceal the more radical claims that Emerson's "literary nationalism" actually maps. In other words, one should not return to this essay under the impression that one already knows what is covered by the term *literary nationalism*, covered in either sense.

The problematic word here and throughout the essay is "literary." It first appears in the opening sentence of the essay:

> I greet you on the re-commencement of our literary year. Our anniversary is one of hope, and perhaps, not enough of labor. We do not meet

for games of strength or skill, for the recitation of histories, tragedies and odes, like the ancient Greeks; for parliaments of love and poesy, like the Troubadours; nor for the advancement of science, like our cotemporaries in the British and European capitals. Thus far, our holiday has been simply a friendly sign of the survival of the love of letters amongst a people too busy to give to letters any more. As such, it is precious as the sign of an indestructible instinct. Perhaps the time is already come, when it ought to be, and will be, something else.[6]

What follows are Emerson's pronouncements about the end of America's long dependence on Europe, as if in the sudden call for American letters, everything might occur like the ultimately simple and natural discovery of a new literature. And yet, the opening sentence above suggests that this is not a new beginning, but rather a recommencement, not an originary event, but its anniversary. What recommences here is the literary itself, presumably after the summer holidays of those students amongst whom a love of letters still survives, but also, after a pause within a larger history. I do not know what a "literary year" is, but let us suppose that Emerson opens with this obscure phrase to signify a history that itself has become obscure. In the beginning was an "indestructible instinct," hence a timeless instinct, equated in the last sentence with "a love of letters," expressed by Greek and Troubadour alike, but lost to and in the present. These students live "amongst a people too busy to give to letters any more." I read this not simply as "any longer" but also as "anything further," as if Emerson were suggesting that the literary as a category needed to be continued rather than to start all over. In fact, as an indestructible instinct, a love of letters can only recommence. Emerson is speaking not of beginnings but of transformations.

The role of the American scholar in this transformation has thus far been twofold. In the first place, he has yet to make the right start. The anniversary of his literary year is one of "not enough labor," where labor is conceived both as work and that to which it might give birth. But this failure is also a forbearance, a refusal to do as Greek, Troubadour, or European have done. In the first two instances, the difference seems to reside within the literary itself, but in a particular way. The American scholar has foreborn to do as his forbears, that is, to recite what has already been written or to compete in games or in parliaments, differences that will become important within the theory of reading that Emerson develops later in the essay. For the moment, though, there is another difference at hand, the difference between those students amongst whom a love of letters still survives and their European "cotemporaries." When Emerson says that he and his fellows do not meet for the advancement of science, readers are not, I think, meant to understand the natural sciences in the strict sense, but rather philosophy as well. It would have been less than sixty years since Kant had published his *Prologomena to Any Future Metaphysics Which is to Rank as a Science*, and Emerson would surely have been aware of the struggle within philosophy to establish a method by which the validity of its statements could be tested. Indeed, as Richard Rorty has suggested, the distinction between philosophy and science is a post-Kantian notion that did not achieve currency until well into the nineteenth century.[7] That Emerson intends philosophy here seems especially plausible in light of a later passage in which he refers to "data for marking the genius of the Classic, of the Romantic, and now of the Reflective or Philosophical age."[8] If the Greeks represent the classical age, the Troubadours the Romantic age, then the present moment represents the philosophical, but the philosophical as yet untried. Having listed the three ages, Emerson adds, "I look upon the discontent of the literary class, as a mere announcement of the fact, that they find themselves not in the state of mind of their fathers, and regret the coming state as untried" (68). In this sense, Emerson again suggests something yet to come for the scholar, something fearsome because it is unknown. At the same time, what makes this unknown possible at all is that the American scholar's holiday has been a refusal of both the literary as embodied in a past age and also of the present, of a certain turn not in literature itself but within thinking which has made of it a science and of letters in turn something insufficient. In this respect, the holiday or forbearance of the American scholar is itself the sign of a love of letters, a refusal to do them the violence elsewhere done to them. It is this dual difference within the history of the literary, this holiday from its former and present modes of expression, that marks the promise of continuing, of adding something further.

None of this, of course, explains what Emerson means by the term *literary*, nor why letters are to be the site of the transformation of American thinking, but perhaps this very uncertainty lodges at the center of his call. Whatever letters have been, their future resides in chance, in the "perhaps" that initiates Emerson's call for transformation. This future may or may not occur, and its form cannot be predicted. Without this chance, without the unknown, there would in fact be no future at all. In this sense, we can say that the very content of letters as Emerson envisions them to come will be open-ended, provisional. This provisionality itself may help to explain why, if the American scholar is to play a further role in the transformations about which Emerson speaks, the final sentence of the passage quoted above leaves the nature of such transformation, and even of what requires transformation in the first place, less than clear.

Nonetheless, as Emerson opens letters to the future, he does so in a specific way. The scholar's holiday is a sign of a love of letters, and therefore of an indestructible instinct, but "*perhaps* the time is already come, when it ought to be, and will be, something else; when the sluggard intellect of this continent will look from under its iron lids, and fill the postponed expectation of the world with something better than the exertions of mechanical skill" (53; emphasis added). In one sense, Emerson is simply suggesting that the holiday should become something else, that it is time to do the work of giving to letters. Syntactically, the implication is that one must do this by transforming one's instinct, but the remainder of the sentence contradicts such a reading, as does the idea that the instinct is indestructible.[9] The implication instead is perhaps that the fragmentariness of the sign, its incomplete character, must somehow complete itself. To give something more to letters would be to move beyond our friendly sign, to a complete investment in letters. And, as the passage indicates, this would entail a new mode of thinking, a transformation of intellect, specifically away from the mechanical, which would mean, paradoxically, a transformation of thinking into the spontaneous or instinctual. Indeed, as Emerson writes at the close of the essay, the fulfillment of the scholar will come when he sees that "if the single man plant himself indomitably on his instincts and there abide, the huge world will come round to him."[10] I want to return to the tension between the spontaneous and the mechanical shortly, but first it should be clear that Emerson is calling at once for the transformation of letters and for the transformation of the scholar, which is as it must be. As the remainder of the essay demonstrates, the two tasks cannot be distinguished.

Since the scholar requires transformation, it is wholly fitting that Emerson casts his own task in the essay as the characterization of the ideal scholar. Having announced the coming change, he begins his argument, "In this hope, I accept the topic which not only usage, but the nature of our association, seem to prescribe to this day,—the AMERICAN SCHOLAR. Year by year, we come up hither to read one more chapter of his biography. Let us inquire what light new days and events have thrown on his character, and his hopes" (53). A topic, of course, is a subject, but here in a double sense. To accept the topic prescribed is not simply to agree to speak on a particular subject, but also to inhabit a place, to take a place as a subject, as if Emerson were assuming for himself in what he is about to do the place of the American scholar. His address, the nature of his particular association with this audience, will exemplify the new chapter of the biography or characterization of the scholar. By insisting that this characterization occurs in relation to his audience, Emerson suggests that his address will be not so much a mere description of a third party or thing as a kind of dramatization or enactment of the scholar's office for the purpose of each individual in his audience. Further, this relation itself characterizes the scholar.

Let me be a little more and also a little less precise about Emerson's relation to his audience here. The fact that Emerson casts his address as a biography or characterization already suggests that his interest is less in a cultural declaration of independence and more in the individual scholar, whomever this might turn out to be.[11] Indeed, "whomever" is just at issue here. According to a vertiginous shift in the pronouns "I," "him," "we," and "you," throughout the essay, the scholar does and does not exist. Emerson sometimes says "I," and sometimes "we." The speaker of this address to "you" is sometimes just "I" and sometimes "we," that is, among the company to whom he addresses himself. Emerson himself, an "I," nonetheless takes responsibility for these scholars, accepts a topic, but insofar as this "I" is one of "us," his responsibility is both an address and a response to that address. An "I" feels responsible to these scholars who are coming and, therefore, responsible before "we" who announce them, "we" who are already what we are announcing, and before "you," the ones whom I am addressing and whom I call to join "us." Perhaps all of this simply amounts to saying that it is as if Emerson, as one of them, addresses them to ask when they will arrive, they and we, who are already here. His address, in short, originates in the very future it projects, or rather, creates its own addressees even as it presupposes the coming of those addressees, if they can hear.[12] One might well question the need to perform such confusion, but surely this is the point itself. These shifting pronouns allow Emerson to move from stating that the American scholar does not yet exist to reading his "biography." In other words, it is this play of pronouns, a play which quite literally creates the possibility of the scholar who at once is and is not yet, that reveals the very nature of the scholar. He is not there before he performs or enacts himself rhetorically. This, not so much because, as the first paragraph of the essay has stated, the scholar has yet to come, but rather because this scholar of the future comes into being by placing himself in the uncertainty of an unknown relation. Call him, then, a scholar of the unknown, a scholar who may arrive and who also has already arrived at the end of the paragraph, which only promises him, providing of course that his "association" allows him to hear this promise. The appeal to the scholar, then, presupposes both his coming and his persistent absence. In this way, Emerson's address begins on a wholly self-authorized ground, one with neither preconditions nor foreseeable ends. The claim at the opening of the essay is thus twofold. In the first place the character of the scholar as genre will be to contain its own conditions of possibility, or, in other words, to be self-positing without preconditions. Emerson's essay itself will have to show its ground; this is the nature of Emerson's exemplification. But since that exemplification itself characterizes the scholar, this same gesture will be a defining characteristic of the scholar himself. He, too, must show his ground.

This taking up of topics, this way of inhabiting them, is one of

Stanley Cavell's main ideas in his essay, "Aversive Thinking: Emersonian Representations in Heidegger and Nietzsche." According to Cavell, Emerson makes the claim in this essay:

> Namely to be providing this incentive of thinking, laying the conditions for thinking, becomings its "source," calling for it, attracting it to its partiality, by what he calls living his thoughts, which is pertinent to us so far as his writing is this life. . . . How can "The American Scholar" represent the incentive of thinking—constitute a sign of its event—without at the same time presenting thinking, showing it? . . . This life must illustrate thinking.[13]

Beginning with the idea that Emerson is placing himself in a particular relation to his audience, Cavell suggests, as he has with a number of Emerson's essays, that part of Emerson's task will be precisely to include in his essay its conditions of possibility, as if to be self-posited and undetermined by anything external to it. For Cavell, a large part of the way in which Emerson goes about this task is to focus on the particular way in which he transfigures everyday words, brings them home, and makes them, and us, intelligible again. This would be the first step for any reader who wished to take Emerson seriously, that is, to show that Emerson means every word he says, that his words are self-authorizing, despite the enormity and outrageousness of certain of his claims. Thoreau was such a reader, and there have been many others, most notably American poets and novelists but also Nietzsche and, more recently, Eduardo Cadava and Cavell himself. This heritage is a tribute to Emerson's generativity, an illustration of the very point Cavell wishes to make about how Emerson provides the incentive for thinking. Such an incentive will happen differently for each reader, necessarily beginning with each word. Indeed those words, as incentives, ask for completion, or rather every individual interpretation. For Cavell, such interpretation hinges on the connection between Emerson and ordinary language philosophy. In fact, it is Cavell who speaks of the transformative potential within Emerson's writing, to reveal Emerson's desire to provide incentive to thinking, and who has done more than anyone else to transform our sense of Emerson, making him into a kind of familiar genius. At the same time, we may have much to gain from making Emerson strange again. There are some very specific rhetorical practices—call them incentives—within "The American Scholar" that illuminate how Emerson imagines thinking to occur, and if these practices bring our words home, they bring them to us from some distance.

In the first place, Emerson himself, in keeping with the emphases of the opening paragraph, does not begin *ex nihilo*, but rather by going further, by adding more because of having first been receptive to other thinkers in particular ways.[14] Just as he speaks for and to his audience because of "the nature of our association," he speaks *from* association as well. Far from the demonstration of some impossible originality, his strategy throughout the essay consists in a receptivity to various influences, a receptivity which, in turn, is to serve as the exemplary model in the formation of the American scholar. Such a scholar will not be the high-Romantic figure he has often been made out to be, but rather a kind of proto-pragmatist. The scholar's virtue will turn out to be not, as has usually been supposed, originality or even intellectuality, but rather an ability to be receptive to and therefore to use what he encounters. Indeed, why else does Emerson devote half of the essay to what influences the scholar if not to suggest that the scholar must be receptive to the thoughts of others. If the state of receptivity is central to the being of the scholar, then in the case of Emerson's own writing, the particular texts and ideas to which he is receptive are equally central.

Emerson is the exemplar; that is, his own strategy defines and exemplifies the role of the American scholar. As it happens, too, the very notion of receptivity is itself part of Emerson's reception. It is not my intention in what follows to provide a source study—it hardly matters if Emerson is responding directly to a particular tradition, to its aftermath, or, as David Van Leer has said, to some idea "intuited from the mind of God."[15] The point is rather to position Emerson within a particular European tradition, because it is, in fact, only in relation to such a tradition that his project for American letters can be understood and that the full originality of his hopes for letters becomes clear. Literary nationalism? Perhaps, but not necessarily as we thought we knew it.

By Way of Jena and Carlyle

The relation of receptivity informs the structure of the essay as a kind of ideal character-sketch of the American scholar. This interest in the genre of the character pervades Emerson's work, from the early biographical sketches he had written two years before "The American Scholar," through an essay entitled "Character" and also in *Representative Men.* The purpose of these works is not to define what already exists but to provide an incentive to become what John Hollander calls "the central figure in the book of one's life."[16] In the case of "The American Scholar," the most important determinant is perhaps Thomas Carlyle, specifically in an 1831 essay entitled "Characteristics," in which Carlyle undertakes to characterize the fully realized potential of humanity as thinking, a move that allies characterization with German *Bildung.* Beginning with the physician's aphorism "the healthy know not of their health, but only the sick," Carlyle distinguishes health as whatever functions "unconsciously, unheeded," whereas sickness consists precisely in a kind of labored, mechanical functioning that everywhere takes cognizance of its functioning.[17] Health thus implies a unity, a lack of the division that characterizes self-consciousness; it is instead a kind of self-evidency. This distinction, which is really nothing other than that between organicism and mechanism, in turn comes to characterize the difference between the true poet and the philosopher of a certain stripe. After a vituperative diatribe against logic and argumentation, Carlyle concludes, "The poet or priest or by whatever title the inspired thinker may be named, is the sign of vigour and well-being; so likewise is the logician or uninspired thinker the sign of disease" (16). The inspired thinker is thus he who unconsciously and spontaneously creates. The philosopher is at best mechanical and merely "manufactures," to use Carlyle's word, with his conscious mind as if it were a tool that could explain itself and everything else. The former is "vital" and "dynamical," the latter, "dormant" and "extinct" when it comes to interior formative force. This is why Carlyle insists that were the inspired thinker to prevail, "in a perfect state . . . except as poetry and religion, philosophy would have no being" (25). Thinking must become *poesis* or making, in short, vital.

As Carlyle insists, these two kinds of thinkers, as well as the differences that characterize them, are "quite separable," but the relation between them is nonetheless synecdochal:

> Of our Thinking, we might say, it is but the mere upper surface that we shape into articulate Thoughts;—underneath the region of argument and conscious discourse, lies the region of meditation; here, in its quiet mysterious depths, dwells what vital force is in us; here, if aught is to be created, and not merely manufactured and communicated, must the work go on. Manufacture is intelligible, but trivial; Creation is great, and cannot be understood. (3)

Among other things, this passage implicitly presents a theory of the spatial and temporal fragment that bears on Emerson's own insistence on signs and fragments at the opening of "The American Scholar." According to its logic, the unity and wholeness of unconsciousness is nonetheless always and only fragmentary. As Carlyle emphasizes, the true genius never knows itself, and this is as it must be, for if genius is precisely a healthy unity and wholeness, then there is no vantage point from which to seize it as such. Since it lies beneath the surface of conscious discourse and cannot be discursively understood or grasped, one can only know it through partial signs. What Carlyle calls "manufacture" is one such sign; it is the surface, as he explains it, of that lower region. But it is a ruined or sick version of that of which it is the sign, much like the attenuated sign of a once-robust love of letters. Another sign is the work of genius itself, and it is for this reason that Carlyle insists throughout the essay that the inspired thinker serves as a sign of what can be. Because of the fragmentary nature of the perfection to which he points, Carlyle stresses that it "has faded away into an ideal poetic dream," as if the present were but a ruin or fragment of the past (3). And yet, Carlyle himself acknowledges that this poetic dream represents "an ideal, impossible state of being; yet ever the goal towards which our actual state of being strives" (8). In this sense, and because this ideality can by nature be known only through fragments or signs of itself, "Characteristics" remains a sketch or blueprint for the future.

Carlyle is typically cranky in this essay, and yet this work represents more than a dispeptic attack. Indeed, Carlyle's essay is a response to a crisis in philosophy that is at the heart of Romanticism itself. Carlyle indicates near the close of the essay that Friedrich Schlegel is an inspired thinker, and indeed, Schlegel lurks throughout the essay. Carlyle would have learned from Schlegel the necessity of characterizing the philosopher and, more to the point, the reasons behind that necessity.[18] Above all, Carlyle's idea about the unification of poetry and philosophy comes specifically, or at least originally, out of a small body of writings produced at the turn of the century by the Jena Romantics, that is, primarily by Schelling, the Schlegels, and Novalis, who in turn associate with other figures such as Tieck, Schliermacher, and Fichte. It is here, at Jena, that literature and philosophy will, for the first time, definitively become one. This, in any case, is the theory developed by Lacoue-Labarthe and Nancy in *The Literary Absolute*, a study that undertakes at once to demonstrate the precise ways in which such unification will proceed and the motivating reasons for which it must do so. If Carlyle traces the symptoms of humankind's illness, then Lacoue-Labarthe and Nancy show how humans fell ill in the first place. It is an etiology that bears strongly on "The American Scholar."

The Literary Absolute takes as its starting point the idea that the concept of literature itself arises as a response to a crisis inaugurated by Kant's critical philosophy.[19] Lacoue-Labarthe and Nancy's presentation of this crisis is brief, so I am going to take the liberty of restating and elaborating upon the Kantian problem to which they point. Examining this crisis in some detail makes apparent why literature and philosophy must become one and how the specific solutions—those, for example, envisioned by Carlyle—bear on the problem at all. As is well known, the Kantian cogito is empty, no more than a logical necessity unifying the manifold of perception. The corollary of the Transcendental Deduction is that I may perceive myself as an object, *and* under the unity of pure apperception, such that an empirical self and the self in itself—as self-consciousness—must be distinguished. The empirical self is knowable and known like any other object of perception, subject to the Ideas of space and time. But the self of pure apperception, the cogito that must accompany all presentations, cannot possibly be known because it is located outside of the Ideas. Consequently, as Kant puts it, "I am conscious not of how I appear to myself, or of how I am in myself but only *that* I am."[20] This conclusion effectively erases the subject known to itself as itself, and with it, for example, the sufficiency of the auto-foundational Cartesian cogito. Even if I do think, thought can provide no knowledge about that being who thinks, about myself. This is simply to say that Kant effectively deprives the subject of any substantive being, of the possibility of presenting itself to itself in an empirically knowable form. The question thus becomes how subjectivity might achieve an adequate, which is here to say, sensible presentation (*Darstellung*) of itself.

One way in which Kant himself and many who came after him approached this loss of the subject was by a complementary strengthening of the moral subject. Such a subject is posited as freedom, with freedom construed as our autonomy to give laws to ourselves, but neither the moral subject nor moral freedom transcend negative definition. Like the immortality of the soul and the existence of God, the idea of moral freedom can, without contradiction, be thought but not known. It is a problematic solution at best, but as Kant famously put it: "I had to abolish knowledge in order to make room for faith."[21] On the basis of this faith, we can give ourselves the law, but because the universality of the law is neither an intuition nor a concept in the Kantian sense, we cannot know our moral freedom and its working; as Kant himself insists, nothing in his argument alters the fact that moral freedom is an Idea of Pure Reason and is, therefore, unknowable.[22] One's moral freedom and capacities to know are thus split between the noumenal and the phenomenal. The moral subject is not the subject of knowledge and in no way escapes the difficulties of the subject as determined in the first Critique.

It is only in the third Critique that the loss of the thinking subject achieves some restitution, and yet, the schematism with which Kant does so is, significantly, only an approximation. Many of the crucial aspects of Judgment have already been anticipated in the Transcendental Aesthetic, and the Transcendental Aesthetic as it appears in the first Critique does at times appear to restore some substance to the subject in the form of the Transcendental imagination, as that which gives unity to objects that may be grasped within the limits of a priori intuition. But such a cognition cannot be thought as a true form of reason, and so recuperates only something like a subject of the cognition of appearances. In the dialectic of the Aesthetical Judgment, however, Kant considers the problem of indirect judgment, which might be called a kind of argument by analogy, characterized "by the transference of reflection upon an object of intuition to a quite different concept to which perhaps an intuition can never directly correspond."[23] By the object of intuition, Kant means the work of art, and by that to which no intuition corresponds, the realm of the supersensible, including the Idea of freedom. In this sense, it is in judging the work of art, specifically the beautiful, that one achieves a representation of his or her own moral freedom; put simply, the beautiful is formally symbolic of the moral. In an act of analogy, the free play of imagination, the ability of genius to give the law to itself as represented in the work of art, becomes a sensible sign of a corresponding faculty in our own natures, a faculty bound up with representing ourselves to ourselves in an act of total freedom. Aesthetic Judgment thus becomes the mode of thinking capable of synthesizing the phenomenal and the noumenal, although only in an analogical and hence for Kant a regulative sense. Indeed, as Kant himself remarks, "This matter has not been sufficiently analyzed hitherto, for it deserves a deeper investigation; but this is not the place to linger over it."[24]

What Kant declined to linger over became the philosophical inheritance of the nineteenth century and, at the same time, marked out the path for the Romantic project that sought to collapse literature and philosophy. As Lacoue-Labarthe and Nancy demonstrate again and again, speculative idealism and the concept of Romantic literature are but two sides of the same coin:

> If the *Darstellung* of the infinite after and despite Kant, constitutes the essential preoccupation of idealism, then Romanticism . . . forms the exergue of philosophical idealism. . . . Purely theoretical completion is impossible . . . because the theoretical infinite remains asymptotic. The actual infinite is the infinity of the work of art.[25]

What Lacoue-Labarthe and Nancy suggest here is that the impetus behind speculative idealism from Fichte through Hegel is the perceived loss of the subject able to present itself to itself in sensible form, a problem wholly determined by Kant's critical philosophy. Henceforth, idealism will work to restore that subject by demonstrating that the auto-production of the subject through its own activity will constitute the closure of the speculative absolute. As Hegel will explain it in the Introduction to *The Phenomenology of Mind*, consciousness no longer aims to find itself immediately, but rather to produce itself by its own activity.[26] It is itself the end at which its action aims, whereas in the role of observer it was concerned only with things, including itself as thing. Romanticism, too, will reconceive the subject as its own auto-production, but, following Kant in the *Critique of Judgment*, it will be auto-production specifically in and through the work of art, in and through a sensible presentation that is but a sign of an interior formative power so that such auto-production can, of necessity, never achieve closure of any kind.

Lacoue-Labarthe and Nancy sketch four ways in which the Jena Romantics attempt this presentation, which, in turn, implies the completion of philosophy, of the aporia opened by Kant, in and as literature.[27] This is not the place to recapitulate their argument, if only because the particular example of Jena bears on Emerson only in the most general way, in terms of the impetus behind it and the larger conclusions it reaches. Emerson takes up these origins and ends, but his path between them diverges from Jena. It is sufficient to say here that all the types of literary production to which Lacoue-Labarthe and Nancy point, from the fragment and character sketch to the very notion of critical perfection in which criticism aims to reproduce the engenderment of the work itself, follow a similar trajectory. In every instance, it is a matter of the subject, here the poet-philosopher or artist-critic, producing itself in the work, which must consequently embody the operative and therefore potential nature of that subject, as witnessed, for example, in Emerson's rhetoric in the opening paragraphs of "The American Scholar." In the simplest sense, this means that the subject is conceived no longer as a complete or static entity, but rather as force, production, and process, all in the sense of the subject creating itself through its activity, which by definition must now be fragmentary.

Jena, in short, represents a version and even the culmination of the German concept of *Bildung*, or self-formation, with which Emerson, and Carlyle with him, would already have been familiar through Goethe. The frequent and typical injunctions throughout "Characteristics" for work, work, and more work suggest that Carlyle himself is "working" not simply with Romantic clichés but with this central informing principle of Romanticism itself. The fully realized human subject is not a preexistent mind that grasps opposed matter, but rather the work-subject of the Jena group, the subject as auto-production. The subject as its own work or self-creation can never be grasped or represented by the mechanical exertions of the mere thinker. Indeed, if Carlyle dismisses what Emerson will later call "mere thinkers" as "sick," then it is because they seek to grasp what cannot be grasped. Carlyle writes, "Could you ever spell-bind man into a scholar merely, so that he had nothing to discover, to correct; could you ever establish a Theory of the Universe that were entire, unimprovable, and which needed only to be got by heart; man then were spiritually defunct, the Species we now name Man had ceased to exist."[28] The implication here is that system building and conceptualization are not only inadequate to the world but also to the nature of the human itself. One is as the other, or as Emerson will have it, one is seal, the other print. Both are, according to Carlyle's lights, fragmentary and incomplete in an essential way, because their informing principle is their own auto-production. No system can ever grasp this vital, operative force because its very nature is to be perpetual and unbounded, present only in and as activity. It cannot be circumscribed by reflection, but only by the perpetual enactment of itself, which resembles the way in which Emersonian "circles" constantly overcome and outcircle themselves.

To achieve its full impact, "Characteristics" should be read against another of Carlyle's essays from the same period, "Signs of the Times," which Emerson read. This work amounts to an articulate and cogent statement of the entire theory of the German *Bildung*, or the self-cultivation that leads finally to culture in the widest of senses. The importance of this essay to Emerson can be measured by the force of a single sentence in "The American Scholar," a sentence offered as a characterization of the scholar's highest office. He speaks of a "revolution . . . to be wrought by the domestication of the idea of Culture. The main enterprise of the world for splendor, for extent, is the upbuilding of a man."[29] To domesticate the idea of Culture would be to bring it home, first perhaps to America, but more literally to the individual who will care for or tend to him- or herself. Similarly, upbuilding, particularly in the context of this essay, should remind us of the etymology of "education," such that the task proper to the scholar, which is to say of the human, becomes his own upbuilding or self-creation. This suggests that Emerson shares with Carlyle the idea that we are ourselves a work, an operative principle that brings itself into being by enacting itself, specifically in the sense of auto-producing a self, although we would still of course need to specify the particular ways in which Emerson envisions this *Bildung* happening. If this is difficult to do, then it is because, as Lacoue-Labarthe and Nancy point out, Romanticism as it develops in and from Jena provides no position from which one might command an overview of the whole, no fixed point from which a system might be set into place.[30] This may be simply to say that the subject of the *Bildung* can only enact itself without grasping itself from an external or originary point. Indeed, it is because philosophy as such can do nothing to initiate, hasten, or maintain this auto-production that Carlyle denounces philosophical thinking as "sick," and also the reason for which he insists on the unification of poetry and philosophy, or the completion of philosophy in and as literature.

Receptivity

If, despite the overt emphasis on *Bildung*, all of this sounds well beyond Emerson and in a key quite different from his own, then it is, at the same time, the very nature of the Kantian crisis that necessitates this difference. Emerson did not simply get his Kant, Schelling, and Fichte through Carlyle and Coleridge.[31] Here Lacoue-Labarthe and Nancy are particularly useful in understanding the vexed relation between Emerson and a certain kind of philosophy. Precisely because theoretical completion is impossible, the subject must now seek its completion, that is, its adequate presentation, outside of the theoretical domain and instead in the work of art itself. From this perspective, it is easier to understand why, on the one hand, Emerson's writing throughout bears the stamp of theoretical idealism, including its roots in Kantian thought, without, however, in the least its will to systematization or discursivity and, to some minds, its rigor. We might read this as Emerson's failure as a metaphysician; however, it may equally evidence his understanding that the self-realization of the human—of the scholar—lay not in philosophy as such but in poetry, or, more precisely, in the unification of poetry and philosophy called for by both Carlyle and Schlegel. Such a unification would, to a philosophical eye, look aggressively antitheoretical, but this very refusal of the theoretical would itself demonstrate and be replaced by the auto-production of the subject.[32] In terms of the medium through which the subject produces itself, one can say that every work would require a putting into practice the production of its own theory in a way that is not theoretical. This production, in both its senses, would be exactly the *Darstellung*, or presentation, sought by both the Idealists and the German Romantics, and a presentation to which no discursive representation can be adequate.

That Emerson is responding to the crisis that sparked the thought of Schlegel and Carlyle alike is clear from the beginning of his commencement essay. It should be no surprise that the biography of the scholar, of Man Thinking, begins not with a philosophical proposition at all, but with a myth about our origin as laborers, a myth that presents at once our illness and its cure. In the beginning, it seems, the gods "divided Man into men, that he might be more helpful to himself; just as the hand was divided into fingers, the better to answer its end. The old fable covers a doctrine ever new and sublime; that there is One Man,—present to all particular men only partially, or through one faculty."[33] This passage elaborates two concerns with which Emerson opens the essay. In the first place, it continues the emphasis on fragmentation introduced in the first paragraph of the essay and takes it a step further. Like the sign of the love of letters in the first paragraph, the image points both to origins and ends. Clearly the fable of the One Man is intended as an image of complete and fulfilled potential. It is a promise of what it would mean to be fully human, but here located as if in a lost past. The old fable anticipates the new, provides an image of what we might yet become. Each of us, as a fragment of the One Man, stands not only for ourselves but also for that from which we are detached. To achieve our end, or what we were originally made to do, we must do what we do as representatives of the One Man, that is, as approximations. By likening this telos to the hand divided into fingers, Emerson suggests, following Carlyle and the Jena Romantics, that the definition of the truly human is the human as production and as making. Taken together, then, the opening paragraphs of the essay posit for the human a proper end or telos as work and production, with the proviso that no work, including that of the subject as a work, is in itself ever complete.

Just as fragmentation is for both Carlyle and speculative idealism the disease *and* the cure, here, too, the scholar fails to achieve himself as an ideal fragment or approximation of the One Man because another kind of fragmentation has taken its place:

> Unfortunately this original unit, this fountain of power, has been so distributed to multitudes, has been so minutely subdivided and peddled out, that it is spilled into drops, and cannot be gathered. The state of society is one in which the members have suffered amputation from the trunk, and strut about so many walking monsters,—a good finger, a neck, a stomach, an elbow, but never a man.
>
> Man is thus metamorphosed into a thing. (54)

Walking monsters, amputated parts, a thing—these designations all but say that we are no longer properly human, a point raised in the opening paragraph when Emerson laments our capacity for no more than "exertions of mechanical skill" (53). Like Carlyle, Emerson distinguishes between an apparently natural, whole, and healthy functioning and a mechanical, divided, and sick functioning. Insofar as we are detached from ourselves, we are mechanical. An elbow or a stomach detached from a body is, of course, of little use. These parts cease to answer their original purposes of being helpful to man. This is no doubt true of the mind as well. A brain detached from the rest of the body would serve no purpose, and a brain as a kind of machine would not be much better. As Fichte asks again and again, why, if humans are mechanisms, would they come to reflect on their own functioning at all.[34] The very fact that we do so makes us more than mechanisms and suggests some ground outside the realm of mechanical cause and effect, the "I."

In "The American Scholar," this is the ground that has been lost, but this is not all. As the quotation suggests, we are, as individuals, merely things dismembered, and as such, we are specifically dismembered from society. The loss of the "I" thus becomes the loss of the "we," so that the cure of the individual would imply the cure of society. Indeed, already, in the opening paragraph, Emerson has suggested that should the American scholar transform himself, undoubtedly, "poetry will revive and lead in a new age, as the star in the constellation Harp . . . shall one day be the pole-star for a thousand years."[35] This formulation anticipates the *poesis*, or making, that returns throughout the essay, and it underscores the prospective and fragmentary nature of that making. But in addition, to liken this *poesis* to the star in the constellation Harp is to suggest that the role of the American scholar is to extend well beyond the literary, or rather that letters will become a privileged site of expression for a crisis that is not merely literary in the usual sense. Among other things, Psalms, sacred songs, are sung to the harp, particularly the harp of David. In Emerson's time, it was still believed that the Psalms had been composed by David, a figure in whom the sacred and the secular are united. David is the great king and also God's chosen. As a surrogate for the American scholar, David suggests that the role of the scholar is to be religious, in the primary sense of re-linking (*re-ligio*) all of the functions that have been divided up among us. He is to be the figure who fulfills us as humans, but this in turn implies a political and a spiritual function. If this is the case, then it is because the Kantian problematic of the division between noumena and phenomena is none other than the division between private and public. The structure of pure Reason may be a law, but since noumena is unknowable, it is wholly private; only phenomena can be shared. To return the subject to the possibility of representing itself to itself would be to bridge the gap between not simply noumena and phenomena but the private and the public as well. In this respect, Emerson's project for the scholar would be the guarantee of democracy itself.[36]

Despite the apparent literary nationalism of Emerson's address, he is not responding to an aesthetic problem per se, but according to the opening fable, to a crisis in subjectivity both private and public that apparently can only be presented at all in a literary form, and that must perhaps be solved on literary grounds. But as Emerson has already insisted, we fail precisely in our relation to letters, and this failure must be redressed by a transformation in our thinking. We cannot fulfill our love of letters until we heal our thinking. Ordinarily, it would be the scholar who would embody a healthy kind of thinking, but in his sick and mechanical state, he degenerates into "a mere thinker, or, still worse, the parrot of other men's thinking." Perhaps even more to the point, since the scholar in the right state, as "Man Thinking," exercises "the highest functions of human nature,"[37] the loss of the scholar points doubly to the loss of the human itself.

This particular problem coalesces in the figure of the hand divided into fingers. The original division of the One Man is as a hand divided into fingers, a kind of useful fragmentation or division. But the hand is equally, as Cavell has pointed out, Emerson's figure for rejecting a certain type of thinking, associated particularly with a Western tradition of thought aimed at grasping, a type of thought that Cavell calls "sublimized violence."[38] Indeed, the etymological root of "comprehend" is exactly to grasp or to seize. It is a mode of thinking that implies a strict opposition between subject and object, that actively seeks to master its "materials" by seizing them. Emerson's association between this mechanical thinking and Kant first emerges in the essay when he discusses the relation between the scholar and nature:

> When he has learned to worship the soul, and to see that the natural philosophy that now is, is only the first gropings of its gigantic hand, he shall look forward to an ever expanding knowledge as to becoming a creator. He shall see, that nature is the opposite of the soul, answering to

it part for part. One is seal, one is print. Its beauty is the beauty of his own mind. Nature then becomes to him the measure of his own attainments. . . . in fine, the ancient precept, "know thyself," and the modern precept, "study nature," become at last one maxim.[39]

By natural philosophy Emerson surely intends something like the Kantian thought that only what can be known empirically can be known truly, and one might indeed read this whole passage as itself Kantian insofar as it emphasizes the correspondence between mind and nature. Within this philosophy, however, the *ancient* precept "know thyself," has been subsumed by the *modern* "study nature," since the phenomenal world is all that can be known. It is thought as a grasping or taking by "a gigantic hand" of what lies "out there." For Emerson, however, this is only a first move, a gesture that initiates self-knowledge. Is it not, I think, a coincidence that in *The Biographia Literaria*, Coleridge remarks that he was taken by Kant's critical philosophy "as with a giantic hand." As much as Coleridge professes to "admire" Kant, he nonetheless confesses within a few paragraphs that it is Fichte and Schelling who made the decisive step of "commencing with an act, instead of a thing or substance."[40] This is precisely the shift that Emerson is attempting to achieve in "The American Scholar," that is, the shift from defining mind or nature as objects to be observed as if they were static mechanisms to mind and nature as relational and ongoing process.

The duality of Emerson's figure of the hand—its oscillation between providing telos as the labor of self-production and figuring thought as comprehension—suggests that our relation to the world is not one of knowing in the usual sense, but of making.[41] One might measure the difference between these two modes simply by tracing out all of the transformations Emerson works on words associated with the hand. Beyond the introductory idea of giving to letters, he speaks of "unhandselled nature," of the world "as plastic and fluid in the hands of God," of the way in which certain experiences cause "currents of life [to] run into the hands," of the "manufacture" of experience into thought, and, at the end, of perfecting ourselves with the work of "our own hands."[42] I wish to point particularly to one example that goes back to a transformation worked on the idea of comprehension itself. Midway through the essay,

Emerson asserts, "In self-trust, all the virtues are comprehended. Free should the scholar be," and a few sentences later, speaking of all dangers that cow us from self-trust, "he will then find in himself a perfect comprehension of its nature and extent; he will have made his hands meet on the other side, and can henceforth defy it, and pass on superior" (65). Since self-trust is equated with freedom, and with reasons "darker than can be enlightened" (66), to say that it comprehends all virtues remakes the containment of comprehension into an open field. Similarly, since the scholar comprehends things, literally encircles them with his arms, only to supersede them, comprehension can hardly be a final grasping of some complete entity. It is as if Emerson were suggesting that done properly, thinking as associated with the hand would answer our end, make us more human, rather than less so, and that the very nature of "more-ness" would have to do with something we cannot yet even envision. In this, thinking anticipates the nature of Emersonian circles, a geometry in which humans are always furthering themselves, becoming other than what they are. The most human, then, would be the most other, and since thinking is but one function of the One Man, and the hand is but one part of the body, this thinking would have to take account of its own fragmentary nature. It would not be thinking as an end in itself, or thinking as the desire to create a complete system that could comprehend all particulars, but say thinking as a manifestation of futurity itself, again, as a kind of approximation of what we might become as we produce ourselves. As Emerson will write later in the essay, "Character is higher than intellect. Thinking is the function. Living is the functionary" (62).

Such rhetorical transformations themselves retrope the nature of thinking, exemplify the way in which philosophy is to become literature.[43] Apart from this, however, as appropriate as Emerson's figure of the hand is for exploring the nature of thinking itself, the physicality of the figure itself remains important. The very fact that Emerson imagines our fall as well as the trouble with thinking in bodily terms suggests that he views the problem of subjectivity in the Carlylesque terms of health and sickness, where health is allied with unconsciousness, and sickness with self-consciousness and speculation. Indeed, this connection is quite clear in the later essay,

"Spiritual Laws," where Emerson writes, "The intellectual life may be kept clean and healthful . . . no man need be perplexed in his speculations. . . . These are the soul's mumps, and measles, and whooping-coughs, and those who have not caught them cannot describe their health or prescribe the cure. A simple mind will not know these enemies."[44] Read back into "The American Scholar," the passage suggests that the transformation of intellect spoken about at the beginning of the essay would be a kind of cure. Our implicit illness also helps to explain why Emerson presents both the One Man and the figure of the hand as part of a fable. Surely Emerson, like Carlyle, is in part suggesting that the idea of achieved humanity is a myth and fragmentation of the fact. Additionally, however, Emerson begins as he does because, like all fables, this one's intent is pedagogical. But it has a twist. One does not "teach" a sick person how to get well; one provides remedies and cures. If health is unity and vital force, and sickness is mechanism, particularly as it infects thought, then figuratively Emerson's own task is to cure us of this mechanism. In this sense, Emerson begins by sketching out an image of the human that consists in a kind of essential incompletion, or incompletion and fragmentation as a positive condition, rather than as illness. His task in the essay is to achieve this transformation or cure.

The idea of cure here must be qualified in that it does not presuppose the intentionality usually associated with cure. The exemplification undertaken by Emerson as our cure is, as becomes more evident in later essays, neither active nor passive, if such a thing is possible. Even in "The American Scholar," the intentionality of cure is in question. If what Emerson calls "letters" in the opening paragraph are to be the site of a cure or transformation, then it is because Emerson's text calls on us to replace active conceptualization with what, in the most general sense, can be called receptive reading. The sort of reading Emerson has in mind can be viewed as a particular sort of receptivity to both external and internal influences. But such receptivity is equally a form of production, say, for example, the productivity that results from Emerson's own receptivity to the many possible plays on the figure of the hand. The German term would be *Witz*, or that process wherein ideas simply fall upon us, producing a kind of spontaneous gesture.[45] *Witz* is the other of conceptual knowledge, its obverse, thought without origin and without a telos and, therefore, without intentionality as such. Another way of understanding this receptivity is to remember that Kant distinguishes knowledge as active and sensuous intuition such as occurs in apprehending a sensible presentation as receptive. In this respect, Emersonian receptivity would overcome the inability of the self to present itself to itself, but not in the sense that it literally represents itself to itself. It would, instead, be our availability, or relation to certain kinds of influence, that constitutes our auto-production.

In order to consider the dynamics of this receptivity more fully, I will briefly examine how Emerson treats the three influences he names: for Emerson, nature, books, and experience are the chief instruments of the scholar's education, or upbuilding. In his remarks on nature, Emerson's point is explicitly to wriggle out of Kant's giant hand. Kant's argument of analogy suggests that the self cannot know itself in itself, and for Kant, no more can be said. In describing the first influence on the scholar—nature—Emerson attempts to show that direct and analogical knowledge are in fact one. He begins with what looks like a version of the Transcendental Deduction: "What is classification but the perceiving that these objects are not chaotic, and are not foreign, but have a law which is also a law of the human mind?"[46] The unity of nature, its laws, reside not in nature itself but in the human mind, such that the perception of this unity becomes a sign both of and for the laws of the mind. To say that only by reading nature do we discern the laws of our own mind is also to suggest two separate realms, the phenomenal and the noumenal. If this seems to be Emerson's direction here, then he changes it by using the word "maxim" to describe the unification of nature, empirically observed, and the self as noumenal construct. The section closes with the statement quoted above: "in fine, the ancient precept, 'Know thyself,' and the modern precept, 'Study nature,' become at last one maxim." According to Kant, a maxim is, in all three Critiques, a piece of procedural advice. To achieve systematic unity, one must find for every condition a further condition and proceed in that way to an ultimate condition dependent on nothing further. Unlike a principle of pure reason, the maxim does not imply that there *is* any ultimate, unconditioned condition, but only bids us to strive toward it. Knowing oneself is not a matter of conclusion.

More specifically, in the context of practical reason, a maxim is a subjective principle of behavior, not necessarily what one ought to do, but the principle according to which one does in fact act. By describing the study of nature and the knowledge of self as unified under one maxim, then, Emerson suggests that one never knows oneself except by analogy. The important point, however, is that for our actions to be intelligible, we must formulate a maxim. A maxim may describe our behavior, but if we have not formulated it as such, with awareness that our actions are freely chosen as expressions of the maxim, our actions would, in Kant's view, remain unintelligible.[47] Emerson has here transposed this idea into a very particular key: if we remain unintelligible to ourselves, then it is because we do not recognize the ways in which we constitute ourselves by interpreting or reading the objects that lie outside of ourselves. Moreover, since this is the condition which ought to lead to all future conditions, we cannot even get started until we recognize this.

The section on nature stops just short of explaining how it is that our receptivity to external influences, say our study of nature, constitutes the self. This Emerson takes up in the most famous of the essay's paragraphs, in which, after stressing that "the theory of books is noble," he proceeds to disparage the book itself. "The sacredness which attaches to the act of creation,—the act of thought,—is transferred to the record. . . . Hence the book-learned class, who value books as such; not as related to nature and the human constitution. . . . We hear that we may speak. The Arabian proverb says, 'A fig tree, looking on a fig tree, becometh fruitful.'"[48] This passage outlines a theme that will remain important to Emerson through "Self-Reliance" and *Representative Men*. Like nature, human artifacts are merely signs through which is received a representation of one's own productivity.[49] The purpose of reading is not to grasp the "meaning" of the book as a thing apart, but rather to see as if in a mirror of our own creative capacities, and so to constitute or upbuild ourselves.[50] At the same time, the specular model is misleading here in that, as the proverb suggests, the point is not to seize on some external appearance, but to appropriate interior, formative force itself. It is perhaps on the basis of this distinction that Emerson evades the idea of cultural competition at the opening of the essay and stresses that "the love of letters" is an "indestructible instinct." Letters will not be a matter of strength or skill, a matter of negating what has already been written, but rather of knowing that we always use previous examples, as well as everything else that lies outside of us, as the means of auto-production.

First, then, in the section on nature, Emerson tells us that auto-production through receptivity defines what we are doing all the time. The section on books attempts to show what, in fact, we are receiving. It is only in the final and perhaps most nebulous section, on the relation between thought and action, that Emerson attempts to give an account of receptivity itself. As in the earlier sections, Emerson begins with the idea that we only come to ourselves mediately, through some kind of other: "The world,—this shadow of the soul, or *other me*, lies wide around. Its attractions are the keys which unlock my thoughts and make me acquainted with myself."[51] Emerson is essentially describing a two-step process here, or so it would seem. We begin unknown to ourselves, locked "dumb" as he puts it within ourselves. We then take the world as another "me," an image of ourselves, which like nature and books, presents us to ourselves. We must say, however, that this relation is formative of the self, rather than merely reflective, because without it we would not know ourselves at all. In a curious way, then, this act of self-constitution by definition seems to remain unavailable to us, for if without this key we cannot unlock or form ourselves, one must wonder who is doing the unlocking in the first place.

In keeping with the idea that the self is not something to be known, but rather to be enacted and produced, Emerson states that "with the business which we now have in hand," "we are quite unable to speculate. Our affections as yet circulate through it. We no more feel or know it, than we feel the feet, or the hand, or the brain of our body. The new deed is yet part of life, remains immersed in our unconscious life."[52] Since only later does this new deed "become a thought of the mind" (61), it would be tempting to read this passage as that from action or instinct to proper thought. One may find he or she has been receptive and produced a work or a thought, but the completed work is not the point. Rather, the completed work represents but a fragment of what produced it. Moreover, if Emerson seems to be opposing thought and action, one should recall that since the scholar is Man Thinking, then for the scholar the business at hand can only be thinking, but thinking as a process situated somewhere between I and the other, thinking as receptivity. This is not speculation, not the mind confronting an object or even itself as object, but rather the mind engaged in an activity wholly experiential and thus unavailable to representation, or unavailable, say, in the very way in which Emerson's juggling of pronouns makes the scholar at once unavailable in certain respects and also wholly available in others. In language that closely echoes Carlyle's dictum that only the healthy are unaware of their health, Emerson insists that thinking as receptivity is experiential or nothing; experiential, as the above passage clearly indicates, means unconscious.

If as Emerson has been suggesting in the previous two sections, thought is a kind of receptivity, then receptivity would be a kind of unconscious state that proceeds all the time apart from will, perhaps much like the indestructible instinct that is a love of letters. Indeed, Emerson likens the effects of receptivity to the mulberry leaf converting itself into satin: "the manufacture goes forward at all hours."[53] This is simply to say that we cannot make ourselves receptive, any more than the mulberry leaf wills its conversion into satin, or any more than we can will ourselves to be healthy. And yet, if we find ourselves so, we will find as well "the impossibility of antedating this act" (61). The suggestion is that the very receptivity which allows the usual kind of thinking to happen is a traumatic state only experienced, hence never presented and, above all, never willed as a project. To go back to the beginning of the essay, if all of our transformations look like beginnings, say even the birth of a national literature, it is because they only will have been available to us as absolute ruptures, known only as absences that mark our start, known then, finally, only through their effects. This is why Emerson insists "thinking is a partial act" (62), a mere sign of what will have been.

This emphasis on the unsayable experience of auto-production marks Emerson's difference from the Romanticism of Jena and points to the very reasons for which we might wish to locate "The American Scholar" in a nationalistic context. If the Schlegels, Novalis, and Schelling insist on the unification of poetry and philosophy, then their emphasis still falls heavily on the aesthetic and the theoretical dimension of this unification itself. For Emerson's Continental couterparts, that unification, and the *Bildung* that it underwrites, may intend more than the literary, but it proceeds almost within a wholly aesthetic and theoretical framework of genres that seems programmatic and intentional. In its insistence on the impossibility of antedating our acts of production, it may be that the way in which Emerson envisions a new kind of thinking owes more to Carlyle than to Schelling or Schlegel. Not only does Carlyle's reconstruction of the Romantic problem in terms of healthy and sick ways of thinking reorient an epistemological and aesthetic problem in a distinctly pragmatic direction, but also it equally suggests that such thinking does not fall within the purview of intention or work as such. What we find in Emerson is that the theoretical dimension of poetry/philosophy and the *Bildung* that accompanies it is replaced by an equal and opposite attention to the actual experience of auto-production itself, an experience that simply goes forward at all hours whether we will it or not.

I will return to this "strange process" at length in later chapters, but for the moment, the experiential and therefore traumatic origins of thought help to put a final focus on the task that Emerson sets for himself and for the scholar. Early in the essay, Emerson remarks, "the one thing in the world, of value, is the active soul. This every man is entitled to; this every man contains within him, although, in almost all men, obstructed, and as yet unborn" (57). Presumably the scholar would become Man Thinking if he but had an active soul, and without it, he is as Emerson puts it, "unborn." In one sense, the passage simply repeats the equation between thinking and achieved humanity, but it refines that equation as well. According to the logic of receptivity, thinking is always "unborn"; it cannot be antedated. But to be unborn means also that one does not yet know how to bear oneself, say in the sense of carrying ourselves, but perhaps more particularly in the sense that one does not know how to *take* oneself. All of which returns to "nation"—yet another identity waiting to be born but also being born. If we have not yet achieved it, then that is because individual and national identity have from the start been one. As at the opening of the essay in the figure of Harp, Emerson explains the relation between individual and national births later in the essay by equating the two: the scholar "then learns, that in going down into the secrets of his own mind, he has descended into the secrets of all minds" (64). This equivalency would be fine were it not for the fact that the most private is precisely what is inaccessible, known only in its aftereffects. This makes of cultural life, of American letters too, a sheer contingency, a kind of unbearable absence.

To be unable to bear oneself marks a kind of failure to acknowledge who and what one is, and because of this failure, one cannot know how to carry oneself, as in carrying oneself forward, into the future. What in all of these instances would one have to learn to bear in order to make it over into the future? Perhaps nothing other than one's unborn state, the very fact that receptive thinking as such with all that it now entails, is something that can neither be explained nor represented, neither willed nor caused. Properly speaking, then, Emerson could do nothing to start us on the path to thinking, or at least nothing that he can tell us as such, anymore than we could start ourselves on such a path. We would simply find one day that we had begun, that we had been beginning all the time: "the manufacture goes forward at all hours." All of our births are contingent, including that of America itself. In the face of such contingency, the curative, exemplary and initiatory claims of the essay can only be read as Emerson's attempt to engender in the reader the very receptivity that gets us started, to engender that which can never be born. To hear this call would mark our willingness to accept the contingency of starting points, a willingness in turn that constitutes nothing other than our responsibility to our own upbuilding. No more appeals to Europe, to its grounding authority, to any other ground but our own, the one which is the site of a groundless reception that happens just the same. This finally perhaps is where Emerson leaves us. In a contingency, a provisionality, a receptivity to which we are everywhere to learn to be responsible. To accept this responsibility would be to have answered Emerson's opening call, to be drawn into the future as a scholar of the future.

What remains uncertain in "The American Scholar" is the particular way in which this cultural revolution can occur at all. Carlyle had written toward the end of "Characteristics" that "the old spell" of mechanism would, at length, be broken by "a new magic word."[54] By taking the place of the American scholar, Emerson promises this word, but he does not speak it. The claim is there—to exemplify the thinking that should characterize the scholar—but this essay has not yet worked out the particulars of such exemplification, at least to the degree that his later essays will. This is simply to say that what Emerson characterizes as the relation of receptive reading has not yet achieved its fullest form. If, however, Emerson's call, a call that presupposes a response, must be characterized as literary, then at this point it is because the self constitutes itself by the reading of what lies outside of it. This may not be reading in the sense one usually understands it, not reading as a grasping of the meaning of a text. But, because the self is structured as it is, all thinking that is thinking will be to some degree literary; thought will always constitute itself as the reading of signs, the encounter with an Other.[55] To return to the opening paragraph of the essay, we might say now that to give to letters would be to give ourselves to them, to lose ourselves in them, there to make ourselves anew in the Other. And it is in this giving, as we come to exist as ourselves for the first time, or again, that we open the possibility of adding something further to letters.

Part Two

The Emersonian Subject: Reading and Transference

Chapter 2 · · ·

From Philosophy to Rhetoric

> *I cast away in this new moment all my once hoarded knowledge, as vacant and vain. Now, for the first time, seem I to know any thing rightly. The simplest words,—we do not know what they mean, except when we love. . . .*
> —Emerson, "Circles"

Letting Go

Despite Emerson's eloquent call for a new mode of letters that will replace philosophy as such, its representative—the American scholar—no more exists at the end of the essay than he did at the beginning. Emerson has been quite clear about what American letters are not, but he fails to delineate what they shall be. It would be typically Emersonian if the American scholar and letters themselves were by definition prospective, but at this point, all that one can really say about Man Thinking is that he is not to bear the image of the traditional philosopher. As "The American Scholar" suggests, by this Emerson means that his thinking is to participate neither in what he elsewhere calls "a paltry empiricism," nor in the forms of conceptualization and system building associated particularly with Kant and his ancestors. We are, in some sense not entirely clear, to let go of philosophy. Such an idea of course returns us to the image of the hand with which Emerson opens his address to the scholar and that, in turn, structures his argument throughout the essay. If taking from letters is associated with the hand divided into fingers in order to close round something, to grasp or comprehend it in a teleological fashion, giving to letters might well be represented by an opposite image, that of an open hand. Such an image does not appear in Emerson's text, any more so than any image of what American letters might be. But is it likely that Emerson, well read in the pre-Socratics, could fail to have known that with a closed hand Zeno represented dialectics or philosophical argument? With an open hand, he represented eloquence.[1]

The subject of this chapter is precisely Emersonian eloquence or rhetoric as performance and persuasion, but before attempting to understand what that might mean and how it might replace a more traditional philosophical project, recall that an open hand can invite or repel. It may be as much a shield as a greeting, a warning as a welcome. I say this at the outset because if thinking as the potential receptivity embodied by the open hand is to replace the activity of conceptualization, it does so in complex ways that imply more than a sequential transition from one discourse to another. Transition is one of Emerson's central tropes, and it is never simple. Perhaps the most trenchant instance occurs in "Self-Reliance": "Life only avails, not the having lived. Power ceases in the instant of repose; it resides in the moment of transition from a past to a new state, in the shooting of the gulf, in the darting to an aim."[2] This passage will become emblematic of the process that Emersonian rhetoric attempts to engender in the reader, but in the meanwhile, it serves as a reminder that Emerson's interest lies neither here nor there, in neither past nor future, but rather somewhere in between, in the interstitial process of moving from one point to another. His project for American letters takes shape as just such a process or trajectory between what are on their own ground reified disciplines or conceptual fields. The difficulty is that the opposition between those disciplines, between philosophy and rhetoric, is not itself definitive for Emerson but merely encloses the transitional process between them.

Emerson himself provides a paradigmatic example of the problems attendant to the transition from philosophy to letters, fittingly, at the close of the essay entitled "Intellect," the penultimate piece in *Essays: First Series*. At the beginning of this essay, Emerson announces, "Intellect and intellection signify to the common ear consideration of the abstract truth."[3] The point of the essay will be to subtilize the common, to revise our notions of what is called thinking so that we no longer see thought as bound up solely with abstract truth. The essay concludes, as might be expected, with a brief meditation on different types of knowing. Speaking of the man who would know "truth," Emerson begins:

> The circle of the green earth he must measure with his shoes, to find the man who can yield him truth. He shall then know that there is somewhat more blessed and great in hearing than in speaking. Happy is the hearing man; unhappy the speaking man. As long as I hear truth, I am bathed by a beautiful element and am not conscious of any limits to my nature . . . but if I speak, I define, I confine, and am less.[4]

In an immediate sense, the passage echoes a number of Emerson's concerns in "The American Scholar." If we must measure the earth with our shoes, then it is because knowledge is to be experiential or nothing; as Emerson insists earlier in the essay, "I would put myself in the attitude to look in the eye an abstract truth, and I cannot" (420).

The turn away from such truth is a turn toward mediation, toward the Other who can yield truth, and indeed, throughout the essay, the emphasis falls on just such mediation. The implication of the first two sentences in the above passage is that once we recognize that knowledge is mediated, something reflected back to us through the circuit of the Other, then we must understand thinking as reception rather than as reaching after, a difference further underscored by the passivity of hearing itself. As Emerson notes several pages earlier, "Our thinking is to be a pious reception. Our truth of thought is therefore vitiated as much by too violent direction given by our will" (418–19). Receptivity implies affectability—that is, the susceptibility to being affected by the Other, and it is for this reason that the later part of the passage shifts the opposition between receptivity and activity into a different register. In the interplay with the Other, we learn that hearing is more "blessed" than speaking, and the three terms—"hearing," "blessing," and "speaking"—continue to figure centrally as the essay comes to its conclusion. If the opposition between receptivity and activity is relocated specifically in terms of speech, then it is because knowing is in the process of becoming the province of rhetoric and persuasion, of the ways in which language affects us, make us receptive to it. This dynamic is, in turn, conceived as making us more, just as the kind of conceptualization that defines and confines makes us less.

Emerson will address this transition more specifically at the close of the essay, but in the meantime, it is worth noting that the connotations of the word "blessing," particularly as it appears in the Hebrew Bible (*berakha*), have always had to do with more-ness and increase, particularly in the sense of "more life." To be blessed, by giving ourselves up to hearing, then, would mean in some sense to be more of who we are. What might otherwise seem like no more than the replacement of one discourse with another is thus complicated by the fact that, as in "The American Scholar," the passage from philosophy to rhetoric subtends the larger trajectory of self-creation, or *Bildung*. The beginning of the paragraph quoted above indicates Emerson understood the connotation of blessing as more life; it is a connotation he then makes explicit at the close of the paragraph and with which he reveals the stakes of the confrontation with traditional philosophy. Echoing the preceding essay in the series, "Circles," he continues in "Intellect":

> Every man's progress is through a succession of teachers, each of whom seems at the time to have a superlative influence, but it at last gives place to a new. Frankly let him accept it. Jesus says, Leave father, mother, house and lands, and follow me.... Each new mind we approach seems to require an abdication of all our past and present possessions. A new doctrine seems, at first, a subversion of all our opinions, tastes, and manner of living. Such has Swedenborg, such has Kant, such has Coleridge, such has Hegel or his interpreter Cousin, seemed to many young men in this country. Take thankfully and heartily all they can give. Exhaust them, wrestle with them, let them not go until their blessing be won. (426–27)

I quote this passage at length because it encapsulates the nature of the Emersonian way of both inheriting and disowning traditional philosophy. At the beginning of the paragraph, the emphasis is on learning and knowledge as occurring by overwhelming influence or reception, both of which proceed by abandonment of current investments. Yet these influences will themselves one day give way to abandonment. In between these two moments, Emerson inserts the striking idea of one's encounter with philosophy as that of Jacob wrestling with the angel for the blessing. Coupled with the mention of Jesus, it is in part as if Emerson is simply suggesting that knowledge, and philosophy in particular, are spiritual pursuits, or rather the nineteenth-century way of inheriting religion. The passage, however, goes further than that.

In the Biblical account, Jacob's encounter with the angel itself occurs as a transitional moment.[5] Having fled the house of Laban, Jacob returns to the Holy Land after twenty years. His first move is to send gifts ahead to his brother Esau, asking for reconciliation and peace. As Avivah Zornberg puts it, "The central image that expresses Jacob's dilemma at this period of his life . . . is of Jacob behind."[6] By "Jacob behind," Zornberg intends something like his temporal lastness and lateness. The last of the patriarchs and second-born, he nonetheless steals the birthright and the blessing from Esau, and now he sends his propitiatory gifts of livestock ahead, along with his servants and his camp, remaining behind on the far side of the Jabbok. Indeed, the classic reading of his position of birth is that of a man whose destiny is deferred. That destiny, however, will accomplish itself as he wrestles with a nameless one until daybreak, finally wresting the blessing from him. Who is this nameless one? Midrashic tradition holds that it is Esau's guardian angel, but also it surely must be an image of Jacob himself, who is in any case Esau's twin.[7] Angels are named for their mission, and this one's mission is to give Jacob a new name, to show him in a face-to-face confrontation how to become Israel. It is perhaps for this reason that in response to Jacob's question, ("Tell me, I pray thee, thy name"), the angel responds, "Wherefore is it that thou dost ask after my name?" Jacob already knows the answer, for he is facing himself in the moment at which he is leaving one identity behind to take on a new one. Evidently, such leave-taking is not possible on one's own. Jacob somehow needs this angel, and even then, the blessing comes hard. The angel only blesses Jacob in order to escape, as if facing ourselves literally means letting go of ourselves. The wrestling match thus becomes an opportunity for self-understanding and -discovery won at the cost of a battle. Not least significantly, this is a battle unfolding on the threshold between private and public identities. After asking Jacob his name, the angel says, "Thy name shall be called no more Jacob, but Israel: for as a prince hast thou power with God and with men, and hast prevailed."[8] Jacob will become a new nation.

So, lateness or behindness, and winning the blessing, means the possibility of being more than one has been by achieving a new and larger identity.[9] I emphasize these two aspects of the Jacob story because I think they bear on Emerson's use of the trope to describe the American confrontation with European philosophy. Like Jacob, Americans, too, as individual readers, always come after when it comes to European philosophy, not just because they are Americans but also because the philosophic conception of truth is something always already there, immutable and universal. In our confrontation with European philosophy, what we stand to gain is precisely the possibility of our own identity as makers, rather than onlookers. This holds both at the personal and cultural levels. Jacob's story represents this moment as the passage from private to public identity, suggesting that for Emerson, an American's individual grappling with European philosophy will lead to an American way of inheriting or disowning that tradition, although at this point, the nature of the passage from private to public remains uncertain.

The central idea is still that philosophy represents the decisive battleground on which the war for identity is to be won or lost. Thus Emerson insists at the opening of the passage that one must abdicate all past and present possessions, including oneself, if one is to make any progress. To win a new name, one must give up the old. And, to make such progress, to win the blessing from philosophy, means to overcome it on its own ground. It is not a matter, as de Tocqueville had insisted, of being ignorant of all of the schools of European philosophy.[10] We must wrestle with it, hand to hand, grasp it, see ourselves face to face in it, to see how we find or fail to find ourselves there. Only then can we let go, just as Jacob lets go of the angel once its blessing is won. It is as if, in this decisive confrontation, one grasps conceptualization itself, thereby overcoming it and replacing it with the receptivity of the open hand.

Nonetheless, Emerson here worries about losing, and indeed, in Jacob's story itself, the outcome is equivocal. Jacob wins a new name, but he is crippled. One might construe this to mean that neither Jacob nor the angel exactly triumphs, but rather that both prevail. For Emerson, the anxiety generated by the conflict with European philosophy manifests itself as a fear of overinfluence. But as he writes immediately following the passage on winning the blessing, "After a short season, the dismay will be overpast, the excess of influence withdrawn, and they [the philosophers] will be no longer an alarming meteor, but one more bright star shining serenely in your heaven, and blending its light with all your day."[11] There is something in our confrontation that unmakes us, but I take this passage to say as well that European philosophy will no longer be a call to arms, a reason to do battle. Having wrestled with it and won its blessing, we will be remade, but we will also have changed it, domesticated it into the common light of our day. To make philosophy part of the everyday would surely mean to make it experiential, to transform conceptualization into living, into something in which we recognize ourselves, see ourselves face to face. The possibility of such a confrontation provides at least one of the reasons that Emerson alludes to Jacob in the first place. Wrestling involves bodily contact, direct experience, as well as an etymological root that includes the idea of twisting or turning. The way in which Emerson figures our encounter with European philosophy involves both.

In the first place, we are not simply to take what the other gives, but rather to experience it, to make contact with it in a direct way—to live it. It is just this dimension of the encounter that makes possible the transition from private to public. If we are not looking an abstract truth in the eye, but taking on the teachings of philosophy experientially, seeing ourselves face to face, then we must each do it individually. As we upbuild ourselves, so we inherit philosophy as part of a collective day. This type of contact implies a subversion, or a twisting of the usual relation between the subject seeking to grasp the object of truth, into a more dynamic process of receptivity in which the subject and its truth might no longer be distinguishable. Wrestling requires two participants who, in their confrontation, are far less separable than opposing sides in a battle would be. Such perhaps would be the American way both of letting go of a European philosophical inheritance and, at the same time, of taking something of it afterward.

The closing paragraphs of "Intellect" make clear that thinking as experience, and particularly the experience of self-understanding, has been Emerson's tangent all along. Speaking of the difficulty of European philosophy, Emerson is simply dismissive: "The Bacon, the Spinoza, the Hume, Schelling, Kant, or whosoever propounds to you a philosophy of the mind, is only a more or less awkward translator of the things in your consciousness. . . . Say, then, instead of too timidly poring into his obscure sense, that he has not succeeded in rendering back to you your consciousness" (427). According to this logic, the reading of philosophy becomes, far from a search for abstract truth, an exercise in self-recognition, just as Jacob's confrontation with the angel leads to self-understanding. But the drift here is negative, for in the remaining paragraph of the essay, Emerson worries over whether or not the type of philosophy with which he has been grappling has anything to do with the laws of intellect at all. He announces his reservation with the statement, "I will not, though the subject might provoke it, speak to the open question between Truth and Love" (427). For Emerson, who has little or nothing to say about love, what could such a question mean? If, however, the subject of intellect provokes this question, it is because philosophy may be the way of Truth, but if truth cannot speak to us, and if we cannot hear it, engage with it, then it means nothing.

To understand what is at stake in the open question between truth and love, we perhaps need to move to the closing sentence of the essay: "The angels are so enamoured of the language that is spoken in heaven, that they will not distort their lips with the hissing and unmusical dialects of men, but speak their own, whether there be any who understand it or not" (428). Aside from an echo of Emerson's earlier dissatisfaction with the ministry, there is also an echo here of the well-known passage from Chapter 13 of Paul's first letter to the Corinthians: "Though I speak with the tongues of men and angels, and have not love, I am become as sounding brass, or a tinkling cymbal."[12] What is missing, of course, in this musical language of truth as spoken by men or angels is precisely love. In the context of the earlier distinction between speaking and hearing, with the latter as the more blessed, Emerson here ironically wrests the blessing from the angels who speak but are not heard and transfers it to those who deal in the hissing and unmusical dialects of men. If this dialect is hissing, then it is perhaps because the language of men, like that of the serpent, entails speaking with a double tongue, that is, in the language of metaphor, of figure, of self-conscious rhetoricity, rather than transparency. Similarly, to speak the language of men must also mean to be heard, and being heard implies persuasion. This leaves us with love. In "Friendship," Emerson had suggested that "our intellectual and active powers increase with our affections,"[13] which is perhaps another way of stating that all of our intellectual progress is through a series of teachers. Truth on its own, say the kind of truth that Emerson presupposes by European philosophy, never persuades us. It is always the Other who does so, always our affections for the Other that lead. And how does the Other do this? It would seem, given Emerson's emphasis on the involuntary nature of hearing itself, through our own passivity, or call it receptivity. But receptivity to what? The answer at this point can only be "rhetoric."

Put another way, if the purpose of letters is a form of self-creation, itself not yet clear, then there is no point in Emerson or anyone else reporting that this is so. To do so would be similar to Descartes having formulated the cogito in the second person. As with the cogito, the project of American letters is one which each reader, each potential scholar, must take up for him- or herself. Indeed, the project consists precisely in the taking up of it, which can only be done by being drawn to it through its rhetorical pull. If the Other speaks to us and we hear it, then the connection is everything, and the connection is established through the way in which the Other speaks and in which we hear. Insofar as this connection must be experiential rather than a statement of what is to be, "The American Scholar" cannot properly be said to constitute part of the project of American letters. It is no more than an announcement of what is to come, a sketch or a blueprint. The actual transition from philosophy to letters occurs later, in *Essays: First Series*, as I have been trying to demonstrate by way of examining the close of "Intellect." But as I have also just suggested, the transition itself eludes discursive statement or else loses itself in such statement. The real work of transition will have to be performed rhetorically, in such a way that the reader can be receptive to it, persuaded by it. Only then will we have let go.

Reading

Transitions necessarily occur briefly, quickly, say, for example, through an allusive moment within a text, or in the turning of a single word. But lest it seem I have placed too much weight on the single reference to Jacob in what is in any case an obscure essay in Emerson's canon, let us return to the beginning of *Essays: First Series*, to the essay entitled "History." The assumption in doing so is that we take the book's title itself seriously, for the *First Series* is just that, a continuous meditation on the nature of letters in all of their senses. It is an explanatory meditation at times, but primarily a serial exemplification of the type of thinking with which we are to replace philosophy, as well as an act of performative rhetoric designed to put the reader on the path of that thinking. Emerson implies as much midway through "History" when he writes in a paragraph comprised of a single sentence, "His onward thinking leads him into the truth to which that fact or series belongs."[14] In short, each of the parts of a series represents a single idea, but the purpose of serial presentation is to foster onward thinking, to give us up, as Emerson has it in "Intellect," "unreservedly to that which draws [us]."[15] This is not to say that a series always proceeds continuously; as "Experience" demonstrates, a series may equally imply discontinuity. In either respect, whether as continuity or discontinuity, *Essays: First Series* is aimed just at onward thinking itself, and particularly onward thinking construed as the activity of self-creation through letters.

To say that *Essays: First Series* proceeds serially in an attempt to draw the reader into onward thinking raises the question of why Emerson begins with an essay entitled "History." The answer must surely be that the topic is somehow necessary for the understanding of the purpose of the series as a whole and, more specifically, preparatory for the lessons of the essay immediately following, "Self-Reliance." There is, of course, in a general sense nothing in the least unusual about Emerson writing an essay on history. He would simply be sharing in the nineteenth-century preoccupation with the use of historical method and, particularly, genealogy, as tools of self-understanding. Whether they be tales of our biological origins, of our economic system, of Western morality, or of individual human development, the historical fictions of the nineteenth century all make the assertion that identity cannot be understood outside of the historical matrix. Indeed, as Emerson puts it in the second paragraph of the essay, "Man is explicable by nothing less than his whole history."[16] In the most general sense, it is from this perspective of history as constitutive of self-understanding that the essay's inaugural position in the series makes sense. Emerson, however, differs from Darwin, Marx, Nietzsche, and Freud not simply by virtue of preceding them, but quite specifically in his use of the genealogical method. One assumption usually underlying this method is that the past informs the present: tell me who you were, and I'll tell you who you are. It is clear that Emerson found this kind of determinism distasteful, and yet, the genealogical method remains important for him for reasons tangential to determinism. From Marx through Freud, genealogies may expose the lineaments of the past in the face of the present, but they also show just how tenuous the links are between origins and ends. Paradoxically, the very connection between past and present that implies determinism also reminds us again and again of the contingencies by which the present became what it is. Rather than a record of natural fact, history thus becomes the medium in which we have constructed ourselves and can do so again and again.

 I take this belief in the constructedness of history to underlie the architectural tropes pervading Emerson's "History." It is not simply that architecture belongs to the material record of culture but also that architecture serves as a reminder of the purpose of reading or writing history as constructed, and therefore as perpetually educative or upbuilding. For the same reason, it should not surprise us in the least that the essay on history has little to do with history as material record and everything to do with the reading and writing of history. In order to understand the nature of Emerson's emphasis on reading and writing, it is important to specify that by history, Emerson intends more than the mere record of events: "There is one mind common to all individual men.... Of the works of this mind history is the record" (237). These apparently simple sentences, both of which express well-known Emersonian truisms, lay the groundwork for the theory of self-creation that takes shape throughout the *First Series*.[17] It is precisely because there is one mind that we can begin to read the record of history at all. Reading, then, becomes an identificatory process, a kind of identification of ourselves with the one mind, or, say, a recognition of ourselves through and as that one mind. As the record of the one mind, the writing of history then is not simply the cataloguing of events or facts, any more than the reading of history would be the grasping or comprehending of such a catalogue. Instead, history becomes a medium in which we find ourselves through the processes of reading and writing, or, as Emerson puts it, "The advancing man discovers how deep a property he has in literature,—in all fable as well as in all history."[18] The fact that Emerson refuses to distinguish between fable and history is simply one more indication that the essay is less about history per se than about reading and writing. If as we advance we learn that we have a deep property in such activities, then it is precisely because they are proper to us, the means through which we define ourselves.

If, however, Emerson does not more straightforwardly entitle the essay "Reading," then it is perhaps because the reading process itself marks our advent *in* history. To say we find ourselves in history is not precisely accurate insofar as finding implies that a self already exists, perhaps in the same way that history implies a past that exists. If everything already has sense in it, if we already exist as particulars identical with the one mind, then history in a sense is a meaningless term. But just as Emerson insists, in an uncanny anticipation of Nietzsche, that "all inquiry into antiquity ... is the desire to do away this wild savage and preposterous There or Then, and introduce in its place the Here and Now" (241), so, too, as the essay continues, it elaborates a theory of reading in which the self, far from already existing, comes into being as it reads. This idea is made explicit early in the essay: "So all that is said of the wise man by Stoic, or oriental or modern essayist, describes to each reader his own idea, describes his unattained but attainable self. All literature writes the character of the wise man. Books, monuments, picture, conversation, are portraits in which he finds the lineaments he is forming" (239). Perhaps the most notable feature of this passage is the ambiguity of the pronouns. In the simplest sense, the passage would seem to be saying that the essayist merely describes himself in his representation of the wise man, but this construction contradicts Emerson's entire drift in "History." We are to esteem ourselves the text, and books the commentary. In fact, the grammar of the sentence allows that in the representation of the wise man, the idea to which Emerson refers may belong both to the essayist and to the reader, so that in either case the identificatory nature of reading alluded to in the opening paragraph of the essay is here confirmed. The shifting pronouns that govern the double sense of this passage thus indicate a kind of process or interaction in which it is impossible to tell whose ideas are whose. Far from being the passive absorption of "material," reading becomes an active experiential encounter defined precisely by the slippages between text and reader. It is in our reading of the other's text that we form an idea—literally, an image—not of what we are, if we are indeed anything, but of what we might become. Yet it is impossible to say where that image originates.

Let me take this a little further. When Emerson says that all literature writes the character of the wise man, he may simply be suggesting that the task of literature is to depict wisdom. But surely he is working as well with a kind of pun on the etymological meaning of "character" as a written thing. Originally in the Greek, "character" designated a stylus, and by extension from the active to passive voice, the marks it makes, as for example in the contemporary sense of the "characters" of the alphabet. But the word was also extended to mean distinguishing characteristic, as that which marks one. It is only later, perhaps with Aristotle's *Rhetoric* that the meaning of "character" extends itself still further, coming to mean not only that which typifies but also that unique interior state or quality that makes one who one is and no other. It is an etymological history that implicitly defines one's characteristic—or, in Emersonian terms, "representative"—self as a written, constructed thing. The written nature of the self is furthered with the final sentence of the paragraph in which reading provides "a portrait in which he [the reader] finds the lineaments he is forming" (239). In this sense, Emerson's insistence that literature writes the character of the wise man is equivalent to the statement that the reading of literature creates or gives birth to character. More specifically, we might say that in our acts of reading, we author or script the lines of the text of our future selves.

The corollary, of course, is that until we learn how to read history properly, we do not properly exist as characters. As Emerson writes in the opening paragraph, "Who hath access to this universal mind is a party to all that is or can be done" (237). Prior to the reading that gives access to this mind, we are evidently limited. We cannot do what can be done. And what can be done, in the terms of the essay, is always something constructed, be it the building of architectural monuments, the writing of literary texts, the making of sculptures, or the making of men. We are to identify ourselves precisely with such activities, not necessarily in the specific sense but more generally as activities involving the construction of things. As we do so, as we learn to read history aright, we identify with those figures who occupy the historical record, not with their creations per se but with their creative activity, just as in "The American Scholar." The implication is that once we begin reading, we pass from some natural chronology—say, history conceived as a mere transcription or record of what we already are, as mere repetition of the one mind—into a perpetual self-construction, the writing of our own characters. This form of self-creation differs from brute chronology or repetition precisely in its reference to that nonhistorical point, the one mind. It duplicates the one mind, but with a difference, the difference being just that consciousness of itself as a form of the one mind. If we manage this passage, then our "annals" would be "broader and deeper," as the end of the essay has it, and "we would trulier express our central and wide-related nature, instead of this old chronology of selfishness and pride" (256). The shift from the attained to the attainable self as it occurs in the reading and writing of history, which is nothing other than the reading and writing of ourselves, thus marks the difference between prehistorical and historical being.

It is here that the connection between self-creation and reading becomes explicit for the first time, and in essence, it is rhetoric that forms the nexus. This is the nexus that will become so crucial for the later pragmatism of William James, Charles Peirce, and Richard Rorty.[19] The self is not something there and given, but rather something arrived at interpretively, or, more precisely, a text that is always giving birth to itself through its interpretive acts. Our concerns for the moment, however, are more immediate, especially in the way that "History" lays out the central principles that will inform "Self-Reliance." In the first place, it suggests that the activity of self-creation is to be understood and undertaken as a form of reading, that is, under the guise of letters. To say so, of course, brings us close to Cavell's understanding of what he calls "Emersonian perfectionism." Cavell in fact deploys the above passage about our unattained but attainable selves as the centerpiece of his very persuasive argument about what constitutes that perfectionism. His agenda entails assimilating Emerson to a philosophical tradition of moral perfectionism that extends from Plato to Wittgenstein, with particular attention to Kant. Cavell lists no less than twenty-eight characteristic features of philosophical texts that participate in such a tradition. Essentially, however, moral perfectionism involves a process in which the self transforms itself for the better with the help of an Other, a transformation, which, in turn, prepares for larger social change as well. According to Cavell's reading, Emerson's work falls into this category not simply because of the emphasis on transformation and upbuilding but also because Emerson's text presents itself as that Other making such transformations possible. Thus the modern essayist in the passage quoted above is Emerson himself. In this respect, Emerson is presenting his own text as the path by which we each, in our reading, begin to move toward our future or unattained selves. Were it possible to quote Cavell's entire commentary on Emerson I would do so, since it informs at every step what I wish to do here. But here is a representative passage:

> Emerson's turn is to make my partiality itself the sign and incentive of my siding with the next or further self, which means siding against my

attained perfection (or conformity), sidings which require the recognition of an other—the acknowledgement of a relationship—in which the sign is manifest. Emerson does not much attempt to depict such a relationship (film may call it marriage, philosophers have usually called it friendship), but the sense I seek to clarify is that Emerson offers his writing as representing this other for his reader.[20]

For Cavell, Emersonian perfectionism is that movement whereby one achieves a new identity—for within any perfectionism, identity is not something one has, but something to be attained—by rejecting one's former self. One does so by reading a sign of one's future self in the text of the Other.

Cavell's interpretation differs from most kinds of reader-response theories in that his interest lies neither in determining the universal operations of the text that enlist the participation of some generic reader nor even in the more psychologized version of American reader-response theory. Instead he focuses more pointedly on what might be Emerson's hopes for both the individual words of his text and each reader. The idea that the text requires the reader's completion and at the same time completes the reader is by no means new. One might think of Roland Barthes's *S/Z* as a primary example, but one need not take any Gallic detours to arrive at similar constructions of the relation between reader and text. Arthur Danto, for example, in an article fittingly entitled "Philosophy As/And/Of Literature," suggests thinking of the literary text in general as a kind of mirror:

> Each work of literature shows in this sense an aspect we would not know were ours without benefit of that mirror: each discovers, in the eighteenth-century meaning of the term, an unguessed dimension of the self. It is a mirror less in passively returning an image than in transforming the self-consciousness of the reader who in virtue of identifying with the image recognizes what he is. Literature is in this sense transfigurative.[21]

What interests me about both Cavell and Danto is that even as they open up the possibility that reading might become constitutive of the self, they tend to ignore precisely how the relation between reader and text works. In a later section, I will suggest that one of the reasons for this evasion has to do with the fact that the relation between reader and text in Emerson itself lies beyond representability, such that one can speak neither of a reader nor a text, but only of relation. That this undoing of the subject and the text is also the foreclosure of the tradition of moral perfectionism about which Cavell speaks must wait for later consideration.[22]

Indeed, as Cavell says, Emerson himself does not much represent that relationship, except to designate it as a form of reading, and one must wonder about the vagueness of the word. What precisely does it mean to say that the self authors itself by way of an encounter with the text of the Other? It is surely appropriate that Emerson calls such an encounter "letters," but as we move from conceptualization to rhetoric, we are also moving from the simple opposition between reader and text, subject and object, to a more complex kind of relation. This is implicit in Cavell's argument, although he never states it as such, an absence revealed in his diffidence about how Emerson's text attracts us to itself in the first place and how we actually then go about moving from our attained to unattainable self. Nonetheless, Cavell provides an important starting point, for if the Emersonian text is to perform the work that he attributes to it, it begins to function more like another subject in its own right—Lacan would say as a subject of desire—than like a static entity waiting to be grasped. Moreover, the fact that the self comes to itself only through the detour of the Other implies a self always other than itself, or at least elsewhere from itself. Indeed, if the Emersonian text were no more than a mirror reflecting a given and fixed subject, then one would be wholly on the ground of early speculative idealism. Although at times Emerson does seem to remain on this ground, the transformative work he posits for his text situates him neither as a philosopher nor purely as a rhetorician. His work does not seek to posit our preconditions, nor, properly speaking, to persuade us of anything. Persuasion, however, will remain at the forefront; Emerson then is a rhetorician with a difference. In other words, the Emersonian project of letters can no longer be formulated simply as the opposition between philosophy and rhetoric. A third term is necessary, and once we are talking about persuasion, about intersubjective relations, or about the absence of subjectivity perhaps implied by desire itself, that term must be psychology.

Alienated Majesties: Beyond Representation

"Self-Reliance" indeed begins by positing a psychological self, but also and first with what we already know in at least several senses. Not only is it Emerson's most widely read essay, the centerpiece of his work (and, therefore, in a sense, the least readable of his works), but also it returns us as well to the problem of the subject present to itself. It does so by reminding us of what we already are. Here is the inescapable beginning:

> I read the other day some verses written by an eminent painter which were original and not conventional. The soul always hears an admonition in such lines, let the subject be what it may. The sentiment they instil is of more value than any thought they may contain. To believe your own thought, to believe what is true for you in your private heart is true for all men,—that is genius. Speak your latent conviction, and it shall be the universal sense; for the inmost in due time becomes the outmost,—and our first thought is rendered back to us by the trumpets of the Last Judgment. . . . A man should learn to detect and watch that gleam of light which flashes across his mind from within, more than the lustre of the firmament of bards and sages. Yet he dismisses without notice his thought, because it is his.[23]

Note first the prevalent images informing this paragraph. Emphasis falls overwhelmingly on vision and speech. Emerson begins by reading verses written by a painter, with words created by a maker of images. The very opening of the essay deals with the visual as it coincides with language. This pattern repeats itself when Emerson concludes with the idea of learning to detect, that is, to see as if from the outside, the gleam of light that flashes from within. A flash is something that we might simply see or fail to see, but once we have detected it, it is recognized thought, something we might formulate in language. Both of these statements, in turn, approximate the idea that the inmost should become the outmost when we speak. What is inmost is precisely what is not spoken, and therefore perhaps no more than an image, if that. By wording or speaking the image, inmost becomes outmost. Language is thus linked with representation in a way that the merely visible is not. Vision and speech here are united in the sense that speech posits or represents that which is as yet merely latent or invisible from the outside, a point that bears also on Emerson's repeated injunctions throughout the essay that we do our work. Emerson's other favorite word for work is vocation—the acts through which we make manifest what otherwise was undone or unspoken.[24]

The passage from latent to manifest is also the passage from private to public, but before one can understand how that passage occurs, it is important to note just how Emerson positions himself in order to get underway. In one sense he would seem to be announcing, here at the beginning of an essay that Nietzsche might have titled "How One Becomes What One Is," that he is working well within the Cartesian tradition of subjectivity. For surely that gleam of light flashing across from within is akin to Descartes's natural light, and if Emerson chooses to represent this as a gleam or flash, then it is perhaps simply to underscore the instantaneous nature of the cogito.[25] Emerson thus opens the essay with the inaugural moment of the subject itself, with the whole question of how the self gets started, and he does so at least in part on the Cartesian model, of the auto-foundation or auto-positioning of a subject presenting itself to itself as consciousness. We should remember that the Cartesian subject only knows that he exists, only confirms the cogito, when he pronounces it to himself, and this is very much part of the pattern of Emerson's essay.[26] The visual is exactly that which, paradoxically, is not represented except as spoken. Thought and speech alone constitute the means by which we present ourselves to ourselves, both in the opening paragraph and throughout the essay. In a central passage Emerson tells us that when his genius calls, he "would write on the lintels of the door-post, *Whim*," a word already inscribed with an etymological history that goes back to "wandering with one's eyes." But "whim" is not simply that internal state allowing one to do as one pleases. It is also a word marking that state. Similarly, when Emerson gets around to asking on what precisely are we to ground our reliance, his well-known answer is a "primary wisdom" called "Intuition." Intuition of course means "to look upon," and were that insufficient, it is nothing other than intuition that furnishes Descartes with the originary act of auto-foundation, wherein he formulates his doubt and thereby knows himself to exist.[27] Like the Cartesian subject who poses before himself by speaking himself, the Emersonian subject begins by trying or wanting to be the subject of representation. What is at issue, or seems to be, is why we let others steal from us that unseen gleam or flash with which we might have illuminated ourselves to ourselves in the first place.

Perhaps, however, the question is less how we have lost something than the possibility of obscurity present in the language of flashes and gleams from the beginning. If the visual here marks precisely what remains unrepresented, then it is because the flash from within can illuminate. But it can also eclipse sight; hence the mystical idea of the "black sun." The light by which the invisible becomes visible is itself invisible in this paragraph. This structure also underlies Emerson's emphasis on speaking one's latent thoughts. In both instances the idea is that there is something we are doing all the time—say, thinking—that nonetheless escapes us. We evidently have latent thoughts and regularly send gleams of light abroad from within, but we do not know it; that is, we do not represent it to ourselves, mediate it in graspable form. In this respect, "Self-Reliance" is less an essay about what we do not have than a description of what we do or are all the time without being aware of it. For just this reason, as David Van Leer has persuasively suggested, the obstacles to self-reliance are merely impossibilities. Consistency may be the hobgoblin of little minds, but properly speaking, a self that is a self at all cannot "consist." Consistency simply implies nonbeing.[28] The idea that self-reliance is a version of the self-existence of the self also helps to explain the shift that occurs about midway through the essay, where Emerson moves from his admonitions about why we fail ourselves to more fatalistic statements about what we are. He writes, "I suppose no man can violate his own nature"; or "A character is like an acrostic or Alexandrian stanza;—read it forward, backward, or across, it still spells the same thing."[29]

Let us not forget, however, that we remain acrostics, puzzles to ourselves. The weight of the opening paragraph remains on the latent and the invisible. It could not be otherwise, for as soon as the self is understood as representational consciousness, as the image wherein we appear to and speak ourselves, the largest portion of our activity will become, as Nietzsche concluded again and again, invisible, or unconscious. It is on this basis that Lacan, for example, can insist upon the thread that connects the Cartesian and the Freudian subjects.[30] In any case, the opening paragraph begins in paradox. On the one hand, as long as the subject remains the subject of representation, it is bound to seek after an image of itself. On the other hand, every such desire, be it for the clear and distinct, or for the inmost to become the outmost, proves only the existence of another place where we are not, that is, the place where things are latent, unrepresented, and, it may be in some sense, unrepresentable.

What Emerson sets up, then, in the first paragraph of the essay is, properly speaking, not simply a philosophical self, not simply the centered, transcendental, absolute "I think" of the cogito, but rather a cogito that thinks me—a psychological self divided into the light of representational consciousness and the other of the unconscious.[31] The central interpretive problem of the essay hinges on how one construes Emerson's stance toward this subject that is split between the known and the unknown, the seen and the unseen, the represented and the unrepresentable, which in turn, bears on the matter of self-reliance as the self-evidence of the self. This ambiguity reaches its most intense pitch in the famous sentences following the passage quoted above: "A man should learn to detect and watch that gleam of light which flashes across his mind from within, more than the lustre of the firmament of bards and sages. Yet he dismisses without notice his thought, because it is his. In every work of genius we recognize our own rejected thoughts: they come back to us with a certain alienated majesty."[32] Typically, these lines are read as stating the central problem the essay seeks to solve, and therefore, as an admonition to reappropriate one's rejected thoughts, retrieving them from their alienation in the Other. To do so would be to reclaim all that is latent, unconscious, and invisible into the light of representational consciousness: "Wo Es war, soll Ich werden."

As such, the idea of alienated majesty underpins nearly all readings of the essay as a whole, that is, all of the readings in which the soul of Emersonian individualism takes shape. Do not reject your own thoughts, rely on yourself, on no other, or, as the epigraph has it, "Ne te quaesiveris extra." One might object that when Emerson later complains, "Man is timid and apologetic; he is no longer upright; he dares not say 'I think,' 'I am,'" (270), he would seem to be equating achieved self-reliance with the transcendental auto-foundation of a Cartesian cogito. We may think, and exist, but we dare not *say* it. I want to return to these lines later, but for the moment, it is sufficient to say that read in the light of representational consciousness, the essay has one task: its goal would seem to be to teach us how to become conscious of our latent thoughts by representing them to ourselves, by consciously making them our own and voicing them rather than waiting for them to return through the Other.

Perhaps, then, Emerson is being careless when he gets started in this same paragraph with the words, "I read." And one must wonder why, when Emerson has been so careful from "The American Scholar" onward to distinguish his idea of thinking from the representational conceptualization of modern philosophy, he would now, in his central essay, attempt to rescue a divided subject precisely as the unified subject presenting itself to itself. The very lines, however, that seem to enjoin us to reappropriate our rejected thoughts point in a different direction when we remember that if the only way in which we know ourselves is through a representation of ourselves, that is, by a kind of posing ourselves before ourselves, then alienated majesty comes to define not the problem but the necessary state of affairs from the start. In this respect, alienated majesty marks the primary instance of the self-existence of the self, a description of what we are doing all the time without being conscious of it. There is, however, one key distinction here: in the instance of alienated majesty, one finds the additional suggestion that without the Other, one cannot get started at all. If I did not first read my thoughts in the text of the Other, I would simply have no thoughts of which to be aware. I could hardly be said to exist.

Properly speaking, then, my relation to the Other becomes the inaugural moment of subjectivity, for what Emerson is suggesting in this opening paragraph is that the imperative of self-consciousness, the auto-foundation of the self, always and only occurs in the act of reading the text of the Other. There is no question of short-circuiting alienation, for without exteriorizing itself first, thought necessarily remains latent and invisible. Why, after all, according to Emerson, do we reject our own thoughts in the first place? Simply, "because they are ours," as if one's own thought is, by definition, always rejected, always elsewhere.[33] That is why those thoughts, whether dismissed or repressed, reappear as the thought of or in the work of genius, the work of the Other. If this were all, we would say that alienated majesty is at once the problem and the solution—a problem so long as it remains an unconscious identification with the text of the Other, and a solution insofar as we recognize that Other as ourselves, even if we first need that Other as a medium in which to collect ourselves. Read, however, against "History," Emerson's apparent chagrin in "Self-Reliance" becomes puzzling. Like "History," "Self-Reliance" is very much an essay about becoming ourselves, but the reading process that oriented that project in "History" seems here to have gone awry. In the earlier essay, the emphasis falls on precisely this apparently dialectical process of reading the text of ourselves through the commentary of others, and there is no anxiety on Emerson's part about the question of to whom the thoughts belong. The example is the gothic cathedral which "affirms that it was done by us, and not done by us. Surely it was by man, but we find it not in our man but . . . we put ourselves into the place and state of the builder."[34] Once we have done so, once we have identified ourselves in it, we, too, are builders, both of the cathedral and of ourselves. This is simply to say that it would be impossible to read any work of genius if the thoughts were not ours to begin with, and we discover it experientially. This is why Emerson insists in "History" that "every mind must know the whole lesson for itself,— must go over the whole ground. What it does not see, what it does not live, it will not know" (240). If the lesson were not we ourselves to begin with, then we could not see or live it at all. History would be no more than "a dull book." If it is otherwise, then it is because the text we read is both ours and not ours, just as the thoughts that return to us in alienated majesty belong to us and do not belong to us.[35] In "History," however, the mediations of reading simply "remed[y] the defect of our too great nearness to ourselves." In "Self-Reliance," this remedy would seem to become the illness. We are not too close, but rather too far from ourselves.

Why the reader in "History" should be any less alienated than the one in "Self-Reliance" is not at all clear, and yet, the tone of "Self-Reliance" is unmistakably admonitory, even as its opening paragraph rehearses all that "History" so calmly asserted. In order to understand this difference we need to understand more precisely what Emerson means by reading, and what he means changes somewhat in the space between the two essays. As Emerson remarks toward the close of "History," "I will not now go behind the general statement to explore the reason of this correspondency [between ourselves and what we read]. Let it suffice, that in the light of these two facts, namely, that the mind is One, and that nature is its correlative, history is to be read and written."[36] In short, Emerson has done no more than to state the mimetic nature of the relation between reader and text, without explaining why that relation occurs as it does. Moreover, it can hardly matter to whom the thoughts belong if they all proceed anyway from the One Mind. The first essay would seem to deal with reading that is a kind of reflective mimesis that works on a specular model. History is simply a mirror for us—one we must recognize as such. Such a construction assumes that the task of Emersonian reading remains always to return us to ourselves as a kind of representation, which is, in turn, a representation of the One Mind. Despite the emphasis on an attainable or future self, reading as presented in "History" implies a preexistent self that must simply be brought back to itself, in which case, one would have to ask if Emerson himself were not siding with all of the philosophers from whom elsewhere he wishes to distance himself. Moreover, it is hard to understand why a self that already exists would need the text of the Other in the first place, why such a subject would subject itself in this way.

I think Emerson himself raises precisely these questions at the close of "History." Having steadily asserted that history is nothing but a mirror, he abruptly asks, "Is there somewhat overweening in this claim? Then I reject all I have written, for what is the use of pretending to know what we know not? But it is the fault of our rhetoric that we cannot strongly state one fact without seeming to belie some other. I hold our actual knowledge very cheap" (256). Emerson's strategy here is to shift the frame of reference, to remind us that even as we read history, we read his essay, and that as such, we have been engaged in an active interpretive and self-creative encounter with his text. That encounter may be mimetic insofar as we find ourselves in that text, but it is before all of that, rhetorical: if we have found ourselves in the mirror of Emerson's text, then it is because his rhetoric has persuaded us to do so, not because we have "understood" the essay and, thereby, ourselves. In this sense, we do not appear before we read, any more than the meaning of the text appears after we read; we are constituted in our relation to it. As the passage jolts the reader back to the realization that he or she does not finally know what the text means, the register of meaning is itself made problematic, and doubly so, because Emerson himself claims not to know what he means. Whose thoughts would here be emerging? Mine? The text's? These questions cannot be answered, because in point of fact, no thoughts are emerging at all, thus suspending the priority of both text and reader. Emerson's rhetorical punctuation of what he calls "fact," which is nothing other than what we conceive our own interpretation to be, cancels any kind of representational or mimetic logic, or at least calls it into question, for as the last sentence of the passage indicates, rhetoric exceeds and betrays representation. The moment that it states a fact, represents something, it is wrong. Its strength is its very slipperiness and changeability. Not only, however, is it changeable but also it operates independently of any "message" it may convey, even when that message seems to mime the reader. In a sense, rhetoric as here conceived does no more than to operate a passage, one without origin or destination. This suggests that Emersonian reading consists less in the stability of a specular mimetic relation and more in the uncertain and almost unspecifiable draw of rhetoric itself, a draw in which it is no longer quite clear whether meaning resides in the text, in the reader, or in both and neither.

Such issues reorient Emerson in "Self-Reliance." When our thoughts come back to us with alienated majesty, when "we are forced to take with shame our own opinion from another,"[37] we do not speak our latent conviction, another speaks it for us, speaks us. And why is this the case? Oddly enough, because the Other always seems to mean more than we do. No sooner does Emerson report that our thoughts return with alienated majesty than he adds, "Great works of art have no more affecting lesson for us than this. They teach us to abide by our spontaneous impression with good-humored inflexibility then most when the whole cry of voices is on the other side. Else, tomorrow a stranger will say with masterly good sense precisely what we have thought and felt all the time" (259). Given the position of the first sentence, the most affecting lesson may be that of alienated majesty, or it may be the apparent lesson of self-reliance: abide by your spontaneous impression. In fact, there is no difference between the two. We are to abide specifically by our impression, that is, by what im-presses us, what comes back or on to us from the outside, and yet, as the passage continues, that "outside" escapes thematization and so cannot strictly speaking be named. If that impression differs from all of the voices "on the other side," then it is perhaps because those voices, unlike the "rhetoric" at the close of "History," can be located somewhere and convey a thought. But we have already been told that the sentiment that a text instills is more important than any thought it might contain, which is perhaps just another way of saying that our spontaneous impression is precisely a matter of feeling, of affect. For this reason the lesson of which Emerson speaks is "affecting." It is what draws us to it, influences us, disposes us in a certain way, and attaches us to it, without, in the least voicing itself as a particular thought, as a representation. In one sense, this passage anticipates the open question between truth and love that Emerson raises at the close of "Intellect." Reading is no longer a specular or mimetic circuit wherein we encounter the truth, but rather it is a matter of being affected by an Other. Here that affect is no longer grounded by the mythical authority of the One Mind. If we are attracted to the work of art, then it is not because that work presents us with a truth, or represents the One Mind, but rather because the work seems to exert a kind of power over us, to affect us in this way. It draws us into a process that can no longer be assimilated to a specular or mimetic model, unless of course we wish to call reading affective mimesis. In what does such a process consist? Nothing other than identification. What we think and feel all along, the Other thinks and feels all along, and it is no accident that this identification proceeds through how the Other "speaks." The implication is that the rhetorical effects of the text, of its speaking, are precisely affective. Conversely, it implicates affect itself as rhetorical effect. We are bound to the text, identified by and in it, because we desire it, and we desire it because of its rhetorical power over us. It is just this strange power that fuels Emerson's admonitory tone at the opening of "Self-Reliance."

But why does this Other affect me? What makes me desire it, or, to use Emerson's word, receptive to it in the first place? How does it achieve rhetorical power over me? I am not sure these questions can be answered at this point. Indeed, we are left in the opening paragraph of "Self-Reliance" with anything but the certainty of clear and distinct ideas. On the one hand, Emerson would seem to want us to learn to make the latent manifest, the invisible visible, but on the other hand, the whole notion of affectivity, which is the very suggestibility or receptivity that Emerson everywhere emphasizes, resists the sort of reappropriation implied in the passage from invisible to visible or spoken. Rhetoric and affectivity consistently cancel representational meaning in Emerson. I think that this is a genuine impasse in much of his work, first because a purely rhetorical reading, independent of any thematic "content" would be impossible, but also because Emerson himself seems to want his readers to do a great many things at once, specifically in the sense of the transitional activities I mentioned earlier. The actual workings of an Emersonian essay consistently, if one can say so, evade the straightforward exposition of discursive thought. That evasion is, as I have been suggesting, their central dynamic. Yet if there is nothing but such a dynamic, then the essays become unreadable. To understand the rhetorical maneuvers within any given essay more fully, then, would itself involve a kind of detour through an Other, that is, a reflection through a discourse that lies outside of the Emersonian essay itself. Without this detour, we would have nothing but the oscillations of our own encounter with the text in a close reading that would remain in constant and, therefore, incomprehensible transition.

Chapter 3 · · ·

Reading Transference

> *A layman... will feel that he is being asked to believe in magic. And he will not be so very wrong, for the words which we use in our everyday speech are nothing other than watered-down magic.*
> —Freud, "Psychical or Mental Treatment"

From Repetition to Remembering

Once I introduce the idea of affect, and affect particularly as a rhetorical effect, I am talking about reading as a form of transference. Reading is not simply a psychological question, but quite specifically a psychoanalytic one. It is not solely a matter of our interpretation of the text but also of our transference to that text, our receptivity to it and its persuasive powers. As is well known, Freud defined transference most simply as "an intense emotional relationship" with the physician that reproduces past relationships.[1] Leaving aside for the moment the whole question of pastness, this affective relation is modeled on a rhetorical form, for as Freud himself acknowledged, affects behave "as though they were written on a page by themselves which would not take any other script." Transferences are "clichés," "new editions."[2] Transference is our characteristic way of putting things, our psychological rhetoric, or, we might say in the case of Emerson's text, our predisposition to find our alienated thoughts in a particular way within the lines of the other. But to say that we form a transference to a text raises a number of problems and questions. In the first place, it involves a distinction not usually brought to bear in applied psychoanalysis. Nearly all psychoanalytic approaches to literature, or to any other nonanalytic object, rely on the reader as interpreter; the reader is in the position of analyst and treats the text as if it contained the contents of the unconscious, be it that of the writer or of the text itself.[3] But as Shoshana Felman has suggested, the analogy between reader and analyst holds good only if one views interpretation as the sole activity of the reader or analyst. No psychoanalysis proceeds in this way, and neither does any literary reading. We are, as Felman points out, also in the place of the patient vis-à-vis the text because it has a certain authority over us that elicits interpretation in the first place: we view the text "as the very place where meaning, and knowledge of meaning, reside."[4] This would be the "relation of transference," the activity of interpretation itself, rather than the content of that interpretation. Analysts may object that one's transference to the text is meaningless, because the text, now in the role of the analyst, cannot interpret that transference. Moreover, it would be absurd to speak of a text forming a countertransference to a reader. Since countertransference is one of the analyst's chief tools in arriving at interpretations, this lack becomes a significant problem. In an analogical sense, however, we might say that the text's resistance to being read constitutes a form of countertransference. Perhaps more to the point, the problem simply evaporates when we remember that Lacan in particular situates countertransference at the level of the imaginary, and therefore as incidental to the practice and aim of the analysis.[5] The first objection, however, that the text cannot interpret our transference, is the very notion that Emerson's text everywhere repudiates. What the text can or cannot do in this respect would depend entirely on our sense of what constitutes transference. I would suggest that Emersonian reading develops in such a way that we can speak of a process that occurs in the reader, a process which is itself the meaning. Reading or transference themselves become measures of the text's interpretation of its reader. This is just Emerson's point in "History" when he writes that we are to esteem ourselves the text, and books the commentary.

The shift from the interpretive to the transferential relation in reading raises the second difficulty in asserting that the reader forms a transference to the text. The concept of transference itself is one of the most disputed grounds of psychoanalysis and has been so from the beginning. In fact, there is not one concept of transference, but many. And although psychoanalysis distinguishes itself from all other forms of psychotherapy through its insistence on the analysis of the transference, the analysis of the transference itself aims at different goals.[6] In order to understand the particularities of the transference elicited by Emerson's text, it is necessary first to situate it as precisely as possible within a strictly psychoanalytic construction of transference and, perhaps more importantly, to differentiate it from this. As Jane Gallop suggests, any psychoanalytic "reading" of a literary text is merely analogical. Even if we move from the interpretive to the transferential dimensions of literary analysis, from thematics to rhetoric, our reading can only "analyze something like a 'transference' at play between reader and text, but it would have to be careful to attend to the specificity of that something, to the specific dynamic of the relation of reading."[7]

Historically, before it became a matter of analytic technique, "transference" first designated the kind of displacement that occurs in dreams. Indeed, all forms of transference, as it was eventually conceptualized, involve displacement.[8] Insofar as it is a displacement, transference applies not only to the analytic situation but also to all of affective life, because affect and idea or representation (*Vorstellung*) regularly sever themselves from each other and take different psychic paths. Ideas are repressed, but never affects. They display themselves with an unwished for, and often inexplicable, exactitude, and never so much as when they have been severed from an idea or representation that has undergone repression. According to Freud, it is just such a splitting between affect and idea that gives rise to the transference in analysis in the first place. Once severed from the idea to which they were originally attached, affects readily displace themselves onto any available object, however inappropriately. It is for this reason that Freud insists transference is primarily "a bit of repetition" (161).

It is just this idea of repetition that doubles back to make of transference something very complex in Emerson's text, but it is nonetheless the place to begin. In the 1914 paper, "Further Recommendations in the Technique of Psychoanalysis: Recollection, Repetition and Working Through," Freud begins with a brief description of various types of remembering and forgetting and reminds the reader that from its inception, psychoanalysis has aimed at enabling the patient to remember. But, he writes, "The patient *remembers* nothing of what is forgotten and repressed . . . he expresses it in *action*. He reproduces it not in his memory but in his behaviour; he *repeats* it, without of course knowing that he is repeating it."[9] In short, the repetition of acting out, which is always fueled by a wish, is simply a failure to represent our thoughts to ourselves. The idea to which the affect was once attached has been repressed, but the affect appears in the present, attaching itself to any available representation, and it does so with no distance on itself. Affect, in other words, is always mobile, whereas the repressed is fixed; hence the statement that the unconscious is timeless, which may be understood in two distinct ways. On the one hand, the repressed representation ignores time and specifically its passage; it persists, unchanged and unchanging, fueling the affect. On the other hand, the affect itself lies outside of time, persisting beyond every successive representation to which it is attached.

The chief instance of such unconscious repetition is, of course, the transference as it appears in analysis. Once in the throes of the transference, the patient relives his past affective relationships, now in relation to the analyst, and the forgetting is twofold. Not only does the patient forget the past affective experience and the representation to which it was attached but also he or she does so by forgetting the analyst as well. The patient immediately effects his desires, regardless, as Freud says, "of the reality of the situation," and all the more so when the analyst conceals himself as a real Other in the name of analytic neutrality (114). What is acted out in the transference is felt and experienced in the present without any mediation or consciousness of the experience as a representation or repetition. The patient, as it were, mimes himself without realizing that this is what he is doing. It is this very mimesis or repetition that makes of transference at once the greatest obstacle to the analysis, a trenchant form of resistance, and simultaneously the chief weapon in the analyst's arsenal.[10] Insofar as the transference constitutes "a bit of repetition," it allows the patient to substitute action for self-representation, but since the forgotten past would otherwise have no representation at all, the transference also serves as the only available means through which the patient or the analyst has access to that past.

Freud fully believed that with the proper handling of the transference, which is precisely the negotiation of its double nature as resistance and representation, remembering would replace repetition; affect would be rejoined with the once-repressed idea or representation thus depriving the affect of its uncanny power in the present. First and foremost, the analyst is to use the transference as its own evidence, that is, as a means by which to point out to the patient all of the ways in which he resists remembering. By bringing an affect into the "playground" of the transference, the patient would exhibit—act out—everything he failed to remember, and this exhibition would constitute the chief form of resistance to the analysis. At the same time, all that remains inaccessible to the patient as he enacts his passions in the immediate scene is precisely "seen" by the analyst, who then returns it, represents it, to the patient in a distanced and therefore accessible form. This is why Freud insists elsewhere, in the very language of specular representation, that the analyst "should be impenetrable to the patient, and, like a mirror, reflect nothing but what is shown to him."[11] As the patient looks into the mirror at his own representation, repetition becomes remembering. This moment also anticipates the dissolution of the transference, for once the patient experiences his affects and rejoins them with the original representation to which they were attached, he understands that his affects are readily transferable to this or that object. The very mobility of his own desires portends a consequent devaluing of the object. As Philip Rieff writes in what is a rather Emersonian mode, "the therapy of all therapies, the secret of all secrets, the interpretation of all interpretation, in Freud, is not to attach oneself exclusively or too passionately to any one particular meaning, or object."[12] This is what Freudian transference teaches, and its goal is the reclaiming of energies bound to the past for service in the present, or, as Freud puts it, "the eventual independence of the patient."[13]

If this version encompassed transference, then one could readily produce a reading of "Self-Reliance." Like Freud, Emerson begins with the idea that transference is something that occurs all the time. In "History" this displacement is benign. It is similar to what occurs in the Lacanian mirror stage; the reader or the child anticipates a mastery he may not yet possess through what is no more than a projected image. So, too, in the dynamic of alienated majesty with the difference that Emerson emphasizes the danger of taking the image for the reality. The text, like the physician in Freud's essay, simply acts as a mirror which the reader first mistakes for a real, external image. To reject one's thoughts is to repress them, and the affect once tied to them now displaces itself onto "great works" in which we seem to see ourselves, but to see ourselves as if captured or alienated in the Other. Our identification in the text no longer involves the simple recognition of ourselves in the Other, but rather a sense that our thoughts have been stolen or appropriated. The text always means more than we do; it is, as Lacan says of the analyst, "the one supposed to know." Felman has pointed out that the stance in relation to the one supposed to know comes quite close to the ways in which readers often approach texts. Just as the patient conveys a message to the analyst, the meaning of which he assumes the analyst already possesses, so, too, the reader makes an interpretation of the text, formulates thoughts he takes to be "in" the text and determinative of the interpretation. Alienation remains the dominant experience; the self remains the same.

This relation between text and reader is what Emerson insistently rejects and works against as illusory. In the course of what in analysis is called "working through," the reader would come to realize that all interpretations come, ultimately, not from the text at all but from him- or herself. This is the consistent pattern throughout "History," where one is to find oneself in history and, up to a point, throughout "Self-Reliance." In the latter essay, transference is simply any attachment one has to anything construed as external authority. Thus our energies are overinvested in representations and institutions dead to us because we no longer recognize ourselves in them: "We first share in the life by which things exist, and afterwards see them as appearances in nature, and forget that we have shared in their cause" (269). In this way, all of our attachments to these external representatives of what was once internal authority prevent us from a free use of energy in the present. We live, suggests Emerson, as if we had a neurotic attachment to the past. It is as if we enact a script written by someone else without being conscious that this is what we are doing. We allow ourselves to be spoken by someone else, without knowing it, or we simply repeat ourselves unthinkingly.

From a psychoanalytic perspective, when we fail to recognize the mirror as such, rather than the image projected into it, transference is occurring, but it remains invisible. In a certain respect, Emerson's mode of overcoming such a situation takes the same path as the handling of the transference in Freud. Rhetorically, his first move is to point to all of the obstacles, both internal and external, that prevent us from knowing why it is that we behave as we do. Consistency, conformity, imitation—these are the Emersonian demons, and the very forces at work in the transference conceived as resistance. What is transference if not our consistency, our characteristic way of putting things? We then behave as if this way of putting things has a kind of external necessity, that is, as if our affective life came as a directive from without, be it from "great works," dead institutions, past ways of acting, or family ties. Hence we conform to their dictates without any thought whatsoever, that is, without any recognition that those dictates are our own. We imitate ourselves, or at least our past selves, as it were. We repeat ourselves without hearing what we are saying, or worse still, we become as Emerson has it in "The American Scholar," "the parrot of other men's thinking."[14] Our consistency and conformity thus become forms of unwitting transference to authority, which, as in Freud, nullifies any free or creative use of ourselves in the present.

Emerson is quite clear about this dynamic throughout "Self-Reliance." Here is a characteristic example:

> The objection to conforming to usages that have become dead to you is, that it scatters your force. It loses your time and blurs the impression of your character. If you maintain a dead church, contribute to a dead Bible-society, vote with a great party either for the government or against it, spread your table like base housekeepers,—under all these screens I have difficulty to detect the precise man you are. And, of course, so much force is withdrawn from your proper life.[15]

What does this passage describe if not Freudian transference, that "cliché or stereotype" that "perpetually repeats and reproduces itself as life goes on,"[16] precluding any kind of change? In analytic terms, one can say that "dead usages" are nothing but buried attachments, buried because we hardly recognize what we are doing half of the time. We are living through or in what Cavell calls our "attained selves." Such selves determine the choices we make in the present, but they are choices nonetheless, dictated by earlier, forgotten desires. By pointing them out, Emerson would be lifting our resistance to understanding the pastness of such attachments, thereby detaching us from them. With each attachment relinquished would come a surge of what Emerson calls "proper force," our own force or power to think and act with relative freedom. Our affects, once tied to dead usages, attain the mobility of which they are capable. In this respect, Emerson would seem to share the therapeutic aim of Freudian psychoanalysis.

In this first approach, one might simply say that "Self-Reliance" is an essay that proleptically talks about transference, about attachment to supposedly external authority, and does so in order to make one more oneself, to free one from that mistaken authority. None of this, however, would explain why anyone would be motivated to change simply by reading Emerson's text, any more than an analyst discussing transference with a patient would compel change. We would still need an explanation of how we move toward our "unattained but attainable" selves; in short, thus far, we are leaving out our transference to Emerson's text. Such an explanation would shift the focus from what the text says to our transference to it. But even then, as long as we conceive of transference solely as the mere repetition or making manifest of the past, we will not understand how the text or the analyst lay hold of their illusory power to interpret us from the start. Part of the difficulty stems from a dual ambivalence in Freud's own "handling of the transference." In the first place, however necessary it may be, transference remains for Freud primarily a stumbling block, one that must be surmounted and replaced by narrative interpretation. We are not to repeat or mime our former affective ties, but to remember them, which means narrating the past, as past, from the vantage point of the present. Mimesis must give way to diegesis, and in this transition, the centrality of the transference itself is forgotten. This particular forgetting in turn allows Freud consistently to locate the analyst outside of the field of transference, thus eliding its relational nature. Despite the fact that transference is nothing other than an intense emotional "relationship," that relationship is for Freud unidirectional. The patient may experience all kinds of affects in relation to the physician, but the physician is to remain entirely neutral and unaffected.[17] Transferences thus become, in Freud's papers on technique, objects merely observed by the analyst, which can then be put into words by that observing analyst.[18] Interpretation should triumph over transference, but this does not answer the question of how analysis compels change.

All of this is well known about Freud's technique, and it amounts to nothing more than the truism that from a theoretical perspective, Freud tends to view the transference in positivistic and representational terms. Hence the emphasis on repetition of some past event, and the possibility of re-presenting it as memory, beyond the vicissitudes of blind repetition. This particular aspect in the Freudian construction of transference is itself part of the Cartesian dynamic that surfaces at the opening of "Self-Reliance." According to Descartes, we must put into words what we are doing; we must speak the invisible flash or gleam wherein consciousness gets started, and this speech is a monologue. Just as we must speak the cogito to get started, so, too, in analysis, we must remember, speak, and narrativize our repetitions or enactments of the past, of precisely that which is already there. Since the physician acts as no more than a mirror, analytic speech comes to be very close to monologue, despite the fact that there are two people in the room. In this speech, as in the Cartesian formulation, we are narrating no more than what is already there, a self that already exists, without knowing it, or in Freudian terms an unconscious that exists without our knowing it. In the simplest sense, the Cartesian cogito and the Freudian transference share a grounding in the belief that speech re-presents something, be it that flash or gleam of consciousness itself, or buried and unconscious wishes from the past—everything already there. Hence, the fact of relationship itself is little more than incidental.

This construction returns us to the interpretation of alienated majesty in which the Other of the text simply represents to us our alienated thoughts, and indeed, as long as we think of Emerson's text as telling us about our transferences to authority, to what Freud calls the third person of the transference, we are still well within the Cartesian and Freudian matrices of transference. This, as I suggested earlier, is in fact the way in which "Self-Reliance" is usually read: as a call to return everything to the light of representational consciousness. We need merely become conscious of those thoughts we already have as our own to "be" self-reliant. We are then conceiving the text as having thoughts, whether of its own, or ours in alienated form. As readers ourselves, to reappropriate these latent thoughts, we simply need to form an interpretation, which finally is nothing other than a representation of thought. The text, like the analyst, would provide the necessary mirror in which we would find our images, only to be dispensed with once we have grasped the image. Our unattained selves would really be nothing other than a once-attained self, now forgotten. The immediate relation between reader and text is ignored. We are still left without any explanation as to how Emerson might induce a reader to change, despite the blatantly motivational rhetoric of the essay.

If the representational nature of Freudian transference leaves the analyst outside of its field, and leaves open more questions than it can answer in relation to Emerson's text, then it nonetheless remains important in two senses. Not only does the representational logic of Freud's thought underpin most readings of "Self-

Reliance" but also, and even more to the point, it reminds us that transference is divided into two moments at every point: it is at once *both* a passionate enactment and the opportunity for interpretation. Freud, of course, privileges the interpretive moment, all but eclipsing the centrality of enactment, as have most schools of psychoanalysis until quite recently. Why else is it called the "talking cure" unless talking itself can be conceived as enactment rather than representation? And yet, what we might call the first moment of the transference, that exhibition or feeling of all that remains before or beyond representation, characterizes nearly every subsequent formulation of the transference from Winnicott to Lacan.[19] Freud tends to think of this side of the transference as affective; as he himself knew, mere recounting, without affect, effects no change.[20]

In fact, it is just this immediate tie that compels the patient to accept the analyst's constructions and interpretations at all. The immediacy of the felt passion in the transference situation, the experiential dimension of it, is the element that compels belief on the part of the patient. As Freud writes, albeit somewhat puzzlingly at the close of "The Dynamics of the Transference," "transference-manifestations . . . and only they, render the invaluable service of making the patient's buried and forgotten love-emotion actual and manifest; for in the last resort no one can be slain *in absentia* or *in effigie.*"[21] By this, I take Freud to mean that all of the talking in the world will not change one's mind or one's characteristic way of putting things. There must be a particular kind of talking. In order for the patient to slay old affective or ideational patterns, first those patterns must be made manifest in experience, which, in the analytic situation, manifest themselves nowhere else than in a certain kind of speech. For this speech, the Other is no longer *in absentia*, but present, here, in the person of the analyst. In this sense, analytic speech is, as Lacan understood very well, a matter of address rather than representation. It performs rather than represents. If such speech represents anything, then it is the speaking subject's relation to the Other, experienced in all of its immediacy. It is not just a matter of the analyst being able to grasp, as if from outside, what otherwise remained forgotten and unrepresented, but rather, above all, a matter of the patient's own conviction wrought from the relational experiences that occur in the analysis itself. This is why an interpretation afield of the patient's transference at any given moment simply has no effect. Transference is, before and beyond all else, an experiential state for the patient, a kind of enactment or mimesis of the self, even if in speech, with no time for reflection or mediation. It is, in short, a state that everywhere resists representation or symbolic reintegration.

It is this dimension of the Freudian transference, rather than the mediations of narrative, that becomes central in Emerson. His text repeatedly attempts to represent this state, a kind of living as he puts it, "in the thousand-eyed present,"[22] as the ideal. Perhaps the most famous passage occurs in the second half of "Self-Reliance" when Emerson writes:

> Man is timid and apologetic; he is no longer upright; he dares not say "I think," "I am," but quotes some saint or sage. He is ashamed before the blade of grass or the blowing rose. These roses under my window make no reference to former roses or to better ones; they are for what they are; they exist with God to-day. There is no time to them. There is simply the rose. . . . But man postpones or remembers; he does not live in the present, but with reverted eye laments the past. (270)

Significantly, the passage begins where the essay itself begins, but with a difference. As in the opening paragraph, Emerson seems quite literally to be attempting to engage us in the cogito itself by pointing out that we have not achieved it. And yet, here, he calls into question precisely that possibility, as if it were not he but we who still yearn after a self present to itself in the Cartesian mode; hence, in a simple sense, the quotation marks around the statement of the cogito. By eliding the "therefore" of the cogito, Emerson reminds his readers that Cartesian thinking is not the same as being, and suggests as well that thinking and being are not causally connected. For Emerson, I do not think and therefore come into being. The moments are presented serially—I think, I am, I think, I am—which is just another way of saying that representational consciousness and unmediated existence must remain mutually exclusive. This perhaps helps to explain further why Emerson places his revision of the cogito in quotation marks, and then reminds us that we fail to say this precisely because we prefer to quote some saint or sage. The suggestion is perhaps that in confiding ourselves to the cogito at all, to the light of representational consciousness, we are always already lost in quotation without even knowing it. The alternative is not between the apparent instantaneity of the cogito and quotation, since there is no difference between them. The real alternative is the rose, which never thinks because it lives in an eternal present.

This of course is the present of the transference itself, that enactment where I always fail to remember or to postpone. I act with an immediacy that reduces everything to the present moment; this is an immediacy exclusive of representational thinking. It is important, however, that in figuring this state, Emerson opposes it to the human. Roses may simply exist, but we are not roses, any more than we are those "babes," "brutes," or "boys who are sure of a supper" that exemplify self-reliance at the opening of the essay. This is perhaps Emerson's way of suggesting that the kind of immediacy or self-evidency that he wishes to engender in the reader constitutes itself not prior to any alienation in the other, but after it, that is, after our encounter with the other. As in "History," the act of reading lifts one out of some prereflective chronology and into the constructions of character. We are not, for example, natural roses, but the experience of engaging Emerson's figure of the rose may cause us to experience the moment of immediacy the rose embodies. In this sense, something occurs within or because of the reading process itself, which is nothing other than our relation or transference to the text.

From Remembering to Repetition: Transference as Performativity

It still remains to examine the nature of this reading process, of the type of transference it entails. As I have been suggesting, however, Freud cannot do much to elucidate the matter because he theorizes transference itself primarily as a problem to be overcome. By contrast, Lacan, for example, by insisting that transference is first and foremost an address, underscores the relational nature of the transference, but in such a way that it becomes difficult to speak of the subjects of the relation.[23] Transference becomes a kind of groundless relation in which neither patient nor analyst exists as a substantial subject, so that eventually transference must run up against the register of the real, of all that remains and insists both before and after, and in spite of, symbolization. The interpretive moment of the transference is subsumed by an endless communication of communication, say a repetition compulsion without content, that itself enacts both patient and analyst.[24] Indeed, it is Lacan who most pointedly reconfigures the interpretive and the enacted moments of the transference by reversing their priority. We might say that the Lacanian subject begins where the Freudian subject ends, and arrives, again and again, where the Freudian subject began. The representational nature of Freudian remembering is the departure for the Lacanian subject, and something much more like the endless displacements of Freudian repetition characterize that subject's endpoint.[25]

The Lacanian concept of the real helps to clarify the very sorts of paradoxes so resistant to discursive explanation on their own ground that we find at the outset of "Self-Reliance." But Emerson, in his turn, puts a focus on this rather resistant idea. The point of theory, in this case psychoanalytic, is not to explain the facts of the text, but rather to solve the problems generated by facticity, here Emerson's resistance to being read. Conversely, that very resistance itself points to the contingency of a theory that might have seemed explanatory. We might just as well speak of an Emersonian theory of Lacan as of a Lacanian reading of Emerson. It is not a matter of laying a Lacanian grid across the lines of Emerson's essays, but perhaps rather of locating various points of intersection. The central intersection occurs in what Emerson calls "reading," and what Lacan calls "the real."

In order to understand more clearly what Emerson attempts to do for a reader, let us return to the idea of alienated majesty and the problem of transference. On the one hand, Emerson seems to want to say that this alienation is a necessary stage along the way, that we never recognize our thoughts, except by seeing them first in the Other. Insofar as one agrees with the statement, it becomes recursive. Emerson is no longer describing what has happened elsewhere and many times before, but instead what happens now, as one reads the text. Emerson's text contains one's thoughts. In the simplest sense, this is part of our transference to his text, but there is more to it. What happens rhetorically is not so much that we are left in alienated agreement, but rather that we are thrown into an inchoate longing to speak our own thoughts before the Other does. I call this longing "inchoate" because by definition the thoughts about which Emerson speaks are thoughts we have neither spoken nor thought at all. They are no more than flashes and gleams yet to come. In this respect, the recognition of our thoughts is the least of the tasks performed by the text.

By this logic, the transference to Emerson's text takes us into the future rather than into re-presentation. This is just the way in which Lacan, in his later stages, understands the nature and purpose of transference. He insists that returning to the subject his own image in any form whatsoever no longer dealienates the subject but constitutes an error. This is "to make of analysis the antechamber of madness." Instead, "that the subject come to recognize and name his desire, that is the efficacious action of analysis," and, we can add, the efficacious action of Emersonian reading as well.[26] As the goal of the analysis becomes to teach the patient to desire, not this or that particular object, but simply to desire, desire now becomes what the analyst is to mirror back to the patient. No longer an identical image, nor the omniscient site of knowledge, nor even a displacement of the symbolic itself, the analyst must give to the patient only that which he does not have: his lack, his desire. (Whose? It is on just this question that desire hinges.) He is to be an empty mirror, showing the patient only his own projected lack or desire, which, in terms of reading is no longer construed as discursive understanding, but the foreclosure of all self-consciousness because it involves a moment never presentable to consciousness as such. The clearest way to formulate this shift is perhaps to say that we are no longer to desire *what* the Other has but to desire *as* he desires, that is, to desire the Other's desire. It is important to note that this is by no means the sort of identification Lacan tirelessly denounced as underpinning American ego psychology, a denunciation, incidentally, that has made it virtually impossible to understand the centrality of identificatory processes in Lacan. Indeed, identification is still at work here, but not in the Freudian mode that constitutes identification as a tie to an object allowing us to appropriate as our own the qualities of that object. The difference can be understood as that between imaginary and symbolic identification. Žižek helpfully delineates these two types of identification: "In imaginary identification we imitate the other at the level of resemblance—we identify ourselves with the image of the other inasmuch as we are 'like him', while in symbolic identification we identify ourselves with the other precisely at a point at which he is inimitable, at the point which eludes resemblance."[27] Once this is the case, the analyst can no longer be the object of desire from whom the patient demands something, because the analyst, precisely as eluding resemblance, exists only as an absence. This would be what Lacan variously calls the *objet a*, the cause of desire, or the "thing" that elicits our desire in an identificatory form. If this type of identification rests on just that point which is inimitable, then it is because desire can only be figured as a lack, as a kind of perpetual displacement: a place we can never occupy as such. We learn, in short, to desire as an Other; while desire is what makes us Other from ourselves. We are not imitating, because there is nothing to imitate. The goal of this second type of identification is to teach one to appropriate this place or cause as one's own, to teach one, paradoxically, to become one's own cause.

Indeed, the lack presented in and as desire leads only to paradox. If our mistake in imaginary identification is the failure to see that the Other has nothing to return, then we nonetheless cannot get started without that mistake. It is not simply a matter of dialectically reappropriating our alienated thoughts from the Other, because the Other has no knowledge, anymore than we do. Nor could it be, as Freud insisted, the reappropriation of unconscious repetition of demand through narrative remembering, for in a sense, we have nothing to remember. Our identification with the Other exists before we do, and yet, it is we who make this identification in a single stroke. In this respect, even if we were to recognize our illusion, the illusion of the transference, of the Other's knowledge, it cannot be bypassed; it is written into the very structure of the relation. This is why Lacan insists again and again that "truth arises from misrecognition." More pointedly, we might say that truth is misrecognition, if not madness, and nothing but. As soon as alienation gives way to desire, the very foundation of the subject is revealed to rest on nothing, on an absence within the self and within the Other, so that properly speaking, we are not dealing with subjects here, with some underlying substance, but instead with groundless subjects, which are no more than a relation.

In many respects, psychoanalysis has always known this unsettling fact about the subject to which it gives rise, even if ignoring the consequences for the subject. Winnicott's transitional space, for example, is one in which we are speaking only of relation because the question, "Did I find this, or did I create it?" must never be confronted. At this stage, the baby or toddler neither opposes objects as a distinct and separate subject, nor lives the hallucination that it has created the world. As Winnicott insists, transitional phenomena are irreducibly paradoxical, and it is just this quality that must be fostered. In some sense, Winnicott wants to locate this experience at a developmentally early time, and so as an experience that will be superseded. But since transitional space is the equivalent to the potential space of an analysis, and since it is ancestor also to cultural space, transitional experience not only underlies later developmental stages but also characterizes full maturity.[28] I use Winnicott here as a main example, but his thinking on transitional phenomena orients the way in which most object-relations psychology, from Klein through Mitchell, understands relation at all.[29]

The centerpiece of transitional experience, at whatever developmental stage, is precisely the kind of absence or lack figured by Lacanian desire. This desire, or what Emerson variously calls our "unattainable self," "genius," "whim," "Intuition," "power," "transition," and "self-reliance," would be the experience of lack as such, the experience of a self without preconditions. The real question, of course, is how the text or the analysis enables one to experience such a thing in the first place. A solution, in both Lacan and Emerson, is to clear away the interference of the imaginary in order that desire may appear. We would no longer beg another's opinion, nor any other thing, for that matter. For Lacan, the analyst would encourage this shift by refusing any identificatory gestures on the part of the patient by remaining an "empty" mirror, a paradoxical idea indeed when we remember that a mirror devoid of any content would be imperceptible, if not an impossible concept altogether. The impossibility of conceptualizing this activity is appropriate, however, because pragmatically this simply means that the analyst is to thwart specular or representational understanding, leaving the patient with the sense, perhaps ineffable, of some inexplicable gap in the Other itself. As a result, the patient creates a fantasy, designed explicitly as a screen concealing the inconsistency in the Other.[30] The fantasy thus appears as an answer "to the unbearable enigma of the desire of the Other, of the lack in the Other; . . . it is at the same time fantasy itself which, so to speak, provides the co-ordinates of our desire—which constructs the frame enabling us to desire."[31] If the desire of the Other is unbearable, it is because it would reveal to us our very groundlessness, itself an unrepresentable experience. The trick would be for the patient to understand that it is not the fantasy *itself* that matters, but rather that the fantasy conceals precisely nothing and merely structures desire. This is called "traversing the fantasy," and it is by no means the end of fantasy. Lacan consistently maintains that beyond fantasy is simply drive, that inhuman real beyond which we cannot go. Traversing the fantasy thus stops short of eradicating fantasy; the crossing is not an act of interpretation that does away with fantasy, which indeed cannot be done away with at all, but rather, the experience of the fact that desire is suspended over nothing, desires nothing.

In Emerson, a similar process begins as the refusal to generate any message sufficient for the reader to be able to identify with it in an imaginary form. Imaginary identification would be what Emerson refers to throughout "Self-Reliance" as "imitation." Read against Lacan, the famous statement, "imitation is suicide," is not simply hyperbole but a statement of fact. Imitation would be just that act wherein I alienate myself in the Other, that moment at which I believe that the Other has it and I do not, so that I disappear, as it were, captured inescapably in the Other. Emerson marks the shift from imitation to desire in the passage quoted above regarding the way our allegiance to dead usages scatters our forces. He concludes, "Under all these screens *I* have difficulty to detect the precise man you are [emphasis added],"[32] as if the very reason we are to give up such allegiances is for the benefit of his desire. I say desire rather than demand, because Emerson does not say what precise man we are to be. He does not offer a model for us to imitate, here or, notoriously, anywhere in the entire essay. It is a critical truism that Emerson defines self-reliance only negatively, and perhaps now we are in a position to understand why. He tells us what not to be or do without providing alternatives, as if his only purpose is to remind us that he wants something different than we want. But in point of fact, we do not know what Emerson wants us to be, and in Lacanian terms, what he wants matters least. The point is that the text wants something, that it offers up instances not of what is desirable, but of desirousness itself, and it can only do so by evading all positively determined representation. The reader, then, unable to imitate any model, comes instead to consist in an identificatory relation or a stance adopted relative to the sheer negativity of the Other's desire, such that the reader can appropriate desire itself as his or her own, which is to say him- or herself as Other.

This is just the gesture we find at the close of "History" as well, when Emerson reminds us that we do not know what he means because he can always reject anything he has said, negate any message we think we have understood. We need his text to recognize our thoughts, but not because of the thoughts the text itself may contain. Finally, our thoughts, insofar as they represent any particular thing, are beside the point. We can generalize this particular rhetorical moment to say that once Emerson has rejected all he has said and problematized the register of meaning itself, he is necessarily committing himself to a different understanding of language, an understanding in which what is meant and what was actually said may be two different things. For the psychoanalyst, this is the language of symptoms, of transference, of slips of the tongue. For the writer, it is something very like style and rhetoric, that is, not so much what the text says but how it constantly exceeds itself in linguistic play. Emerson's text, in its refusal of logical argument, intense punning, attention to etymological roots, and stylistic excess in general, bespeaks an understanding of the Other in language. Its meaning can be said to originate neither in the writer nor in the reader. The point could never then be to try to match up what was said and what was meant. Insofar as Emerson evades discursive statement and representational logic, he is inviting the reader to attend to the sentiment rather than the actual thought. Attending to the sentiment is, in part, an interpretive activity, or at least it can become one, and then we are back in the position of the analyst. But first and foremost, our attention to the sentiment requires our ability to be affected by the text, our suggestibility, or else we would remain unaware of that sentiment. I want to examine this suggestibility more closely in a moment, but here, it is sufficient to point out that in a certain respect, the reader has no choice but to attend to sentiment in Emerson's text. The stylistic excess itself thwarts discursive understanding thereby leaving the reader either in frustration or in desire.

A frustrated reader, let us say a latter-day Henry James Sr., who simply throws up his hands and exclaims, "Oh you man without a handle," will simply not read Emerson's text; historically, there have been many such readers. As Cavell points out, Emerson's text has been repressed in our culture, by which he means specifically that American philosophers have ignored the foundational nature of Emerson's work.[33] It would be precisely the philosophers who would be frustrated by the stylistic excess of Emerson's text, who would take that excess as a mark of Emerson's lack of philosophicality; there is no "thought," they claim, in Emerson's text. But for a different kind of reader, say, one invested in a transference to Emerson's text, the rhetorical evasions, the half-silences, and the twistings and turnings become something else: manifestations of desire that elicit the desire to read and interpret, not for any particular content, but for the sake of the experience itself.

In this respect Emerson's language is what Nietzsche describes in his *Course on Rhetoric* as a language that "does not intend to instruct, but to transmit to others a subjective emotion and apprehension," or what Freud might have called the expectant faith characteristic of the positive transference itself.[34] Its goal, if we can still speak of goals, is to communicate a state of faith, or what Emerson has all along called "receptivity." It is just because Emerson has no intention to instruct us in the Nietzschean sense that he insists we read for the sentiment, and not for the thought at all. Thought implies intentionality—"what I mean to say is. . . ." If Emerson suggests that we bypass thought, then it is not simply because reading for the thought co-opts our originality. It is also because he understands that something always exceeds representation and consciousness, or we might say in Lacanian terms that desire always exceeds both itself and its object.

But let us not forget that if "sentiment" is that which exceeds representation, it is also that which falls short of representation. Constituted as nothing but lack, it cannot be stated as such so that our encounter with that desire in the text consists of discovering that like the text, we are always looking for something else. This dynamic helps to explain why Emerson calls alienated majesty our most affecting lesson. The lesson is not the content of the thought that we come to recognize, but rather the process of affection that affects the reader, the very process of desire itself. In a sense, it is just this process that Emerson's text works to create in the reader, although by now it should be clear that we can speak of "reader" and "text" only in quotation marks. The process that occurs can be attributed neither to text nor to reader, but only to a kind of identificatory relation in which the difference between self and Other evaporates. The dynamic of alienated majesty thus changes considerably. The text does not affect me because I feel something for it, nor even because it communicates a sentiment to me through its rhetoric. By excluding the possibility of representation, it obliterates the very distinction between text and reader and operates only as a passage between them. It affects me with my own affectivity, that is, with my own receptivity. In what would be a kind of rhetorical hall of mirrors, Emerson would be attempting to do nothing but make us receptive to our own receptivity.

The main thrust of Emerson's rhetoric would, then, be to locate us in such a place that we might give ourselves up to unmediated, unreflective acts of receptivity, or, as Emerson just as frequently calls it, genius. We do so not by imitating the genius of others, but by passively receiving, in the act of reading, the feeling of genius, of creativity, of intuition as our own. We can no longer speak of such a subject as the Cartesian *hupokeimenon*, or underlying substance, but it may still be a subject appropriately figured by a gleam or a flash. It would consist in a kind of fleeting or transitional spark or excess caused by the act of reading itself. This spark, paradoxically, comes from nowhere and resists every attempt at domestication. Such resistance is perhaps clearest about midway through the essay, when Emerson arrives at what he calls "the highest truth on this subject [of self-reliance]." This truth, Emerson claims, "probably cannot be said," doubtless because he is referring to just that state which always resists representation. The "nearest" Emerson can "approach" it is this:

> When you have life in yourself, it is not by any known or accustomed way; you shall not discern the foot-prints of any other; you shall not see the face of man; you shall not hear any name;—the way, the thought, the good, shall be wholly strange and new. It shall exclude example and experience. You take the way from man, not to man. . . . Fear and hope are alike beneath it. There is somewhat low even in hope. In the hour of vision, there is nothing that can be called gratitude, nor properly joy.[35]

We take the way from man, from our constitutive alienation in the Other, from that first moment in which we see and represent ourselves to ourselves in a specular logic. If on that way we no longer see a face, not even our own, then it is because we confront there the absolutely unrepresentable fact of our desire itself. To say "confront" is perhaps misleading insofar as it implies that we face ourselves, when Emerson is quite clear that we see nothing of an Other or of ourselves and that this moment is unassimilable to experience, or to domestication of any kind.

What Emerson presents here is a figure for the Lacanian imperative not to give way on one's desire. In this persistence, there is a kind of ruthlessness, raised above everyday passions and feelings. Doubtless this very ruthlessness explains the frequency with which Emerson denounces familial relations in the course of "Self-Reliance." In any case, it is just such a figure that provokes in the reader the whole question of Emerson's desire, a question precluding imaginary identifications and eliciting our own desire as such. The "hour of vision," as Emerson calls it, is not something we "know" but something that we do, without any reflection and, therefore, without will or alienation. It is as if in the moment of reading, we are that Other who desires, and that Other is ourselves.

Ruthlessness, then, is also passivity. Indeed, at the turning point of "Self-Reliance," Emerson abruptly reminds readers that "to talk of reliance is a poor external way of speaking. Speak rather of that which relies, because it works and is. Who has more obedience than I masters me" (272). The self is defined here not as some ultimate power, but instead as that which relies on something else. Even more to the point, that which relies because it works and is remains unnamed because it is nothing other than the groundlessness that emerges in the work of reading the text. This work is an obedience, which as Cavell suggests is ours to Emerson's text itself. It reminds us that in Emerson, "obedience" nearly always has the connotation of work as repetition, the "pounding" as Emerson has it in "Fate," on a single thought until "we learn at last its power."[36] If this obedience masters us, then it is perhaps because in the repetitions and working through that are characteristic of Emersonian reading, we learn that the text's power is *our* power, or say that it is no one's—everywhere at once and nowhere that can be specified. Receptivity, then, is obedience in that it can be neither evaded nor willed. We only will have found ourselves affected by a sentiment; ours or the text's, we can no longer say. This is the way of reading, of the receptivity it engenders, and it lies not *before* language but *after* it.

Emersonian receptivity would fall into the category of what Lacan calls "the real," perhaps the brute, presymbolic reality whose existence we can only posit by its effects, but therefore, the real also as a kind of leftover or remnant of representation itself. It is what remains after we have read for the thought, after we have acknowledged the lack in the text and in ourselves. Here, I think, Emerson reminds us of a crucial dimension of the psychoanalytic experience frequently overlooked by analytic theorists, especially in relation to Lacan. In a Lacanian analysis, the analyst would attempt, in the ways described above, to "hit the real," to bring it forth so that it could be integrated into the chain of signification. The process is dialectical in that the unsymbolized elements of experience are gradually and increasingly brought into the signifying chain. This in fact is how the statement "that to recognize and speak his desire, that is the efficacious action of psychoanalysis" is often interpreted—as a move from the impenetrability of unmediated desire to the representation of it. For Emerson, I am not sure this is the case. The whole lesson of alienated majesty would be much more to throw us into what Bruce Fink has called "a real after the letter,"[37] where I am the Other, and the Other is me, not in some alienated form, but rather in a complete identification precluding any representational logic or speech whatsoever, that is, in the original moment of the Freudian transference where I act without presenting myself to myself. At just this point, I am most myself. Lacan coined a word for this state—"extimité"—to designate that thing in me more myself than I am. It is a piece of the real, at the very center of the subject that cannot be symbolized or represented, and which arises not before, but after representation. Emerson thus reminds us that Lacan himself remarked on occasion that neurosis is maintained in speech and that the very narrative of memory constituting "the talking cure" may in fact be the most trenchant resistance of all. To be receptive rather than resistant would, contrary to expectation, be to dwell in what Lacan calls "the real," to dwell free of discourse, and of the Other, able simply to act without mediation.[38]

The Subject in the Real: "Whim"

It might seem, then, that the Emersonian subject is finally a wholly private subject, devoid of any content that it could present to or for another, let alone to or for itself. But the subject free of discourse nonetheless distinctly remains a speaking subject, which is to say, a fully public subject. This public subject differs from the social ego of the imaginary in several important respects, but to understand this difference, we need to return to "Self-Reliance." In fact, we can follow the entire trajectory of the subject, from its inception as an ego to its rebirth in desire and as a fully public being by way of the first few pages of "Self-Reliance." One of the most notable features of "Self-Reliance" is the incessant manipulation of pronouns. Emerson begins the essay literally with the word "I," but goes on for the next three pages shuttling between an identificatory "we" and a third person "he." "We recognize our own rejected thoughts . . ."; "they teach us . . ."; "these are the voices which we hear . . ."; and so on: these are Emerson's invitation to identify with his thoughts, which, however, also means that they are our thoughts. We are, as it were, finding our rejected thoughts in his text but finding them as our own insofar as we continue reading the essay. We see ourselves in these words as we would like to be seen. This identification belongs to the imaginary, and it is punctuated by the symbolic every time Emerson shifts into the declarative third person. "A man should learn to detect . . ."; "he knows what that is which he can do . . ."; "he knows how to speak . . .": these are Emerson's authoritative pronouncements, a reminder that we are, despite our projections and identifications, subject to the literal progression of the words of the essay, words which present themselves or which we take as knowledgeable and authoritative. These statements, too, present us to ourselves as we would like to be seen, but they also split us into observed and observer. We are that one whom Emerson describes, but insofar as we identify with the text, we are now in the position of describing ourselves in this way. In short, we are moving from imaginary to symbolic identification.

After three pages or so, however, Emerson shifts back to the opening "I" for several pages, not now as an invitation to identify, but more in the sense of recounting a personal story that pertains only to him. We are not part of this story. It begins, in fact, in the autobiographical mode, with Emerson's allusion to his rather devout Aunt Mary Moody and her fear that her nephew might be receiving his impulses from the Devil. The idea of obeying one's impulses, which itself embodies the receptivity the essay seeks to teach, culminates a page later in a passage I earlier quoted: "I shun father and mother and wife and brother, when my genius calls me. I would write on the lintels of the door-post, *Whim.* I hope it is somewhat better than whim at last but we cannot spend the day in explanation. Expect me not to show cause why I seek or why I exclude company."[39] This passage, perhaps better than any other in the essay, both exemplifies Emersonian reading and implicates us in it. Moreover, it allows us to glimpse the fully public nature of that process. Most frequently this passage is simply taken as one more instance of Emerson's profound solipsism. Indeed, it is here, where "Whim" appears, that we can most clearly understand why it is that speech represents not a reality—not something that could be shared, but only a fleeting subject. Since that subject is nothing but whim—say, lack or desire—every word it speaks negates itself as referent and puts in the place of the referent desire itself, a manifestation of lack, of nothing. Quite literally, Emerson himself disappears when his genius calls, marking his absence with a word that itself remains absent from meaning. We do not know what Emerson's "Whim" means: "We cannot spend the day in explanation," and if we fail to understand what "Whim" means, Emerson warns us not to ask. He will not say why he excludes or includes company, for example, the understanding and participation of any particular reader, because he himself does not know. He can only "hope" that his genius is more than whim.

Yet, significantly, whim is not something that emerges unbidden from within, but rather as the receptivity to a call; it is a stance within an acknowledged relationship, much as reading, with all that now designates, takes shape in response to the rhetoric of the essay. In one respect, we are dealing here with the individual at his most private, or, in any case, at his most proper. Genius singles me out, calls me and not someone else; as Emerson writes elsewhere, "A man's genius" is "the quality that differences him from every other."[40] My receptivity to this call is precisely what makes me more myself than I am, "extimate" with myself, as Lacan would say. But the fact of singularity here cannot be conceived as an inappropriable interiority. "Whim" neither conceals anything nor marks a hidden interior. It is just to the point here that Emerson writes it on the lintel of the doorpost, neither inside nor outside, but in the passage between, for the writing of "Whim" is this passage and nothing else. One would have to say, then, that what is most proper to oneself absents one from oneself and from the Other, but nonetheless remains wholly public. For if Emerson's refusal to explain himself seems to exclude the reader, he does nonetheless present his disappearance for the reader's benefit. Why else bother to mark his departure in words at all? This is to suggest that although the real of genius, that ineffable experience, can never be represented, its very impossibility can be marked, and in fact, it is just this genius that gives rise in the first place to the necessity of representation: "When my genius calls . . . I would write . . . *Whim*." In this sense, Emerson reminds us that the very experience he attempts to engender in a reader is not simply the failure of that reader's self-representation, but the acknowledgment that we are this failure, this series of endless displacements that never arrives at its destination or always overshoots it. Like Emerson himself in this passage, the reader is nothing but the failure of representation, not so much as an interior fullness unable to express itself, but rather in that this failure or limit marks the subject's positive condition. The point is not to abolish this negativity, but rather to experience how its violent and disruptive power itself enables me to achieve identity—"Whim."

Emerson's response to the Kantian problematic of representation operates on grounds wholly foreign to Kant. In a characteristic gesture, Emerson makes of the problem the solution. His deficiency, as he puts it, becomes a redundancy.[41] The place marked by "Whim" is not some transcendent, Kantian *Ding-an-Sich*, persisting somewhere beyond representation. If it were, then we would still remain the lost victims of representation itself, phenomena alienated from noumena. The whole notion of the unrepresentable still resides at the extreme horizon of representation itself. "Whim" is not the mark of that horizon, not simply the Kantian negative representation, but rather a concrete embodiment of that horizon conceived as positive condition. The unrepresentable in this way paradoxically achieves representation: since the subject is now nothing but the impossibility of its own representation, the only way to represent it is through the failure of representation.

To recognize oneself in and to speak or interpret from this paradoxical nonposition comes very close to what Lacan calls "full speech," purified of all reference and constituted only as an address to the Other. Such speech is, of course, full of nothing. It would be our activity of interpretation and the creativity that sparks it, free from the demand that we or the text "mean" something. The goal is to speak, but to speak nothing, to move beyond the objectifications of representational language in order to learn to speak without the intention of signifying anything, where speech is now understood as no more than the manifestation of a lack, a manifestation of desire.

A wholly private self, then? Perhaps, and yet still, it is manifestation, a communication of communication, for the reader, should the reader take it up. We can, in fact, go as far as to say that insofar as Emersonian writing exemplifies and instigates such speech, it is the very creation of the subject. As Borch-Jacobsen has pointed out, the speech of the subject of desire consists in something very close to the Austinian performative utterance, and as such is constitutive of the subject:

> "Full speech," like the Austinian "performative," does not "constate" or represent anything prior to its enunciation. On the contrary, it instigates (one could even say *creates*) a reality, which is, moreover, purely linguistic since it resides uniquely in the act of its enunciation. . . . Psychoanalytic speech, as such, insofar as it returns speech to its performative essence, thus implements the paradoxical "realization of the subject" by creating him *ex nihilo*.[42]

To my knowledge Freud at no point conceives the transference as constitutive of the subject. Its primary importance is as an analytic tool; at its worst, it is a stumbling block. In Lacan, however, the dual emphasis, first on the necessity of alienating oneself, one's desire, in the Other, and second, on learning to speak nothing but a performative address, characterizes subjectivity at its peak. This is as much as to say that the vicissitudes of the transference constitute our true subjectivity. And so it is with reading. Not only do we need first to alienate ourselves in the text of the Other but, above all, we also need it to instigate those fleeting moments in which whim can appear. This is what happens when Emerson's genius calls; Emerson's text, in turn, is to serve as that call for his reader. Insofar as I am receptive to that call, I perform myself. Since that performance is nothing other than the transferential relation to the text, we might say that in Emerson, the goal is precisely *not* to dissolve the transference, especially because we would no longer be speaking of particular transferences. It would be only in our acts of reading that we could constitute ourselves by becoming our own cause.

Transference, at least as conceived here, would mark the transition from or passage between the private and the public. This passage in turn implies an ethic. It is far too complex a task here to do more than briefly sketch an ethics of psychoanalysis, but perhaps it is sufficient to say that those ethics—Freudian, Lacanian, or otherwise—subtend the therapeutic goals of freedom and responsibility, although not perhaps conceived in the traditional sense. Psychoanalytically speaking, I am never free, in the sense that my decisions always occur before or beyond me, and yet, they are mine. To say that the patient is to learn to become his or her own cause means that although I seem to be answering for choices I never made, I nonetheless assume responsibility for those choices. This responsibility beyond choice no doubt underlies the entire Lacanian project of thwarting discursive understanding. It is not enough for me to understand any one thing, nor to communicate a determinate message, for this kind of understanding always and only produces itself as a form of alienation and bondage. Becoming one's own cause means taking it upon oneself to produce oneself in and as one's speech, not to convey any kind of message, but rather to speak oneself as no more than an address that seeks no specifiable response, to perform oneself without the guarantee of an audience.

The task of the next chapter is to explore such an ethic more fully, but I mention it here because it bears on the public dimension of Emerson's writing.[43] Emerson says, "My life is not for a spectacle," by which he no doubt means he can neither will to take on this role nor tell us about it. He, after all, has nothing to say—nothing except "Whim"—and he cannot guarantee our receptivity. He does not perform for anyone, and this is not the refusal of the solipsist, but instead the very condition of Emerson's responsibility. His acknowledgment that he cannot guarantee the reader's response, contained in the word "Whim" itself, is *his* responsibility. What his text does is no more than a repetition of that state of original faithfulness once marked on the lintel of the doorpost in *Deuteronomy*, now figured as "Whim," a sign or mark of what one is, without the assurance that anyone will read it. In this respect, the genius that calls me to write "Whim" is what Emerson at the beginning of the essay calls "the inmost," or "that gleam of light that flashes from within" when we read. And indeed, "the inmost in due time becomes the outmost." Why? Because as he has it later, "character teaches above our wills." His life is not for a spectacle, not designed for the other's recognition, but it is always available for the Other to read and most worth reading precisely when it has nothing to say. What the text does then and what it provokes in the reader remain always beyond representation, but also before representation in that this provocation itself engenders the necessity of representation. All of our acts of genius, of whim, absent us from ourselves and from any mediation whatsoever. However, in a sense, it is precisely the absence of mediation that provides for the future and endless possibility of representation.

We can say, then, that the performativity of the text, its very resistance to representation, thus marks its public and ethical dimension as well as that of the reader. As Emerson writes in the much later essay, "Culture," "The saint and the poet seek privacy to ends the most public and universal: and it is the secret of culture, to interest the man more in his public, than in his private quality."[44] That public quality is what Emerson elsewhere terms "representativeness," not in the sense of re-presenting anything that exists, but rather as a kind of relation in which the writer, or any representative person, simply exhibits him- or herself. This exhibition is without thought, without mediation, and always for an Other, a potential reader, and yet does not assume that Other in anyway. Thus, and only thus, he draws us on to become our own representative selves by identifying with what can never be stated, only performed. Then, and only then, are we dealing with culture, with that Other who makes us so much ourselves that we become representative. Not of some past, not of anything that we could ever have represented to ourselves. The most private has become the most public, and perhaps it always was.

Part Three

Transfers of Reading:
Toward an Emersonian Politics

Chapter 4 · · ·

Settling Accounts: "Experience"

> *To the proximity of the most distant, to the pressure of the most weightless, to the contact of what does not reach us—it is in* friendship *that I can respond, a friendship unshared, without reciprocity, friendship of that which has passed, leaving no trace.*
> —Maurice Blanchot, The Writing of the Disaster

What Counts? And Who?

Barbara Packer's wonderful chapter on "Experience" in her book *Emerson's Fall*, has made it impossible to approach this essay without considering the problematic relation between the opening section, separated absolutely by a white space on the page, and the remaining sections. That is to say, one cannot approach this essay without asking about the problematic relation between grief, but grief unfelt, and those rather cold and abstract lords of life who comprise the essay's topics. It is as if the essay cast its own "curse of Kehama" on the reader, locked in a question about the relation between emotion and thought that cannot be answered. Or rather, it can only be answered by tipping the balance, as two of the essay's best interpreters have shown us. Sharon Cameron has persuasively argued that grief generates the topics of the essay, which in turn mark an incomplete work of mourning, the partial working through of a loss that cannot be immediately acknowledged and so must be deflected into every other aspect of life. The essay becomes an exercise in preservative repression and, therefore, resists the philosophical concern with skepticism by which it has usually been appropriated. Like Cameron, Stanley Cavell also begins with the idea of grieving, but finds that grief is figurative, rather than structural, a way of expressing precisely the stakes of skepticism as they appear in the body of the essay, a body that attempts to inscribe itself with the fantasy of giving birth. Ultimately, according to Cavell, the essay would teach us to mourn the world's passing and to generate from this loss new conditions of possibility for experience.[1] I find both of these interpretations highly persuasive, and yet, taken together, they duplicate the problem of the essay itself, the dissociation between emotion and thought. Either we must ground this split psychologically, as Cameron does, or philosophically, as Cavell does. It is a question of economy, of what counts between two accounts, and of the economy of the essay itself.

I am not sure that we could ever settle such accounts without accounting first for the fact that the entire essay, from the start, delivers itself over to questions of economy. Economy—from the Greek root *oikos* and all of its derivatives—pertains to the management of a household and to the meaning of "household" itself. From the moment of beginning, the essay is palpably obsessed with figures of counting, of settling accounts, of settling as inhabiting and being at home, of property and possession, of the familiar and the family.[2] Here are some of the opening sentences:

> Where do we find ourselves? In a series of which we do not know the extremes, and believe that it has none. We wake and find ourselves on a stair: there are stairs below us, which we seem to have ascended; there are stairs above us, many a one, which go upward and out of sight. But the Genius which, according to the old belief, stands at the door by which we enter, and gives us the lethe to drink, that we may tell no tales, mixed the cup too strongly, and we cannot shake off the lethargy now at noonday.... Ghostlike we glide through nature, and should not know our place again. Did our birth fall in some fit of indigence and frugality in nature, that she was so sparing of her fire and liberal of her earth, that it appears to us that we lack the affirmative principle, and though

we have health and reason, yet we have no superfluity of spirit for new creation? We have enough to live and bring the year about, but not an ounce to impart or to invest.³

Just what is the grievance here? In the first place, we are not at home in our world; we cannot account for where we are, and more, we are estranged from even ourselves. We do not inhabit our world; rather we haunt it. This loss is compounded by, or accompanied by, our inability to count, literally those stairs on which we wake to find ourselves, but perhaps more to the point, our experience itself. Nothing counts anymore, or at least we cannot account for it, a loss in turn attributed to an insufficient bequest from nature. She gave us so little property, so little of our own at birth, we now have nothing to invest, and so we cannot settle our accounts. We no longer know what is proper to us. All of this is very unsettling, all the more so because it is not just a matter of individual losses. As in all households, we are dealing here with a group, a community of sorts linked by familiarity, similarity, a family model or model family. Emerson does not ask about himself alone, but about "we"—where do *we* find ourselves—and laments within a page, "Our relations to each other are oblique and casual." This formulation implies a common place we might inhabit together, as, say, a family inhabits a household; but this is the place we lack. Our Genius, the spirit of our place, has miscalculated the mixture in the cup, and now, without a common place, nothing is familiar anymore. In this incalculable economy, this no-place, the familiarity of the household, of all of the relations proper to it, are simply unfamiliar, or inhospitable. Every roof, as Emerson puts it a paragraph later, "is agreeable to the eye, until it is lifted; then we find tragedy and moaning women, and hard-eyed husbands, and deluges of lethe" (472).

This question about place, an apparently spatial figure, is temporal as well, for the opening paragraph suggests that we certainly do not find ourselves in the present. In the second paragraph of the essay, Emerson explicitly marks the temporal key sounded above: "In times when we thought ourselves indolent, we have afterwards discovered, that much was accomplished, and much was begun in us. All our days are so unprofitable while they pass, that 'tis wonderful where or when we ever got anything.... We never got it on any dated calendar day" (471). As in the opening paragraph, the question is one of economy. We cannot calculate our profits and losses, except retroactively. The meaning of a given experience is never in the present, always and only available after its event, which is simply to say that experience itself, as in "The American Scholar," is structured as a trauma, an absence, unregistered at the time, accounted for only later. Indeed, if we are strangers to ourselves in the manner suggested in the opening paragraph, then it is just because our Genius gave us the lethe to drink, because of the traumatic nature of experience itself, available and constructed only in a later accounting. Or perhaps nothing is accounted for at all, since we are dealing precisely with an instance of effect preceding cause.

In either case, and because both may be the case, this is just the structure of transferential reading we discovered at work in "Self-Reliance." Before meaning can get started, before I receive anything, I need to presuppose it in the Other, and yet, this presupposition is nothing but an error. Whim, reception, emerge retroactively where they always were, in a reading process that has no ontological status apart from the acts constituting its reality: "I" perform myself over an ontological abyss, only to recognize later where "I" was. Properly speaking, I receive nothing from the Other at all, because the Other has nothing to give that I could ever have represented to myself.[4] That is why Emerson writes "Whim" and refuses to explain, leaving nothing but an exposition that we may or may not take up. At the same time, I must anticipate my reception through an encounter with the Other to receive anything at all. This is why, as we saw in "Self-Reliance," receptivity is really nothing but the way in which I am affected with my own affectibility in a groundless process that nonetheless grounds me. In other words, Whim, or here, experience, is not some transcendent, or to use Emerson's word, "unattained" state we are unable to represent to ourselves. It is already included in our perspective and goes forward all the time, but this is precisely what we cannot know. Hence, all of our days seem unprofitable *while* they pass. It is this very traumatic non-trauma that allows one to understand the Emersonian emphasis on the centrality of experience. It is not simply a preference for experiential knowledge that underwrites Emerson's project, but rather a recognition that experience is the very condition, itself conditionless, of the possibility of knowledge.

It is, I think, just this logic that precipitates Emerson's meditation on the unnamed Waldo and underlies the organization of the economic figures of the essay. In the paragraph prior to the introduction of Waldo, Emerson continues with the theme of being unable to count. "How many individuals can we count in society," he asks, adding, "The pith of each man's genius contracts itself into a very few hours."[5] Society is general but the individual is particular; if one can count no individuals in society, then this is only to say that the singular and particular can never be counted without thereby generalizing and falsifying them. As in the opening paragraph, however, it is not simply a question of number, but of what counts. One can count no individuals, because no individuals count, perhaps because in counting them, one necessarily overlooks that which counts most—their absolute singularity. Perhaps, too, they don't count because, as Emerson puts it later in the essay, they "dodge the account" (474). They fail to settle their accounts. This multiple reflection prepares for the arrival of Waldo, who cannot be counted, who seems not to count, and who has failed to settle his account in a number of ways. In the first place, Emerson likens his son to "a beautiful estate,—no more" (473), and its loss touches him just so: "If tomorrow I should be informed of the bankruptcy of my principal debtors, the loss of my property would be a great inconvenience to me, perhaps, for many years; but it would leave me as it found me,—neither better nor worse" (473). If Emerson figures the loss of his son in these blatantly economic terms, then it is because he finds Waldo has left him nothing. His death seems not to count so that quite literally Emerson can say toward the end of the paragraph, "Nothing is left us now but death." Waldo bequeaths nothing but himself, nothing but his death, and fails in some sense to settle his accounts.

Emerson claims that this leaves him as it found him, claims continuity, but to say that Waldo bequeaths nothing suggests a rupture in continuity as well. In a will and testament, the Other speaks from beyond the grave to the living, transfers his property, what was proper to him, now to others. In "Experience" this form of continuity is lacking, a problem figured in Emerson's failure or refusal to name or to count the son. To count is to enumerate, and so to name. Not only does Emerson literally leave this son unnamed but also, in doing so, he fails to name himself as well. "Waldo," a name long in the family, had been Emerson's preferred designation for himself. This apparent equivalency, however, itself fails when Emerson says of his son's death, "It does not touch me: some thing which I fancied was a part of me, which could not be torn without tearing me, nor enlarged without enriching me, falls off from me, and leaves no scar" (473). Typically, this statement is read as the culmination of Emerson's unacknowledged grief, a sign of his melancholy, but this reading hardly makes sense. Freud, we should remember, distinguishes melancholia from mourning on the basis of identification. In mourning, the ego acknowledges its loss and carries out the work of mourning by de-cathecting itself from the object. In melancholia, it is just the opposite. The ego refuses to acknowledge its loss and instead identifies with the object, setting it up internally so that the love relation need not be renounced.[6] In the paragraph in which he introduces Waldo, far from identifying himself with the lost son, Emerson is saying precisely that he has lost his son but not himself. He is in short denying the identification characteristic of melancholy by acknowledging an absolute loss.

If the loss seems not to count, then it is only in the sense that it might have counted at all as a point of identification between the two Waldos. In fact, Emerson has already attempted and denied this identification several times in the opening paragraphs. Our dislocated state at the opening of the essay leaves us "ghostlike," and yet, Emerson says explicitly, "our life is not so much threatened as our perception." As if to imitate another's death, we "court suffering.... but it turns out to be scene-painting and counterfeit," and finally, "grief too will make us idealists."[7] The death of the Other that we might have felt teaches us only that we do not feel, or are not in feeling with—sympathy—the death of the Other. These reversals suggest that the similarity implied by identification is a fiction. No one can bequeath anything to anyone because of an impassable barrier between them. What death shows Emerson is the radical separateness of individual identities, identities that therefore can never be counted or named because of their absolute singularity. As he notes just before introducing the death of his son, "Souls never touch their objects. An innavigable sea washes with silent waves between us and the things we aim at and converse with" (473). The singularity of each person appears most radically in the fact that no one else's death can be my death. The son's death is not his death, and this is why the father does not name the son, a son whose very name might suppose or create an impossible commensurability.[8]

Perhaps, in another sense, the absence of the name figures a more radical sense in which Emerson cannot name, identify, or represent himself, because he cannot name the Other. In the later essay, "The Ego and the Id," Freud suggests that the identification characteristic of melancholia in fact structures all identity. The ego, as it turns out, is nothing but its identification with lost others: "The character of the ego is a precipitate of abandoned object-cathexes and . . . contains the history of those object choices."[9] The trouble with this claim is just the problem central to Emersonian receptivity: that process in which I am affected by my own affectibility. In both instances it is a matter of the ego requiring an Other in order to come into being, and yet, the ego must also precede that Other in order to be attached to it.[10] This temporal knot is indissoluble. Identification, like the transference itself, follows the logic of retroaction and reveals the self to be grounded on nothing and therefore unrepresentable to itself in its constitutive moments. The absolute marker of such a state would of course be nothing other than my death, that moment that can happen only to me, and yet, the very moment that I can never and will never represent to myself except analogically. The loss of the Other, his or her death, precipitates my identity, my consciousness of self, and yet, it can only be a consciousness of my own otherness from myself. It is precisely when death presents itself as not mine that the impossibility of representing its meaning in turn suspends the possibility of self-representation as well. The death of the Other is itself unrepresentable, as will be my own, as in fact, is all of our "experience." Indeed, the thwarted identifications of the opening paragraphs suggest that Emerson would perhaps like to get hold of his own death through the death of the Other and, therefore, get hold of all the experience that seems to escape him.

But that this is precisely what cannot be done. One's very unrepresentability, one's own self-inadequation, makes impossible any such further equations or commensurations.

Not only does this help to explain why, according to the opening paragraphs, we cannot find ourselves but also why Emerson's grievance takes its economic form. The subjectivity, if it can still be called that, developed in Emerson's theory of reading is the destruction of the foundation of *oikos*—of similarity, of being at home, of managing accounts, of familial and, therefore, natural relations. It should be one thing to lose one's debtors, and quite another to lose one's son. As it turns out, however, this apparently organic relation that Emerson fancied could not be torn from him without tearing him, the very bond that was thought to be most indissoluble and the most natural, only proves the ultimate fragility of every other bond, the discontinuity of every soul with every other and with itself.

In this respect, "Experience" would seem to be less about the conditions of possibility of experience itself, than about the consequences of experience without preconditions, particularly as they pertain to the possibility of community. Emerson seems to be raising a whole series of questions related to the possibility, not of experience in general, which somehow all the time seems *to have* occurred, but particularly of the failed experience of community. Once experience is structured as it is, once we realize that we will always be waking only to ask where we have been, what becomes of community, and community in all of its senses? If familial bonds, the most natural thing in the world, show themselves to be fictive, what of those figurative bonds of our figurative household? If we are each irreducibly singular, unidentifiable with each other and with ourselves, then what becomes of all of those other bonds predicated on our similarity or equality—democracy, for example? How can experience as we find it bequeath us a politics that was always predicated on, first, the autonomous reason of the individual and, then, on a family model of similarity among such individuals rather than singularity? Given the death of even family bonds, how can we then settle this matter of America? Whatever made us think it was settled in the first place? How might we come to be at home here again, or for the first time?

The body of the essay may be read as addressing this whole pack of questions through the opening question: Where do we find ourselves? It is not simply a matter of finding but also of what is to be found. If we were to find *ourselves*, that is, find a "we" or a community at all, then where and how would we do so? On what basis can we now build a community? Each of the topics of Emerson's essay explores the topos of a particular place, as if in each section, Emerson were asking, "Is this the place where we might find a 'we' and found a community?" Each topic thus becomes the possible condition of community, although none for long, and the reasons for which Emerson both chooses his places and for which he leaves them become equally instructive in attempting to answer these vexed questions of how we might find and found a community.

The Atopical Place of Community

In the opening section of "Experience," Emerson takes up the linked issues of illusion and temperament, linked because temperament makes of our lives an illusion: "Life is a train of moods like a string of beads, and, as we pass through them, they prove to be many-colored lenses, which paint the world their own hue.... Temperament is the iron wire on which the beads are strung."[11] If illusion were no more than colored lenses, one might remove the glasses to see things truly. But according to the logic of the passage, illusion is woven into the very structure of identity; temperament determines what one can see, passing as it does like an iron wire through the very center of the moods that make up life. In fact, were it not for the iron wire, the beads would simply scatter, so that temperament, illusion-generating though it may be, guarantees consistency. Such a structuring principle is, moreover, invisible in itself; it "shuts us in a prison of glass" (474), in two senses. Not only would we fail to see the prison walls as such but, because we could not see them, we would not realize that temperament separates us from everything outside of us. The illusion particular to temperament thus would be the mistaken belief that we could know others at all, itself a specific form of the general belief that we could ever see in any way except the way that we do.

In all of these respects, the section on temperament comments on the issues raised in the opening section of the essay and questions temperament as a ground for community. Like death, temperament should, as a prison of glass, separate us each from the other insurmountably, but this is not in fact its immediate effect. In the first place, Emerson begins by figuring both death and temperament as instances of natural and universal meaning. We all have temperaments and we all die. Moreover, because of the apparent naturalness and universality of both conditions, we assume that we "know" the meaning of each. In the case of death, there had been the assumption that in this final moment alone, "there at least, reality will not dodge us" (473). With temperament, it is a matter of determining a person's character and fortunes "by such cheap signboards as the color of his beard, or the slope of his occiput" (475). Without such assumptions, our lives might have no consistency whatsoever. We would be, as it were, without foundations—death as senseless, character as aberration.

Thus the inescapability of temperament might, like that of death, seem to guarantee community itself. Oddly enough, however, the very tropes designed to guarantee this possibility foreclose it:

> I saw a gracious gentleman who adapts his conversation to the form of the head of the man he talks with! I had fancied that the value of life lay in its inscrutable possibilities; in the fact that I never know, in addressing myself to a new individual, what may befall me. I carry the keys to my castle in my hand, ready to throw them at the feet of my lord, whenever and in what disguise he shall appear. I know he is in the neighbourhood hidden among vagabonds. Shall I preclude my future, by taking a high seat, and kindly adapting my conversation to the shape of heads? (475)

If one were to follow the lead of the phrenologists, those decipherers of natural and given meaning, then one would never, properly speaking, speak to anyone. The universality promised by phrenology, perhaps like that promised by natural death, turns out to be nothing but the erasure of the particular Other and, therefore, of the possibility of any communication whatsoever. This implicit emphasis on the particularity of others shows itself in Emerson's uncharacteristic feudal trope. Uncharacteristic, except that the feudal hierarchy here introduced turns out to be wholly contingent and based on nothing that we could surmise prior to its event. It is not, as in feudalism, a matter of all relations being extrinsically determined, but rather a provisional and contingent hierarchy occurring beyond choice or will on the basis of individual particularity. As Emerson makes clear, without such contingency, there is no futurity at all. Emerson thus concludes this section with the idea that once we recognize the trick of temperament, "we hurl it into its own hell, and cannot again contract ourselves to so base a state" (476). Temperament is not our state, not the place in which we might find ourselves or found a community.

Having ripped the ground out from under illusion and temperament as possible foundations for community, Emerson seeks that which precedes or founds illusion—a still more prior ground. The "secret" of illusoriness is succession, and in this section of the essay, the universal and universalizing force of temperament that precludes true community finds its opposite. Far from proving the universality of anything, succession marks the absolute particularity of objects and, more to the point, of desire itself. Emerson begins with a meditation on books and pictures: "Each will bear an emphasis of attention once, which it cannot retain, though we fain would continue to be pleased in that manner" (476). This lament is nothing other than an inverted echo of the plaint at the opening of the essay that all our days are unprofitable while they pass. The retroaction of meaning suggests that we cannot will our experience, just as our fleeting attraction to objects means that we cannot will the futures of our desire. We may wish to continue to be pleased after a manner, but because desires change, we must recognize experience and desire as beyond both choice and accountability. These are wholly contingent. This model of experience not only absents us from ourselves by revealing the unconsciousness of every decision but also, equally, from any permanent relation with others. The succession of our desire thus necessarily occasions mourning:

> The child asks, "Mamma, why don't I like the story as well as when you told it me yesterday?" . . . But will it answer thy question to say, Because thou wert born to a whole, and this story is a particular? The reason of the pain this discovery causes us . . . is the plaint of tragedy which murmurs from it in regard to persons, to friendship and love. (477)

If we knew why we didn't like the story, then we might be able to account for our desire and for relation, thereby preserving them. It is, however, the unique particularity and dissymmetry of every object, every Other and ourselves, that forces the non-reiterability of relation and precludes any accounting whatsoever. We can no more account for the Other than we can for the Other within ourselves. Thus the Other is always being lost, and with this loss comes the loss of all relation—of persons, friendship, and love. If there is a weariness in the tone of this section, it is perhaps because once again Emerson finds that the very structure of experience itself precludes the possibility of a community based on general similarity: on the ground of this section, there is "no universal applicability in men" (477).

What sounds as a lament in this section, however, occasions an optimism in the next section. If succession shows us that desire, experience, and relationship have no foundation by which to account for themselves, the section on "Surface" advises that we simply give up trying to account for them. Here, "the chief good" of life "is for well-mixed people who can enjoy what they find without question" (478). This renunciation, however, brings a new responsibility:

> It is not the part of men, but of fanatics, or of mathematicians, if you will, to say, that, the shortness of life considered, it is not worth caring whether for so short a duration we were sprawling in want, or sitting high. Since our office is with moments, let us husband them. . . . Let us be poised, and wise, and our own, today. Let us treat the men and women well: treat them as if they were real: perhaps they are. (479)

I take Emerson to be suggesting here that the calculations—say, counting—of these metaphorical mathematicians are inhuman. They are not the part of men because our lives if lived cannot be calculated and counted, cannot be accounted for. In fact, we never do know whether we are sitting high or sprawling in want, but this structural opacity in our knowledge by no means exempts us from a responsibility toward our actions. Our office, that is both our natural function and also our service, our duty, and literally the place in which we work, has to do with moments lived serially, as in that series of stairs that has no discernible beginning, no foundation. To husband moments would be to accept that retroaction is the economy of experience and so to plant oneself firmly in each moment without trying to calculate its cause or value.

"Office," however, in the sense of a duty or a service, also implies a relation to others. It is because our office is with moments that we must accept the radical alterity of the Other, but in contrast to the previous section, Emerson here begins to sketch out the possibility of relation without relation, of a community based on the absolute separateness of the Other. The somewhat shocking statement that men and women perhaps are real marks less Emerson's skepticism than his acknowledgment that one cannot know other people. This separateness, however, might itself engender a new politics and a new justice: "Amidst this vertigo of shows and politics, I settle myself ever the firmer in the creed, that we should not postpone and refer and wish, but do broad justice where we are, by whomsoever we deal with, accepting our actual companions and circumstances, however humble or odious" (479). Earlier in the section, Emerson had already remarked upon the unreliability of "party promises," of politics as they are practiced. The economy of party politics is such that there is always an inside as well as an outside, always an inclusion as well as an exclusion. There are those "like us," and then all the others. If this politics produces a vertigo, then it is because its claims, the very claims by which it creates an inside and an outside, are nothing but "show." What looked like natural affinity, say among party members, is actually based on nothing, or at least on no more than the collective illusion that we know ourselves and others. A broader justice would not calculate its recipients on the basis of similarity or difference, but rather would deal with whomsoever our companions happen to be in all of their irreducible otherness. Surface, then, would seem to mark a place in which a new kind of community, one based precisely on separateness, might take root. Here Emerson "settles," as he says above, as one settles a household; here we might find ourselves.

And yet as Emerson himself acknowledges at the opening of the next section, "How easily, if fate would suffer it, we might keep forever these beautiful limits, and adjust ourselves, once and for all, to the perfect calculation of known cause and effect" (482). Twice in the section on "Surface," Emerson has spoken about the balance between power and form, but the emphasis throughout is on form. To do "broad justice" may be to recognize the alterity of the Other in a formal or structural way, but it ignores particularity, that is, the unique and incalculable power of every individual. Our companions may be Other, but they are also particular others, just as the loss at the beginning of the essay is of this particular son, so particular that he cannot be named.[12] As Emerson writes near the close of the section, the balance of the surface or formal justice he has outlined is always upset because "everything runs to excess . . . nature causes each man's peculiarity to superabound."[13] It could never, then, be a question of just any justice toward just anyone, for this would be nothing other than the inverse of a community based on temperament, based on the particularity that is universal, and, therefore, not a true community at all. One way in which to understand the change in tone and stance at the end of the section is as a rejection of the Hegelian Other. It is not a matter of finding the Other of sameness, the alter alternative to a politics of *oikos*, but of finding the Other beyond *one's* Other. Since the alterity of the Other resembles my own alterity, we are no longer speaking of individual and determinate subjects who might have individual and determinate Others. The potential community of the section thus reveals itself to calculate a structure, not foundationless at all, but rather based on a belief that the Other would remain Other in an always calculable way. Hence, it is not genuinely Other; it is not particular.

Paradoxically, it is not at all surprising, then, that the following section, on "Surprise," devotes itself nearly entirely to the undoing of calculation, be it of the positive, negative, or neutral kind. Not only does Emerson begin by saying that we might wish to keep our limits and live within calculation but also he goes on to insist that this calculation would "quickly bankrupt" us, that "nature hates calculators" and that "the results of life are uncalculated and uncalculable" (482–83). In one sense, such statements are no more than a reformulation of the experience of retroaction, for here, the loss of ourselves, of others, of experience itself, becomes the promise of futurity canceled by the calculations of the previous sections. Typically, we are counseled neither to remember nor to expect, to live by surprise, but now "we thrive by casualties. Our chief experiences have been casual" (483). The accidentality of our experience, the fact that its meaning is always contingent, is itself a casualty or loss, perhaps much like the death of the son and the loss of community that this portends. But every loss recognized and mourned becomes an occasion for futurity. If we thrive on the loss occasioned by the casual, then it is because it is precisely this loss that leaves open the possibility of the future.

In this respect, the section does not become a ground for community, but instead a groundlessness that might allow the future to arrive. This groundlessness is akin to the "perhaps" that opens the space for the American scholar to enter; that is, it equates the incalculability of the Other with the incalculability of the future itself. This is the Levinasian future, the one always to come: "The future is not grasped, what befalls us and lays hold of us. The other is the future. The very relationship with the other is the relationship with the future," which is perhaps also to say that we can do nothing to will this future or this relationship, nothing whatsoever to foresee it.[14] This relation forms a possible community, which becomes clear at the close of the section when Emerson writes, "The persons who compose our company, converse, and come and go, and design and execute many things, and somewhat comes of it all, but an unlooked for result. The individual is always mistaken."[15] If the individual is always mistaken, then it is because that individual cannot calculate the effects of his or her actions; and so is not an individual in the typical nineteenth-century sense of the word. At the same time, the very impenetrability of those actions, hence their privateness, always has an undesigned public effect. They become part of an exchange without teleology, or at least without discernible teleology, but exchange nonetheless. It is as if Emerson were here suggesting that community can, paradoxically, occur only when the individual resigns his or her will and decisiveness, not in favor of some public good, but precisely to make way for the genuine futurity of the unknown in which we might come to exist together.

In the following section, "Reality," Emerson explicitly takes up the question of the futurity generated by all of our casualties. In one immediate respect he would seem here to be contradicting all that has come before. He opens by suggesting that rather than exalt chance or contingency into a divinity, we should maintain a belief or an expectation in the eventual accomplishment of the future. If this seems to falsify the illogic of retroaction characterizing every other section of "Experience" as well as the ungraspability of the future itself, then it is only if retroaction is viewed as part of a natural cycle, that is, if our expectation is viewed as having a teleology. By likening our trajectories to the "coetaneous" growth of an embryo, Emerson would seem to be arguing for such a natural teleology, which, if pushed to its extreme, moves from growth to birth, to life, and to death, only to begin again. The analogy, however, proves inaccurate, for just after remarking the coactive growth of the embryo, Emerson continues, "Life has no memory. That which proceeds in succession might be remembered, but that which is coexistent, or ejaculated from a deeper cause, as yet far from being conscious, knows not its own tendency" (484). If our lives are like embryos, then it would be only in the sense that if one moves back to the origin itself, then all is mystery. If one moves forward, then only the most general tendencies of growth and death can be predicted. Hence nothing can occur in succession, nothing can be remembered, and nothing determinate can be expected, which is perhaps to say that now, finally, always and only now, anything can be expected. By erasing the possibility of any natural teleology, Emerson would thus be instituting the deferrals of retroaction, the casualties of experience, as the very guarantee and structure of a more genuine futurity.

On closer examination, futurity, it seems, always arrives in the form of the Other. Emerson continues in the section:

> Do but observe the mode of our illumination. When I converse with a profound mind . . . I do not at once arrive at satisfactions, as when, being thirsty, I drink water, or go to the fire, being cold: no! but I am at first apprised of my vicinity to a new and excellent region of life. By persisting to read or to think, this region gives further sign of itself, as it were in flashes of light. (484)

This passage reiterates the central motif of "Self-Reliance" about the way in which the self comes to itself, or, perhaps more accurately, goes from itself. The flashes of light, those éclats that occur in the relation of reading, always defer our satisfaction because they proceed as if from nowhere in at least several senses. In the first place, these flashes are neither representational nor teleological. To say that I am thirsty or cold means representing to myself a determinate desire or lack and, therefore, being able to specify the precise means of fulfillment. I am thirsty, therefore I drink; effect follows cause. Here, however, desire seems to proceed from the Other, from my encounter with the Other, and yet this cannot be entirely the case since the Other is only just approaching. As the impossibility of specifying who persists in reading or thinking indicates, no identity holds the place of origin here. Desire, then, like succession reveals itself as a groundless process, sprung from nowhere, and therefore incapable of teleological satisfaction, all of which helps to explain why Emerson figures this process in terms of proximity. Emerson neither arrives at satisfactions nor does the Other finally approach. He simply finds himself in the neighborhood of the Other, who communicates nothing except the nearness of an approach, its own or Emerson's, equally and unspecifiably. If the Other offers him- or herself up, then it is neither out of will nor choice. It is a matter of receiving what the Other offers simply by virtue of being near, of being open to it, without in the least being able to will what one may receive or when, any more than one can will one's offers. In this respect, both offering and receiving occur prior to any conscious decision, outside of signification itself.[16]

The destruction of natural teleology, however, is not simply the destruction of signification. The approach of this "new and excellent region of life" prompts Emerson to speak of the way in which every expectation is "felt as initial, promises a sequel," which, however, recedes as suddenly as it approaches:

> I do not make it; I arrive there, and behold what was there already. I make! Oh no! I clap my hands in infantine joy and amazement, before the first opening to me of this august magnificence, old with the love and homage of innumerable ages, young with the life of life, the sunbright Mecca of the desert. And what a future it opens! I feel a new heart beating with the love of the new beauty. I am ready to die out of nature, and be born again into this new yet unapproachable America I have found in the West.[17]

The "august magnificence" of which Emerson speaks here is what comes upon him when he opens himself up to the Other. This relation is neither chosen nor willed; it is not something Emerson makes, but can only applaud. To clap is neither to grasp nor to let go, but perhaps to mark the perpetual approach and retreat of august magnificence. The syntax of the sentence beginning "I clap . . ." indeed leaves open the referent of all of the clauses. Is it I, or the august magnificence, that is old with love, young with life, a sunbright Mecca? Whose heart is beating with the love of a new beauty? The sentences do not tell us because the whole figuration of approach and retreat marks a proximal relation, rather than a departure point or a destination, an I or a you. This perhaps helps to explain the somewhat curious reference to Mecca, a reference suggesting that this relation of contingent proximity implies a particular kind of community. Mecca, of course, figures a desirable place to go, especially one where we go together, a place outstandingly frequented by the followers of a particular religion or pursuit. But even were one to complete the pilgrimage and arrive at Mecca, one would still not have arrived if only in the sense that Mecca itself is a figurative place that marks an absence. It is as close as one can get, but it is not the place itself—"and what a future it opens." In this respect Mecca is a figure for the futurity of community itself, community that is always about to arrive and always retreating. Perhaps, equally to the point, Mecca is the sacred place of a religion decidedly absent in nineteenth-century America and, hence, truly Other. This otherness at once reinforces the genuine futurity of proximal relations and underscores the absolute distance between every Other, that is, their irreducible alterity.

How does such a future open? Precisely, it seems, by moving beyond the natural order of relation. As Emerson looks toward this future, he finds himself ready to die out of nature and be born again in this new, yet unapproachable, America. To die out of nature would be not simply to die, but specifically to move beyond the natural cycle of birth and death, of the cyclical teleology implied by the embryo at the opening of the section. In short, to die out of nature is to be reborn, or at least one hopes it is a rebirth, into the mere contingency of retroaction where nothing is remembered and nothing expected, the very contingency of origin that has suspended the indivisible identity of the self. If this experience prompts Emerson to speak of a new, yet unapproachable, America, then it is perhaps because the annihilation of natural meaning, much like the annihilation of natural relation, liberates us from the law of memory and opens the way for the creation of new forms of life *ex nihilo*. In terms of community, say the America to come, this might mean disowning apparently natural bonds, all of the bonds implied by *oikos*, in an appeal to bonds. As nonnatural and beyond will or choice, such bonds would be without preconditions of any kind, and they would always, by definition, be to come. Dying out of nature, like the death of Waldo in the opening pages, is indeed the death that makes both ourselves and others Other—unknowable—and, thus, destroys signification. But it is also the death that makes a new community, a community without community, possible. If, however, there is no individual subject present to itself, neither then can there be any collective totality so that this possible community is not today, or even tomorrow, and maybe never. We are not speaking here of a future or of a community on the verge of fulfillment, suffering only the necessary delay caused by any approach. Emerson's use of the word "yet" does not, I think, mean "still" in the sense that one day, some particular day, we will be able to approach this new America. Once we have died out of nature neither you nor I can do anything or will anything that could make this community happen. It will always be to come, hence new and yet unapproachable.

In another sense, however, it is unapproachable because we are already there; in fact, it is happening all the time. Emerson closes this section:

> The spirit is not helpless or needful of mediate organs. It has plentiful powers and direct effect. I am explained without explaining, I am felt without acting, and where I am not. Therefore all just persons . . . refuse to explain themselves, and are content that new actions should do them that office. They believe that we communicate without speech, and above speech, and that no right action of ours is quite unaffecting to our friends, at whatever distance; for the influence of action is not to be

measured by miles.... If I am not at the meeting, my presence where I am, should be as useful to the commonwealth of friendship and wisdom, as would be my presence in that place. (486)

The idea that I am explained without explaining, that I can communicate without speaking, should remind us of "Whim" on the lintel of the doorpost, but perhaps now we are in a better position to trace its public implications. The whole moment of "Whim" is one in which Emerson not only absents himself from others but also in effect from himself, because Whim is produced by the genius who calls, by that Other who affects me in spite of myself and yet not in any way that could be represented. It should be clear by now that this pre-originary affectibility that makes "Whim" appear in the first place forever precludes reflexive self-presence. Hence one could never explain oneself or communicate that self to some Other so that one is, as the passage puts it, most felt where one is not. If this dynamic follows the logic of Lacanian transference and institutes a particular sort of non-subject, it equally brings into play the institution of a particular form of community traceable from Nietzsche and Bataille through Levinas, Blanchot, Nancy, and Derrida. Without attempting to negotiate this trajectory and all of the differences within it, I would say that each of the others begins with the very idea developed in Emersonian reading, that is, of a self present to itself only in absence and, in fact, most present to itself in the absence occasioned by a groundless affectibility. This idea can be read as the annihilation of the subject and, therefore, of community. At the same time, even as it traces the contours of an unrepresentable singularity, it reveals the possibility of a new community both to come and always here. As Emerson's formulation above suggests, the fact that I am felt where I am not means that my absence from myself, most absent when my action is most direct, nonetheless exposes itself, offers itself, for the Other all the time. This is why Emerson has emphasized earlier the trope of proximity, but it must be understood, as this passage insists, that proximity cannot be reduced to literal distances, nor to the mere representation of some neighbor. It can perhaps only be thought, as Levinas has it, as an obligation prior to any commitment, a communication preceding intentionality, without speech, as Emerson says.[18] (This is the relational non-relation Emerson will later designate as "representativeness.") More immediately, however, we should note that if this communication is "useful to the commonwealth of friendship," it would not be in the sense that now we have some common kind of being or common place, but quite the opposite. It would mean no longer having any place—actual or ideal—for substantial beings, but rather sharing the very finitude that absents me from myself and makes me present to others, who in turn present themselves to me in their very finitude and irreplaceability. The departure from myself becomes the approach to the neighbor.

    Lest it seem that this form of sharing constitutes a social bond, Emerson concludes the body of the essay with a powerful meditation on what he calls "Subjectiveness." Here we find "the rapaciousness" of a new power, "the great and crescive self, rooted in absolute nature." This section, however, should not be read as it often is—as a description of the wholly solipsistic individuality born of idealism. Throughout the section, the emphasis is on the incommensurability of every individual. The self of which Emerson speaks, "supplants all relative existence, and ruins the kingdom of mortal friendship and love. Marriage (in what is called the spiritual world) is impossible, because of the inequality between every subject and every object."[19] Here is the fulfillment of the plaint murmured earlier by the discovery of the incalculability of one's changing desires ("The reason of the pain this discovery causes us . . . is the plaint of tragedy which murmurs from it in regard to persons, to friendship and love" [477]). If this is the case, then it is because this self is not merely an inimitable nuance that would be added on to a being belonging to some kind or genus of the human and thus common to many inimitable individuals, making reciprocity possible from the first. Not only does Emerson suggest that for each subject there are only objects, thus differentiating every singular being not just by degree but by kind, but also he goes on to claim that the soul is not "twin-born, but the only begotten . . . admitting no co-life." This is no longer the soul as part or parcel of some universal One Mind, no longer the formulation of a self common to me and the Other. This soul is not an instance of souls among souls. Indeed, as the passage makes clear, and as the following section on moral relativity confirms, the "I" is the very exclusion from any possibility of comparison. And yet, even as it admits no co-life, Emerson is quite specific that the soul is "begotten." In this respect, we are precisely not dealing with the indivisibility of the individual in the usual sense, but rather with that self other to and from itself, endlessly divided and recurring, begotten in a past that will never be present, enacted, then, too, in every moment. As Emerson asks midway through the section, "How long before our masquerade will end its noise of tamborines, laughter and shout, and we shall find it was a solitary performance?" (489).

In a curious respect, this particular section of the essay enacts the very sort of retroaction about which the entire essay speaks. The question about solitary performance arises on the trail of the famous image of a puss chasing its tail, which is as it should be, because the question of singularity and its effects returns full circle to the beginning of the essay which, in some sense, was already its completion. For it is just here, in the solitary performances that we are, that it must be asked again: What kind of community could we ever achieve, and where? Indeed, the singularity of which Emerson speaks ruins the kingdom of mortal friendship and love, which is precisely where Emerson began, but with a difference. If mortal or natural friendship can no longer exist, then perhaps friendship as mortality can. As we saw at the beginning of the essay, the death of the Other reveals his alterity, as well as my own within myself. However, these very losses may themselves destroy one kingdom, one communal place, so that another may arrive. This is not a community of similar identities, of anything rooted in the idea of *oikos*: it is not familial, natural, given, present, accounted for in any way, but precisely the loss of these things. In fact, we can go so far as to say that this loss *is* community, an impossible possible community, a community without community. I, says Emerson, am not my son, but the son's distance is indeed the father's distance from his son, and from himself. In this sense, all of the failed identifications that mark the beginning of the essay are themselves the recognition of community itself, for paradoxically, loss and mourning mark the only available passage from private to public, from singularity to generality. They would do so, however, only as the possibility of joining incommensurables in the strange process described by the arc of the essay: I am like the Other because death reveals the way in which we are each always exposed to the alterity that we are for ourselves and that we are ever making of each other.[20]

At the end of the opening section, Emerson writes, "I take this evanescence and lubricity of all objects, which lets them slip through our fingers then when we clutch hardest, to be the most unhandsome part of our condition."[21] We might read this now, retroactively, as asking, given the incommensurability of selves, both to one another and of each within itself: Do I clutch after the Other, including the Other that I am, as in the opening paragraph of the essay, or is it, as the passage implies, this very clutching that most distances the Other? This has perhaps been the central exemplification of the essay, to let go of the other on every ground, to show the atopicality of relation, the absolute resistance of every singularity to any generality. There is no place for community, no common ground as such. If community appears at all, then it will be in a giving up of bonds in an appeal to bonds that are not attachments, not natural, not thematizable, or representable in anyway whatsoever. One can say that not only does the essay resist community as a communion or fusion of individuals into a higher "We" but also that it resists any philosophy of immanence, universality, or transcendence that would turn an "I" into a "We."[22] As Emerson discounts each of the topics or places in which he sought to found a "we," he finds only that there is never any foundation for this "we," never any philosophical account that could count singularities and add them into a general sum. It would never, then, be a matter of trying to decide between grief and philosophy, emotion and thought, because the entire essay works to subvert the priority of either. The singularity that grief occasions is itself the groundless ground of community. And as it turns out, community is the bondless bond of affectivity that occasioned grief from the start.

"Where Do We Find Ourselves?"

> Illusion, Temperament, Succession, Surface, Surprise, Reality, Subjectiveness,—these are threads on the loom of time, these are the lords of

> life. I dare not assume to give their order, but name them as I find them in my way. I know better than to claim any completeness for my picture. I am a fragment, and this is a fragment of me.[23]

Thus Emerson begins the final section of the essay, by retroactively naming all of the places he has visited, conferring meaning now and also refusing to do so. One finds oneself in fragmentation, in the collectivity of fragments that remains incomplete. Typically, Emerson leaves unclear whether the naming or counting of the places he has been comes of running up against them, as if they were in his way, or whether perhaps he has simply named them after his fashion. In a sense, it hardly matters, because tomorrow will change the meaning of today, so that no picture can be complete. Emerson here does no more, then, than confirm what the whole essay has worked to show: true futurity can never arrive in the form of a complete picture, with edges flush against the present. It may seem at this point, as the essay closes, that Emerson necessarily declines all responsibility, not just for the essay itself but also for himself and, therefore, for community of any kind, leaving it to nothing but chance.

But this confirmation is more than a repetition, for it leads to a reflection on the possible nature of responsibility given and for this future. Having remarked that he is no longer the novice he was fourteen years ago, and more significantly since it marks the birth of the now dead son, seven years ago, he imagines someone putting a question to him: "Let who will ask, where is the fruit?" (491). The question may be read as asking a number of things. It is in one sense, given the allusion to Waldo, a return to the beginning of the essay, a question about what Emerson has learned from his son born in that space that has made him no longer a novice. Equally, it asks how this individual moves beyond the private sphere of his loss and into the public, and specifically, how this individual contributes to the community. In any case, the question occasions what are perhaps the most well-known lines in the essay:

> I find a private fruit sufficient. . . . All I know is reception; I am and I have: but I do not get, and when I have fancied I had gotten anything, I found I did not. I worship with wonder the great Fortune. My reception

has been so large, that I am not annoyed by receiving this or that superabundantly. I say to the Genius, if he will pardon the proverb, *In for a mill, in for a million*. When I receive a new gift, I do not macerate my body to make the account square, for, if I should die, I could not make the account square. The benefit overran the merit the first day, and has overran the merit ever since. The merit itself, so-called, I reckon part of the receiving. (491)

This is Emerson's final refusal to account for anything, to calculate gains and losses, to square his own account and so, too, the final ruin of economy and *oikos* in all of their senses. Indeed one would have to ask here as well if Emerson were not simply declining responsibility for everything—for producing a public fruit, for "getting" perhaps in the sense of earning a dollar, for making use of what was given him, for the way in which he has spent his life itself, and finally, for community itself. As the first sentence makes clear, this is an escape from the relations or networks of society, say, its economy. In this respect, it echoes Emerson's determination to shun father and mother, wife and brother, when his genius calls. Similarly, here Emerson is declining not responsibility as such, but rather the responsibility that traditionally comes of freedom, traditionally conceived. In this economy there is a strict bookkeeping, in which liberties compensate for responsibility, say, for example, in which a public fruit would justify what otherwise might appear to be no more than dawdling. In this economy, I am responsible only for what I have done, for my intentions, my actions, my projects. The whole essay, however, and the passage itself work against such a logic of cause and effect. To say he has never gotten anything means, among other things, that he cannot specify the source of his reception, his beginning, when he got what he has. He cannot, in fact, even count how much he has been given—it may be a mill or a million, and perhaps there is no difference since retroaction would always cancel the possibility of counting at all. Nonetheless, the passage insists that his being (I am) is nothing but a reception, an openness to what comes from the Other. For all of the reasons the essay has demonstrated, this reception undoes the possibility of any intentionality, of ever deciding or acting on the basis of our "free will." As the close of the passage suggests, it is not a question of benefits received for merits shown. The self is, as it were, on absolute loan from the Other, with no accounting possible.

Emerson's response to the bookkeeping of debt and loan, responsibility and freedom, private and public may indeed imply a solipsistic vision of absolute abandon and freedom from constraint. He treats all he receives as gratuity, all as if he could spend as freely as he receives. This might mean only that we can all be worlds unto ourselves, with private economies. If, however, this reception escapes the reduction of singularity into a generality that undoes all responsibility, then it is finally because it is given as and to a singular being. It is given to Emerson as irreplaceable for, in fact, it creates his irreplaceability. Since Emerson himself cannot account for this reception, he cannot escape it; he, and no other, is still in debt, which is to say that experience is what happens all the time; it happens to me, to you, to each of us irreplaceably. Experience is what makes each of us irreplaceable. The only response to such a debt can be a prodigality, for it is just this prodigality that constitutes responsibility, a responsibility before any debts are incurred, before decision, before even freedom, and it cannot be otherwise. In acknowledging myself as Other, as precisely on loan and therefore always mistaken in any decision or freedom, I am enjoined to do the same for the Other, to put myself in the place of the Other; I am the Other in the double sense. I, you, all of us, occupy this position. Hence, a private fruit alone would be sufficient. It could never be a question of doing as I do on the assumption that the Other would recognize my action in some particular or expected way, that I could specify the Other in this way, for this would be the very cancellation of the alterity that is community. I cannot repay debts that were never incurred at any given time and for no given amount, but I can be responsible in the place of the Other, paying gratuitously, with no guarantee that my payments are necessary or even received. I take responsibility for the Other's response and, therefore, absolute responsibility for my actions, even though and in fact because they lie beyond will and choice.

This sense of responsibility may prompt Emerson to speak of the loss of his son in the opening pages as "caducous," and links the death of Waldo with the question of community. In organic terms, "caducous" signifies a limb that falls off when it has served its function, as, for example, the way in which Waldo simply "falls off" of Emerson. But "caducous" also refers in Roman law to a bequest that has lapsed from the donée, a peculiar situation in which the law of continuity, law itself, is suspended. Perhaps it is not so much that Waldo has left nothing, but rather that Emerson himself refuses the bequest, realizing from the start that the Other had nothing to leave, nothing for which the donée was not already in debt even before the bequest was made. No binding testaments are possible because one cannot witness oneself or the Other in such a way that guarantees the destination of the testament. The legal meaning of "caducous" puts testament beyond law and thus undoes the organic meaning in two senses. In the first place, it suggests that the continuity of organic relations, say familial relations, undertaken because they are natural, given, or even obligatory, are not finally guaranteed in any way. To undertake a relation for the sake of duty or law, as Kant would have us do, is to negate the very possibility of relation itself. And, precisely because this is the case, it is our responsibility to refuse any such relations so that others can take their place. The responsibility of this relation without relation, of the other myself to the Other is endless, can never be calculated, and it is this very impossibility of calculation that makes it responsibility in the first place.[24]

What Emerson calls "experience" is nothing other than this responsibility, which takes us back to the etymological root "experience," *per*, a root it shares with "peril." Our experience is a risk, an adventure into an unforeseeable future, but a future for which we are nonetheless responsible at every step. Could this risk that entails a community without community, relation without relation, ever become the basis for that particular community that is democracy, one that would still resemble what we mean by that word? The close of the essay offers a provisional answer at best. In the final paragraph Emerson imagines another interlocutor, asking him this time, "Why not realize your world?" This question, like the first asking "Where is the fruit," reminds us for a final time that we are always answering for questions that were never posed by anyone at any time. Fittingly, both instances return us to the question of community; and both answers are similar to Emerson's writing of "Whim" on the doorpost. To say that a private fruit is sufficient, or that no, I need not realize my world, does nothing more than mark one's finitude and alterity. None of the three statements attempts to put an inside outside, to make the private public, to communicate some piece of information that could be taken up in a direct exchange. We can say instead that they are testaments with a difference: a bearing of witness to his own otherness, a testament made possible by the death of Waldo; and above all the very creation of community itself. For before and after all, they are nothing but the communicating of communication itself, an opening on to openness, of oneself in all of one's otherness, with no guarantee that they will be taken up and, therefore, in absolute responsibility for the Other now finally as Other. These questions and answers have no place in, as Emerson claims, "our talking America," in which "we are ruined by our good nature and listening on all sides."[25] They do not describe a space in which we feel like the Other in sympathy or similitude, a space of consensus, but rather that space between us. This space that marks our otherness—and our connection—is also our future, that of community itself. A community of such spacings would occur only in that which interrupts and fragments it, never here, always here, and always to come.

Chapter 5 · · ·

From Exemplarity to Representativeness

> *Human character evermore publishes itself. The most fugitive deed and word, the mere air of doing a thing, the intimated purpose, expresses character . . . your silence answers very loud.*
> —Emerson, "Spiritual Laws"

The Evasions of Representativeness

To describe Emersonian reading according to a transferential model is, of course, to point to the therapeutic intent of Emerson's writing. In "Self-Reliance" that intent is directed primarily toward the individual, whose very "cure" entails the passage from private to public, or, perhaps more accurately, inscribes the most private as the most public. As the Emersonian text leads the reader into a performance of the most private, it simultaneously engenders a self that is always social, always public, and, finally, always exemplary. In "Self-Reliance" this exemplarity is left implicit, its nature and consequences unexplored. It is marked by nothing but "Whim" and the possibility of its reception. "Experience" pursues the consequences of such a possibility, but even as it posits the singularity marked by "Whim" to be the basis of community, the interchange among singularities remains abstract. The very goal of Emersonian writing and reading is to set this interchange in motion, to elicit the exemplary by way of the private, and yet, since our responsibility as it emerges at the end of "Experience" is something we can neither will nor evade, a question remains.

In essence, it might be phrased as a question that arises within the structure of responsibility as to whether or not we can be responsible for our responsibility. This is to ask whether or not there is anything beyond a structural possibility linking private and public, which in turn raises the question of the political. Can the subject who emerges in the act of Emersonian reading realize its public nature in anything more than a structural fashion, as a politics, practical or theoretic. The close of "Experience" would seem to suggest that our singularity, even as it defines community, can never be realized in any way. In a statement perfectly consistent with the entire concept of community as developed in the essay, Emerson writes, "I know that the world I converse with in the city and in the farms, is not the world I *think*. I observe that difference, and shall observe it. One day, I shall know the value and law of this discrepance. But I have not found that much was gained by manipular attempts to realize the world of thought."[1] In one respect, the passage simply reasserts Emerson's distrust of philosophical thinking as an instrument that might achieve anything. Its *manipular* attempts cannot realize the very world to which it has given rise in the first place. And yet the irreplaceable singularity to which the essay keeps returning is certainly part of the world Emerson "thinks," so that when he opposes such thought to his conversation with the world, he is not simply denigrating philosophy. If the world of thought is the site of genuine community, then conversation points toward practical politics. Throughout "Experience," Emerson's multiple references to political issues are figured in terms of conversation and consensus. To oppose the world of thought to the world with which he converses is to raise a double problem. Singularity as such ruins the very possibility of the kind of consensus on which liberal democracy is based; however, consensus without true otherness is hardly worth the name. Emerson may have envisioned a new form of community, but he is shrewd enough to ask here whether such a community can be political in any way, with politics now defined as the actual ways in which our community is at stake. All he can say is that he will observe the difference between the world of thought—say, community as he has envisioned it—and the world he converses with—say, practical politics—but he cannot turn one into the other.

In this chapter, I propose that the series entitled *Representative Men* is Emerson's attempt to come to terms with that difference by exploring the ways in which this community without place might still take place. As a piece of writing, *Representative Men* is more diffuse, less read, and less powerful than "Experience," so that it may seem perverse to insist upon these essays as pivotal in Emerson's attempt to realize a politics as part of the project of American letters. Indeed, the political aspect of *Representative Men* evidently escaped many of Emerson's contemporaries. Concerned that the essays were merely autobiographical, less sympathetic reviewers denounced as political detachment what would have been from Emerson's perspective inevitable self-commentary. Between the time Emerson delivered the lectures and published them, the political and religious revolutions of 1848 had shaken Europe. As Edward Emerson points out in the introduction to the *Centenary Edition*, a number of reviewers, particularly in England, were baffled by Emerson's indifference in the wake of these upheavals.[2] But even if had Emerson known nothing of Europe in 1848, his apparent indifference may have masked political despair: he would have been familiar enough with the profound economic, social, political, and moral crises of early to mid-nineteenth-century America. At times, Emerson does seem to evade these crises. As for himself, his greatest personal ambition, one he only partially realized, was to be a poet. This literary ambition, however, may also be read as the result of his larger ambition for American letters. As "The American Scholar" makes clear, American letters entails an entirely new social function for the poet or writer, a function that would bridge the realms of literature, culture, and politics and perhaps make them indistinguishable. The mediating function is one registered in Hawthorne's hopes for romance, in Whitman's Preface to the 1855 edition of *Leaves of Grass*, and in Thoreau's account of his stay at Walden Pond. In Emerson's work, its possibility is most frequently designated with the word "representative," and *Representative Men* is perhaps its fullest exploration.[3]

Each of the essays in *Representative Men* locates its subject in an explicitly political context. The first essay, for example, on "Plato; or, the Philosopher" reopens the whole question about the relation between poetry and philosophy and its political context. If Plato is the first figure that Emerson treats, then it is because Plato is our inescapable origin in a double sense. Among philosophers, Plato is foremost: "Out of Plato come all things that are still written and debated among men of thought. . . . Plato is philosophy, and philosophy, Plato."[4] By placing Plato first, Emerson acknowledges the traditional privilege of philosophy and lays the foundation for the other essays; without philosophy, we would have no mysticism, no poetry, no politics, and so on. No sooner, however, does he announce that "philosophy is Plato" than he adds, "a philosopher must be more than a philosopher. Plato is clothed with the powers of the poet, stands upon the highest place of the poet."[5] Leaving aside the fact that this sentence explains, or excuses, Emerson's own rhetorical practice, one is reminded immediately that the quarrel between poetry and philosophy is lost and won on the battlefield of rhetoric. It is a quarrel about the nature and capacities of language. When Emerson concedes that Plato is finally not a poet, but only because he subordinates his poetic gifts to ulterior purposes, one is further reminded that the quarrel between poetry and philosophy, even as it stages itself within Plato's work, takes place specifically in a political context. If Plato is representative for Emerson, then it is because the political implications of the quarrel over language are precisely what inform Emerson's own quarrel with traditional philosophy. From the outset of the essay, Emerson's focus is on Plato as the foundational figure of Western culture. In reinterpreting Plato as the poet/philosopher, Emerson is thus raising the question of what might constitute the appropriate foundations for our culture, in this case, not the West in general, but most particularly nineteenth-century America. Emerson thus challenges the traditional privilege, not so much of philosophy itself, but of philosophical language and the way in which it might or might not function in a democracy. What Emerson admires about Plato in particular is not finally some absolute and irrefutable truth that Plato discovered, but rather the emphasis on dialectical conversation through which each interlocutor is brought to formulate and assess the truth for himself and then to be responsible for it. Who would ask more of any citizen of the Republic?

Each of the following essays in the volume furthers Emerson's sense that representative figures, whatever else they may do, serve as exemplary citizens. The skeptic, for example, in his talent for balancing all positions, becomes a "bad citizen" in the sense that Socrates was a bad citizen, or in the way in which Emerson advocates we all become bad citizens in "Self-Reliance": "The wise skeptic is a bad citizen; no conservative; he sees the selfishness of property, and the drowsiness of institutions. But neither is he fit to work with any democratic party that ever was constituted; for parties wish every one committed, and he penetrates the popular patriotism."[6] The skeptic, then, weighs the actual practice of institutions and dissents from their verdicts without withdrawing his participation in their constitution. He considers all things. In this, the skeptic is an ideal representative, both of himself and of how an ideally responsible citizenry might behave. And, as in the essay on Plato, Emerson links this function of the skeptic with his own writing: surely he knew that "essay" derives from the Latin *exago*, "to put in the balance and to weigh."[7] Emerson continues with the theme of the writer as citizen in "Goethe," an essay to which I will return in some detail below.

By contrast, both Shakespeare and Napoleon serve as examples of the way in which representativeness as usually conceived can become opportunities for leveling and demagoguery. In all cases, the quality of representativeness broadly attracts political considerations. In order to understand in a detailed way why this is the case, and the precise reasons for which Emerson insists on the political ramifications of his figures, one needs to examine the concept of representativeness itself. In the introductory essay, "Uses of Great Men," Emerson would seem to mean by "representative" something very like exemplar or model. Representative men are exemplary individuals, in the sense fixed by Plutarch and handed down all the way to Emerson's friend Thomas Carlyle and the high Romantics: "Behman and Swedenborg saw that things were representative. Men are also representative; first, of things, and secondly, of ideas."[8] As such, the representative serves a pedagogical function, but it would be misleading to think that what is imitated or learned is some particular line of action or conduct. Emerson's representatives are not Carlyle's heroes, despite the charge of some British reviewers that *Representative Men* was little more than a pale imitation or re-presentation of *On Heroes and Hero Worship*. Recall the line from "Self-Reliance": "Imitation is suicide." Indeed, even as Emerson evades Carlyle and the entire tradition behind him, his use for the representative moves well beyond the usual notions of imitation or mimesis that attach to representation in an aesthetic or moral sense.

"Uses of Great Men" makes clear that the purpose of exemplarity is not some exterior reproduction or copy of a given model, but, on the contrary, an appropriation of what at this point we might call a formative power that makes us representative or exemplary of ourselves. Emerson's comments on Shakespeare provide a good illustration of the difference between these two modes of representation. Of Shakespeare he writes, "His mind is the horizon beyond which, at present, we do not see" (137), and this in at least three senses. Quite literally, Shakespeare re-presents, in the traditionally mimetic sense, such a great range of humanity in the figures who people his plays that one cannot imagine any human types beyond them. In the second place, Shakespeare the individual is himself representative of the most that the poet, in general, can be. He shares with all of Emerson's other representative figures the fact that he embodies the most fully realized potential of his function. Thus, in the most important sense, Shakespeare as the fully realized poet is representative or indicative of our potential for "infinite invention" (138), that is, of creative process itself. To take Shakespeare as an exemplar, then, would not be to attempt a second *Hamlet* or *Othello*, nor even necessarily to write anything at all. It would perhaps be to appropriate inventiveness itself, or, put in a more Emersonian fashion, to recognize our own alienated inventiveness by seeing it first in Shakespeare. But equally and more generally, it would be to become the fully realized version of oneself, whatever one happened to be.

Emerson's apparently unlikely comparison between the poet and the French inventor, Louis Daguerre, underscores this difference between mimetic exemplarity and representativeness and sends us back to the dynamics of reading sketched in "Self-Reliance." According to Emerson, Shakespeare

> is the chief example to prove that more or less of production, more or fewer pictures, is a thing indifferent. He had the power to make one picture. Daguerre learned how to let one flower etch its image on his plate of iodine; and then proceeds at leisure to etch a million. There are always objects; but there was never representation. Here is perfect representation, at last; and now let the world of figures sit for their portraits. (144)

The comparison is doubly suggestive. In the first place, daguerreotypes could not be reproduced, so that, strictly speaking, they are not copies, but rather likenesses, which show us that the object or original and its representation are separate entities. Like Shakespeare's characters, they provide, more than a mimetic copy or representation of some model or object, an example of the process of invention itself, and each one repeats this process in a singular fashion. This is to suggest that representativeness would consist in singular repetitions, rather than in re-presentation in its usual sense. Its nature is to be performative in the Austinian sense.

Insofar as representativeness evades mimesis or re-presentation, and therefore happens singularly each time it occurs, it is one of the sides of Emersonian reading that appears in "Self-Reliance." Like the self generated through reading in the earlier essay, the representative man has nothing to do with representation as copy, but rather lies always beyond mimesis. Equally to the point, however, the analogy between this process and that of daguerreotypy highlights that representativeness is not the ex-pression of some interior quality. A daguerreotype is a two-dimensional image, and the image is the meaning. It does not conceal some inner depth; it is all surface. So, too, it is with representativeness. It implies nothing of will or activity; it does not express an interior formative force: "We take a great deal of pains to waylay and entrap that which of itself will fall into our hands. I count him a great man who inhabits a higher sphere of thought, into which other men rise with labor and difficulty" (5). The idea that representativeness is something that simply falls on one may remind us of the German *Witz* that characterizes thinking as receptivity as early as "The American Scholar." Here, it underscores the way in which representativeness lies beyond will or choice and, therefore, beyond a simple correspondence to or mimesis of an internal state. One simply is representative by virtue of being most wholly oneself, for this in fact would be the very quality or state that representativeness seeks to convey. The representative man is he who simply performs or enacts himself beyond any mere consciousness of what he is doing; he does not tell us how or what he does, but simply demonstrates himself in his full potential. This demonstration or performance conceals nothing.

This is why, as Emerson concludes the paragraph on Shakespeare and Daguerre, "no recipe can be given for the making of a Shakespeare" (144). On the one hand, this formulation would seem to ally Emerson with Kant, when in the third Critique Kant insists that one genius does not imitate another, but rather goes to his sources.[9] The figure can be offered up as representative, but this representativeness is nothing that can be named, and it is not transmissible as such. The representative man does not convey a message or exemplify anything but himself, and according to the logic of Emersonian reading, this would be because he cannot even represent a "message" to himself; he simply is. If, however, representativeness is not some kind of unitary interiority, then neither does it refer back to or re-present synecdochically some preexistent general whole. There is not a genus of the representative to which we all potentially belong as individual instances. In this respect, Emerson is perhaps at some distance from Kant in that there is no "source" of representativeness. In the simplest sense, Emerson implies this by presenting different representatives, but each in such a way that by the end of the essays, we cannot precisely say what any figure has represented; yet we would not mistake one for another.

It may seem that the very reasons for which representativeness is not mimetic amount to the paradox that the representative man is entirely private. He cannot be compared, he does not transmit a message, and he cannot be copied. And yet Emerson is quite clear that representativeness is nothing other than the inescapably public relation that characterizes Emersonian reading. Just after noting the way in which the representative labors not to be representative, he adds, "His service is of like sort. It costs a beautiful person no exertion to paint her image on our eyes; yet how splendid is that benefit! It costs no more for a wise soul to convey his quality to other men. . . . Men have a pictorial or representative quality, and serve us."[10] Emerson does not ally representativeness with the pictorial in order to underscore what would be the usual representational nature of the exemplar. Instead, the representative is pictorial because, as we have already seen, the act of being representative occurs on an interface or surface that conceals nothing, and because it lies beyond will and choice. But far from this unintentionality making of the representative a wholly private figure, it marks his relation to us. This otherness from himself, and nothing else, is his "service." Representativeness, then, is constitutively relational, necessarily in two senses. On the one hand, it initiates just that process wherein we learn to appropriate our own unrecognized potential by way of an Other who represents it to us. As Emerson puts it in "Uses":

> We have social strengths. Our affection towards others create a sort of vantage or purchase which nothing will supply. I can do that by another which I cannot do alone. I can say to you what I cannot first say to myself. Other men are lenses through which we read our own minds. Each man seeks those of different quality from his own, and such as are good of their kind; that is, he seeks other men, and the *otherest*. (5)

In its sociality or reciprocity, representativeness teaches neither a particular moral position nor a type of behavior, but instead the enacted possibility of a transformed version of the self. If this tuition would seem to occur in a specular, identificatory or mimetic fashion, the specular imagery here is overturned by the idea that we only read our own minds through the otherest of others. This is perhaps simply to say that the possibility of our transformation lies beyond the horizon of representation. Reciprocally, the Other contains this possibility for us precisely by being other. If it transforms us, it is by presenting itself *as* singular alterity, as an unappropriable otherness that can only be marked as a limit. By exposing itself as the otherness or singularity that lies on the other side of representation, it calls each one of us in a singular fashion and, therefore, as singular beings. We are called to identify, but to identify precisely with that which is irreplaceable, to identify, then, in what we earlier called a symbolic way.

As in "Self-Reliance" and "Experience," reading is figured here as an act whereby we come to experience our own otherness as such, an experience that can never be conveyed or spoken. As we read our representatives, whomever they may be, and technically they may be anyone at all, we recognize our own alterity to ourselves, as well as to literal others. This division within the self, its otherness from even itself, comes to the fore in "Experience." In order to understand it as more than a structural possibility, more than something we do all the time without even knowing it, it is perhaps necessary to take two detours, one conceptual, the other particular. By reading Emersonian representativeness against the tradition of exemplarity, and with Hawthorne's depiction of the scarlet letter, we may better be able to understand its particular nature.

Two Exemplary Detours:
The Example, and the Scarlet Letter

Examples themselves are traditionally construed as detours or pauses from the essential matter at hand. Kant in fact notes in the prefatory material to the *Critique of Pure Reason* that examples have been excluded from his exposition because they are merely contingent additions.[11] Doubtless this is because examples take up a certain amount of time and energy in writing, but also perhaps Kant declines to include them because they are a tricky business. At once highly particular, incidental and reductive, it is their function to illustrate the general with no slippage. They are presumably interchangeable with other examples, merely ready to hand; therefore, they are instances of a generality without importance in and of themselves. Yet this is rarely the case. Take, for example, the ball of wax that Descartes introduces in his second *Meditation*. The fiction is that it is literally ready to hand, there on his desk, a particular piece of wax. The wax, however, is mentioned not for its particularity, but rather for its illustrative purposes. Once the illustration has been made, the wax is forgotten. At the same time, the ball of wax has a way of escaping the reductive purposes it is meant to serve. It may continue to illustrate the general point Descartes wishes to make, but it does so precisely by transforming itself into something else. It is introduced in its solid form, redolent of the honey it contained and of the flowers from which it has been extracted, definable in shape and size, capable of giving off a sound if struck. But, "now, as I speak, a flame is brought near to it; its lingering savour is dispelled, the scent vanishes, its colour changes, its shape is transformed, its size increases, it turns liquid, it becomes hot, almost too hot to touch, and though you knock on it, it will give back no sound. Is it the same wax?"[12] Here we have the example as a whole new ball of wax. It is not simply an example, as Descartes would have it, of our certainty or lack thereof of material bodies, but serves further as an example of the very mutability of exemplarity itself.[13]

Individuals, of course, are no less complex than objects. As exemplars, they are supposed to be fixed, to illustrate a general, unchanging idea or principle, and to be the best of their kind. Moreover, they risk no slippage in the sense that because they are the best of their kind, their value is supposed to reside in their clarity.[14] Their meaning does not reside in the vicissitudes of interpretation because they themselves are illustrative interpretations. All of this is exactly what Emersonian representativeness works against. The example as rhetorical figure is particularly to the point in Emerson because it is usually taken to mark the comfortable passage between the abstract and the particular, between philosophy and experience. If exemplarity makes of this passage a smooth transition, then representativeness shows it to resist all transition, or else to require no transition whatsoever. No representative belongs to any larger kind, and representatives become so at all only by exposing themselves to being taken up in singular ways by singular readers. Thought and experience become the same thing. In this sense, Emerson's interest would lie less in the fixed, reductive, unchanging nature of the example, than in its possibility for slippage. It is only because we each have the capacity to represent ourselves and in fact do so all the time, because we are always transforming ourselves individually in an exchange with an Other, that Others become representative for us. This is, of course, how receptivity works as well. The Other exists merely in a sense to make me receptive to my own receptivity, just as the representative makes me available to my own representativeness.

The difference between exemplarity and representativeness might be construed as one more move on Emerson's part to grapple with or capture philosophy for America. If this is the case, however, it is nonetheless more than a philosophical move. Exemplarity would be just that trope underlying the usual way in which the relation between private and public is construed for and in a democracy. Like the example, the individual is taken to be the type of a genus, individual perhaps, but interchangeable with all other individuals, without slippage. We can all stand for each other and, in the most literal sense, elect representatives, because ultimately we are each homogeneous parts of a greater whole. Exemplarity is synecdoche. By contrast, representativeness might best be understood as metonymy, as the contiguous relation of nonanalogical parts. The question, of course, is how nonanalogical parts are or can be related at all; this is a question that bears particularly on the kind of consensus supposedly undergirding democratic functioning.

In order to understand how such a refiguration of exemplarity might lead to a politics, let us move from the example of the example to a particular exemplification that bears not only on representativeness but also on the most pervasive rhetorical figure in American Renaissance writing—the symbol—with more than rhetorical consequences. The scarlet letter in Hawthorne's romance is usually read as being a sign of something else, and yet, Hawthorne works against such an understanding in a number of ways. In the Customs-House sketch, Hawthorne imagines the letter as a "mystic symbol" that conveys some "deep meaning." However, in the course of the narrative he then constructs, it becomes something quite other.[15] It begins as a surface manifestation of Hester's soul; the Puritan community brands her with it to mark her inner state. Part of its purpose, of course, is also to mark her as an outsider, as other than those of the community. As it turns out, this otherness is far more radical than the community could have predicted. Hester is not simply other than the positive collectivity of the Puritan community but also she is wholly unpredictable in her effects. As she fulfills her own unstated imperatives, which are unknown even to herself, the meaning of the letter changes, but not because Hester wills it so. She simply does as she does, without the intention of changing anyone's mind about anything, including her own. The letter thus becomes, far from some outer sign of an inner state, a wholly external site of potential interpretation. The letter marks only an absence of determinate meaning, an indetermination underscored by its intimate connection with Pearl who is said to embody it. The point, however, is not indeterminacy as a sign of an interior fullness of meaning. Hester wears the letter on her chest, on the surface, and it hides nothing. It simply marks Hester's difference and otherness, both unrepresentable except through her actions, all in full view, and which themselves engender the meaning of the letter. Indeed, every attempt to install a tropology organized according to surface and depth fails. This is Hawthorne's failure to write romance in the Customs-House sketch, it is the patriarchs' failure to elicit a meaning from Pearl, and it is Chillingworth's immense failure with Dimmesdale. Dimmesdale, too, believes that he hides everything, but Hawthorne severely calls this belief into question at the close of the romance. When he gives his election speech, nothing is revealed because nothing is hidden. Dimmesdale, after all, says that he is the worst sinner of all; it is only the community's obsessive will to interpret that allegorizes and so obscures the meaning of what he says. Pearl alone has understood that even from the beginning Dimmesdale hides nothing. She knows who he is, asking as she does at midnight on the scaffold, when he will be her earthly father, and in a similar gesture, she fetches and returns the letter that Hester casts off in the forest in her encounter with Dimmesdale. For Pearl, Hester is indistinguishable from the sign that constitutes her identity.

Insofar as the letter remains on the surface as a mark of singularity and otherness that cannot be represented except in its immediate performance, a performance beyond all tropes of surface and depth, and therefore beyond symbolism, it resembles the Emersonian concept of representativeness. In addition to demonstrating that meaning occurs only in its offered enactment, in a display or performance, Hester especially underscores the idea that representativeness has nothing to do with instances of a generality. The letter is explicitly designed to cut her off from the commonality of the community. She is not a type or instance of a larger whole, even if the letter does occupy the interface between Hester and her community. Although the people of the community bestow the letter on Hester, in a curious sense she is more at home with it than they are; as she embroiders it, and displays it, these acts link her with her community. It is important, however, that none of Hester's acts is presented by Hawthorne as designed to elicit an effect on the community, in part, as I have suggested, because Hester herself does not know what she is up to. The one intentional act she undertakes, fleeing with Dimmesdale to England, would separate her from the community and is brought to a speedy and unhappy conclusion. The implication is that our acts of will and decision always remove us from community. The letter lies beyond Hester's will, both in the sense that it is originally imposed upon her by the community and also that its meaning takes shape only in the unpredictable interchange between herself and the community. Neither the community nor Hester can be said to originate or control this meaning. Its signification emerges, instead, precisely at their interface or spacing.

The importance of this spacing may help to explain why Hester does not flee the community, first, or finally. She is not like the others in the community, but merely exists with those others. Because she stays and because she wears the letter in the presence of others, the letter exists as the site of possible communication. It is, after all, a letter, a written thing, which is the very nature of representativeness itself insofar as it designates more than the structural relation between the private being and the public sphere. *Representative Men*, even in its very title, insists that although representativeness may lie beyond representation and signification in every sense, it nonetheless occurs and is given to us only *as* representation. It must be marked, if only as a limit; now we might think of such marking or writing as our responsibility for responsibility. This is the meaning of "Whim," that word that still and only marks itself for some potential reader, some Other who will take it up as the sign of something offered. Representativeness may not be transmissible as the content of something being re-presented, but it is nonetheless a communication in the sense of offering itself, without effort or intent—a communication of communication, as "Experience" has it. Like the scarlet letter itself, representativeness is on the surface as an evidency of a possible relation to it. If the writing of such a sign, a writing that is representativeness itself, constitutes a realization of responsibility, it is because the failure to mark it in some way means the foreclosure of the possibility of relation. To experience representativeness, to read it, is to experience the fact of its being offered to and for our representation of it.

Un-writing the Community

I take this to be the reason that five of Emerson's six representatives are writers of one kind or another—literally those who publish or make public. More generally, the idea that representativeness must mark itself as limit in order to be available at all may help to explain why Emerson chooses as his representatives figures who are already clearly well-known figures and also who can be named in terms of a vocation. On the one hand, the very obviousness of his choices emphasizes the fact that these representatives have displayed themselves in such a way as to invite our attention. They have been called to do something irreplaceable and, as such, call us in our irreplaceability and singularity. On the other hand, and even because of this, we may neither agree with Emerson's particular designations, nor may we agree that these figures are the best examples of their kind. Indeed, it is difficult even to specify to what "kind" they belong. It is, after all, not entirely clear what precisely about Plato, for example, makes of him the exemplary philosopher. The tension between the obviousness of Emerson's choices and the vagueness of the figures themselves serves to underscore the fact that representativeness is not communicable as a content, but that it nonetheless takes shape as a communication.

The otherness that forms the basis for such a community would mean that we would have to rethink the nature of democracy itself and the writing that might sustain it. Such a democracy could no longer be a system resting on the possibility of remainderless consensus, but would be instead the aggregation of unassimilable singularities. If representative democracy as it is usually construed founders on questions of difference, then this would be democracy as the very recognition of difference—democracy with difference as its necessity. If, however, such a democratic community can become the basis for a practical politics, then it is only perhaps in the sense of resisting everything that might bring such an aggregate itself to completion. If each individual is other from itself, then so, too, the community must remain other from itself. To exist at all, community must be written, marked, but neither it nor its writing can complete themselves as a project. This knowledge may have guided Emerson's earlier sense in "The American Scholar," that American letters must be fragmentary and, therefore, in the open-endedness of the future. Here, in *Representative Men*, Emerson registers the same resistance to the closure of communication at the end of each essay. Great men are "magnets" who attract us to them, but "the more we are drawn, the more we are repelled."[16] Consequently, having examined the greatness of a given representative figure, Emerson proceeds to find fault. Plato has no system; Shakespeare's life is undistinguished; Napoleon is petty. The actual flaw is in one sense less important than the suggestion that no representative is *the* representative. At best we have partial and fragmentary indications of a vocation, that is, of a work exposed and calling to us. Such work consists in the very actions that have made a particular figure representative in the first place. However, in order to maintain itself as Other, and therefore as the very call for community itself, a representative must not be completed or unitary.[17]

    In this respect, the actual flaw of Emerson's representatives, at least of the five writers, is perhaps of great importance. These flaws are not simply a generic interruption of exemplarity, rather they are quite specifically related to incompletion itself: Plato has no system; Swedenborg inadequately expresses himself; Montaigne, who has no precise flaw, nonetheless writes "on every random topic that comes into his head; treats everything without ceremony."[18] Similarly, Shakespeare has no importunate topic and dissipates his genius in the popular form of theater, and lastly, Goethe,

> this lawgiver of art, is not an artist. Was it that he knew too much, that his sight was microscopic, and interfered with the just perspective, the seeing of the whole? He is fragmentary; a writer of occasional poems, and of an encyclopaedia of sentences. When he sits down to write a drama or a tale, he collects and sorts his observations from a hundred sides, and combines them into the body as fitly as he can. A great deal refuses to incorporate.[19]

Goethe is the very representative of representativeness. More than any other figure, he demonstrates how work that is vocation, that marks one as singular and calls to each of us in our singularity, hence, the work that is the realization of community itself, must abandon itself before completion. He reveals representativeness as the very interruption of exemplarity, as written, exposed, and public, but also, as risk. In exemplifying the rupture of his own exemplarity, Goethe stands as a reminder that writing itself is not a practice we can define as interruption, but rather, that interrupted, it nonetheless goes on. In this respect, representatives could never be originary figures for anyone, but only exposed absences that make true community possible in the first place. Such absence must be marked as the limit at which we might meet. If Plato the philosopher is our origin, then Goethe the writer is our future, a representative of what we might yet become.

Since he is "the philosopher of . . . multiplicity," and his "second part of Faust, is a philosophy of literature set in poetry," he stands also as a representative of the fulfillment of what Emerson has been calling "letters" from the start. As such, he illustrates Emerson's hope for his own writing, for his self-election as the potential American scholar. Indeed, there is not a single passage in *Representative Men* that more accurately describes Emerson himself than his closing words on Goethe's inability to incorporate his writing into a system. Piecing together his lectures and essays from the voluminous repository of thought and quotation that is his journal, Emerson, too, works in fragments. Montaigne is likely Emerson's ideal, but

Goethe is his truest representative, as he himself seems to have known. Nearing the completion of *Representative Men*, Emerson compared in his journal certain Concord residents with his representatives. Himself he paired with Goethe, a correspondence extending well beyond shared compositional practices. The fragmentariness that Emerson attributes to Goethe should remind us that the writing of community, what we have been calling "representativeness," is never finished. Indeed, it is all we have. The actual practice of such writing, rather than its outlined potential, is now what remains to be explored in a final chapter.

Chapter 6 · · ·

Measures of Silence

> What provokes one to look at all philosophers half suspiciously, half mockingly, is . . . they all pose as if they had discovered and reached their real opinions through the self-development of a cold, pure, divinely unconcerned dialectic . . . while at bottom, it is an assumption, a hunch, indeed a kind of "inspiration"—most often a desire of the heart that has been filtered and made abstract—that they defend with reasons they have sought after the fact.
> —Nietzsche, Beyond Good and Evil

Emerson's "Fate" and the Construction of America

From "The American Scholar" through *Representative Men*, Emerson's project for American letters insists upon the centrality of language and reading in the auto-constitution of the subject. Such a subject is more powerfully self-authorizing and self-contained than its Enlightenment counterpart, but at the same time, it cannot escape the social dimension of the reading strategies through which it creates itself.[1] When Emerson relocates meaning within the reading self as the interpretive circuits that create that self—if it can still be called that—he suggests language is responsible for what one is, rather than reflective of it. From one perspective, this view of language marks the shift precipitating the crisis of idealism so often remarked upon in studies of Emerson's epistemology.[2] Perhaps a more important consequence is that as meaning comes to depend on one's particular situation in the world, the language that one chooses, and that prevails, makes all the difference.

In its final form, the power of language becomes the language of power.

This slippage in the registers of power underlies what may be the most vexed issue concerning Emerson's place in American culture. Critics from Richard Chase forward have made commonplace the idea that America's most canonical mid-nineteenth-century authors, particularly Emerson and Melville, remained silent on the political and ideological questions of their day. More recently, a whole generation of new Americanists has begun to examine those silences as potential forms of ideological articulation.[3] But the differences between the old and the new Americanists are perhaps smaller than they seem. Whereas the old Americanists celebrated Emerson's evasion of sociopolitical life in favor of his claims for a transcendental self, the new Americanists have begun to explore the ideology that informs Emerson's radical individualism, without for a moment questioning the entrenched nature of individualism itself. Bercovitch, for example, as well as a number of other critics, want to hear in Emerson's silence about collective life not merely an evasion in favor of other interests, but rather a type of ideological positioning and closure that inadvertently insures the continuity of collective values by insisting upon the individual. In this view, resistance to ideology and dissent are already part of a collective consciousness and serve to reinforce it. Still, there is no great distance between Tony Tanner's observation that the Emersonian self ends before social reality begins and Bercovitch's claim that Emerson "establishes the absolute dichotomy of self and society."[4]

Whatever else their differences may be, this parallelism between Tanner and Bercovitch indicates that old and new Americanists share a belief in Emerson's refusal to acknowledge the connection between the private individual and the public context. Either way, one is left with an Emerson who seems peculiarly unaware of the ways in which a particular construction of the self generates and structures the lineaments of social power. Certainly such a view appears justified by the Emerson who writes in "Experience," "In this our talking America, we are ruined by our good nature and listening on all sides."[5] More shocking is the Emerson who in "Self-Reliance" dismisses the popular philanthropies of his day with the question: "Are they *my* poor?"⁶ But perhaps the most problematic example of Emerson's stance on the relation between private and public life occurs in the late essay "Fate." Written in 1851 and published in 1860, "Fate" rigorously attends to the ancient philosophical knot of freedom and fate while managing to keep all but silent on the issue of chattel slavery. This omission is perhaps doubly disturbing since "Fate" appears as the first essay in a volume entitled *The Conduct of Life*, as if Emerson were suggesting that the initial step in our conduct should be to remove ourselves from the life around us, rather than to live it. No one has quite known what to do with this piece of writing, and for the most part, it remains in the margins of critical discussion, ignored or barely tolerated.⁷ Martha Banta, who is generally sympathetic to Emerson, nicely sums up the critical consensus when she explains away the matter by announcing, "The older Emerson got tired more quickly over the span of an essay, and was increasingly apt to make tomfool pronouncements."⁸

Banta's remark points up how Emerson's career is frequently divided into phases marked by both biographical and intellectual crises; and "Fate" is perhaps rightly read as indicative of just one of those moments.⁹ At the same time, although "Fate" remains a central marker in the development of Emerson's thought, it also stands as a continuing commitment to his larger and more permanent hopes for the efficacy of American letters. As the nature of letters in "The American Scholar" suggests, nation building begins with self-building, but there is a sense in which the passage from the one to the other, from private power to public effect, remains theoretical in most of Emerson's work. Indeed, in the foregoing chapters here, as the Emersonian subject becomes irreducibly social, it does so only in a structural and projected way. The question lingers regarding whether or not the Emersonian rhetoric that generates such a structure has any efficacy in a pragmatic sense. I suggest that if elsewhere the project of self-creation seems limited to the private individual, "Fate" stands as Emerson's firm and pragmatic testament to the inescapably public and pragmatically political dimension of that individual. The essay troubles us for the reason that, in order to accomplish its political aims, it must keep silent on the very issues it attempts to address. Like the Emersonian text that enables us to experience what otherwise remain our own alienated thoughts, "Fate" does no more than to draw its readers into acts of interpretation that are solutions to what Emerson will call "the question of the times" in the first paragraph of the essay. How it does so, and to what end, are the subject of this chapter.

The immediate form that this silence takes is, of course, the persistent abstraction of the tension between personal liberty and fate. In this respect, "Fate" is perhaps the one essay that seems to contradict the recurrent rhetorical moves through which Emerson elsewhere collapses the distinction between literature and philosophy. Still, whatever our misgivings about an essay that appears to address the abstract questions of freedom and necessity while remaining silent on the historical reality of slavery, Emerson nonetheless opens the essay by stating his intention to deal with practical things. Having attended a lecture on "the Spirit of the Times," Emerson concludes:

> To me, however, the question of the times resolved itself into a practical question of the conduct of life. How shall I live? We are incompetent to solve the times. Our geometry cannot span the huge orbits of the prevailing ideas, behold their return, and reconcile their opposition. We can only obey our own polarity. 'Tis fine for us to speculate and elect our course, if we must accept an irresistible dictation.[10]

The anecdotal tone here is misleading because the paragraph's two central tropes—geometry and dictation—at once prefigure the essay's entire argument and recast the potentially private nature of the question, "How should I live?" Ostensibly, the paragraph generates an opposition between our own polarity, say, our private dispositions, and dictation, or large, impersonal, and given meanings. That opposition becomes more complex if we attend to the final two sentences of the paragraph closely, and I want to return to those sentences shortly. For the moment, however, the importance of "dictation" is that it underscores the etymological meaning of "fate" as that which is spoken, *fatum*, usually as a sentence of doom delivered from the gods, and further back as *moira*, or the Greek term for "fate" where it means our sentenced portion or lot. We should remember that Emerson could have titled the essay "Ananke," or

"Necessity," both of which terms he frequently uses. But "fate" is the more apt word: its quiet emphasis on speech is central throughout the essay in which both limitation and freedom turn out to be bound up with language-as-saying in a very particular sense. As the opening paragraph unfolds it announces the essay's subject, not only as the tension between individual desire and its limitation but also, more specifically, as that between what each of us would say for ourselves and that which is spoken for us, dictated to us from a source seemingly not ourselves.

The tone of this speech becomes clearer when placed within the context of the geometrical figure that grounds the opposition between polarity and dictation. The reconciliation of individual desire and the dictates of something beyond the personal pragmatically provides the foundations for the possibility of a liberal democracy. In this geometrical figure, Emerson is precisely questioning those foundations. My guess is that Emerson borrows this figure from the twelfth chapter of *The Biographia Literaria*, where Coleridge introduces geometry as an example of how philosophy might go about finding foundational truths. Geometry, argues Coleridge, does not demonstrate its primary construction or foundational truth, but rather postulates it, because the primary construction—here, a cyclical line—is self-evident. The cyclical line, according to Coleridge, serves as a foundational truth in geometry, because

> it is at once undetermined and determined; undetermined through any point without, and determined through itself. Geometry therefore supplies philosophy with the example of a primary intuition, from which every science that lays claim to evidence must take its commencement. The mathematician does not begin with a demonstrable proposition, but with an intuition, a practical idea.[11]

Whether or not Coleridge's geometrical analogy practices good philosophy, his interest in the question of what is determined or undetermined seems consonant with the necessity/free-will polarity within which Emerson works in "Fate." The figure also provides a more specific pretext for understanding the agenda of the essay, and given that Emerson employs it twice more in the course of the essay, its use cannot be wholly incidental. A cyclical line, of course, not only provides the foundation of geometry but also spans an infinite number of points, which seems to be just where our geometry fails. In saying, then, that our geometry cannot span the huge orbit of prevailing ideas, it is as if Emerson were arguing that our philosophy, whatever it might be, had not yet found the foundational or self-evident truths that justify its primary construction. But Emerson's interest here is not in some abstract philosophizing; he, after all, states his interest to be in the question, "How should I live?" and he declares the question within the context of speaking for ourselves versus being spoken for. I want to read Emerson's lament about our imperfect geometry to state that we have not yet found—or, founded—the foundational truths that made our primary construction or original constitution possible, because our voices are not yet our own. It is as if America did not yet exist.

America's particular foundational truths, those with which it declared its independence and brought itself into being, were precisely those that guaranteed the reconciliation of the individual and the universal, the private and the public: "We hold these truths to be self-evident, that all men are created equal." The trouble is that the words with which Americans brought themselves into being, America's foundational truths, are not self-evident unless they are acted upon as such. Emerson makes this lack within America's words quite clear later in the essay: "Nothing is more disgusting than the crowing about liberty by slaves, as most men are, and the flippant mistaking for freedom of some paper preamble like a 'Declaration of Independence' or the statute right to vote, by those who have never dared to think or to act."[12] The suggestion here is that all Americans are slaves insofar as they have failed to think for themselves and to act on those thoughts. Americans have substituted "windy conceits" (954) for "the conduct of life." The implication is that, as a nation, America has not yet constituted itself because Americans have not yet learned how to act on the thoughts expressed in their words. If they had, then all men would be treated as equal and no tension would exist between the private good, say those whose interests demand the continuation of slavery, and the universal good of equality as put forth in the words through which Americans initially constituted themselves. If Americans are to constitute themselves finally, as a nation, each individual as equal must represent him- or herself in terms of the universal, that is, in terms of the truths held to be self-evident: that all people are created equal, even if such equality is based finally, as "Experience" has it, on the incommensurability of singularities.

It would be misleading, however, to think of the "foundational" as something natural or given. Emerson does not suggest that the form of society is no stronger than its philosophical foundations. Instead, those foundations are no stronger than the present form of cultural life in which they are embodied. In this pragmatic view, truth is a matter wholly contingent on the willingness of each individual to represent him- or herself in terms that make good on the words he or she uses. To represent oneself in this way can only occur in a kind of speech that resists dictation, a speech that actively voices one's individual and equal consent or dissent to the conditions of a system that has been laid, however contingently, as a foundation. We—Americans—fail to do this when we cease to lend our own voices to the continuing constitution of the nation, when, for example, in disagreement, we withdraw—or perhaps even secede—instead of voicing active dissent, not on behalf of our own individual interests, but rather on behalf of the universal or self-evident truths that we ourselves have brought into being.[13] Thus, in remarking upon the American failure to speak in this way, Emerson serves up his peculiar statement that Americans are "incompetent" to solve the times: originally from the Latin word *competentia*, meaning "meeting together, agreement," competence would be the condition in which, regardless of one's individual position, one still consented to be an active member in the ongoing constitution of America.[14] To be incompetent to solve the times would be just that disunited state in which disagreement with one another failed to take account of the system that Americans hold in common and their responsibility in its ongoing constitution, whether by consent or dissent.

Taken in this way, Emerson's concerns in the opening paragraph are twofold, at least. In the simplest sense, he seems to be suggesting that the fact of slavery all but negates the self-evident truths on which America was founded. By locating the meaning of fate as that which is, before all, spoken, he also suggests that words are all we have for this foundation. The words through which Americans originally constituted themselves are their only authorization, in both the sense of creating and also in lending authority. (Like Coleridge's geometrical postulate, our words were authorized by nothing beyond themselves; in this way they alone become self-evident.) They were the words that we spoke; they were not dictated to us. More to the point, the words do not authorize us so much as we authorize them in a continuing willingness to think and to act on their terms, with full awareness that such terms cannot be justified in any absolute sense. They can only be performed. Like selfhood as it is sketched in "Self-Reliance," nationhood is not something that happens once and for all, but rather, a that state exists only in its present saying. This is what I take Emerson to mean when, midway through "Fate," he writes, "The population of the world is a conditional population: not the best, but the best that could live now."[15] "Condition" is a word Emerson employs many times in this essay. It can, of course, mean many things and, as in this sentence, many at once. In one sense, Emerson reminds us that each individual and the nation as a whole are conditional, in the grammatical sense of "contingent." But contingency is itself a condition or limitation, a fact from which we learn that we always depend on ourselves, on our willingness to authorize ourselves. Because of this contingency, our fate or condition, at least as a nation, is precisely one of con-dition—*a saying together.* To say that our condition is con-dition is to suggest that we exist as a nation only in our saying of it; quite literally, our birth as a nation was an act of performative speech. If the truths Americans hold to be self-evident are no longer so, if Americans have not made good on the very truths on which their nation was founded, then it is because they have abandoned their words and their part in their continuing authorization.

The Operations of Ideology

I will put aside for a moment the question of why Emerson raises these issues so indirectly—perhaps it is a question, anyway, that cannot be answered until one understands how one lost one's words in the first place. Already, the final sentence of the first paragraph of "Fate" has named the difficulty: "'Tis fine for us to speculate and elect our course, if we must accept an irresistible dictation." With his choice of the word "elect," Emerson quietly insists democracy is a fantasy when we fail to lend our own voices to our ongoing constitution and, instead, accept a script in which we have no part. This is not, however, to say that someone else necessarily writes the script. Our own polarity may be at odds with dictation, but that opposition itself is complicated by the grammatical possibility that obedience to our own polarity is equally a dictation that deprives us of freedom. In one respect, this is Emerson's interpretation of the Kantian imperative that we choose the law for its own sake: freedom is linked to the autonomy of reflection, but autonomy finally implies giving ourselves the law. Emerson, however, takes Kant's formulation a step further, by suggesting that even reflection is no guarantee of freedom. We may think that we choose our own way, that the only limitations we face are external, but the opposition begins earlier, and within, as an obedience to an internal dictation. Echoing Emerson's earlier thoughts on alienated majesty, "Fate" suggests all apparently external limitations are no more than one's unconscious obedience to constructions of one's own making. Indeed, Emerson opens the essay by saying as much:

> It chanced during one winter, a few years ago, that our cities were bent on discussing the theory of the Age. By an odd coincidence, four or five noted men were each reading a discourse to the citizens of Boston or New York, on the Spirit of the Times. It so happened that the subject had the same prominence in some remarkable pamphlets and journals issued in London in the same season. (943)

"It chanced," "by an odd coincidence," "it so happened": these phrases remind us that large and general meanings like the Theory of the Age and the Spirit of the Times, things as apparently given as the atmosphere or air, are not natural, inherently true, and simply waiting to be discovered; rather they are the product of chance and coincidence, or perhaps more accurately, just one more "windy conceit." It is we who create the Theory of the Age and we who determine its authority—and this is precisely what we fail to see. So it is with fate, too, for later in the paragraph, the Spirit of the Times simply becomes that which we are incompetent to solve.

The true subject of the essay is thus not so much the Providential Fate of the Middle Ages, but rather the unconscious belief that masquerades as natural and total law. Insofar as fate is of our own making, we might say that this is an essay written against itself. Its goal is not so much to overturn fate as to teach us to recognize the contingency of the very structures we now find immutable. This is what I take Emerson to mean when, in the very curious conclusion of the essay, he calls upon us to build altars to the Beautiful Necessity, "which rudely or softly educates him to the perception that there are no contingencies; that Law rules throughout existence, a Law which is not intelligent but intelligence" (968). To say that there are no contingencies is not to insist upon the power of fate, but rather to claim that the process of intelligence or thought is itself the rule. Nothing is left to chance or coincidence because everything finally is a construction of our own making. Or, everything is left to chance and coincidence because such constructions are contingent in the sense that as created by intelligence, rather than dictated by fate, they can be recreated. Their existence has no more authorization than our own consent to them.

Refigured in this way fate, or "dictation," turns out to be something very like the "alienated majesty" of "Self-Reliance." It is a kind of unconscious thought that achieves its power by appearing first as a directive from elsewhere. Finally, this unconscious thought must be recognized as coming from nowhere, its source fabricated only after the fact of its appearance. As Emerson will write later in the essay, "Fate, then, is a name for facts not yet passed under the fire of thought," or, "So far as a man thinks, he is free" (953). By opposing thought to fate, Emerson suggests only a process, for example, thinking in the most general sense of becoming conscious enough to see that we are always writing our own script even when we accept it as dictated to us and, therefore, unchangeable. Thought, as Emerson claims late in the essay, "dissolves the material universe, by carrying the mind up into a sphere where all is plastic" (956). As in Emerson's earlier work, this kind of thinking might be characterized as self-creative, a position from which, by engaging ourselves with the text of the other, rather than accepting terms already dictated to us by ourselves or others, we create our own minds. This project, part of

Emerson's call for a new mode of letters in "The American Scholar," naturally bears on the individual, with the difference that here, Emerson's subject has shifted from the nature of that individual to the vicissitudes of belief itself, to our construction of "the theory of the Age."

It might still be tempting to read "Fate" as no more than a philosophically oriented version of the transferential structures that determine individual identity as early as "Self-Reliance." But given the broadened scope of the later essay, and particularly in light of the political implications of the opening geometrical figure, it proves productive to think of "Fate" as Emerson's tacit exploration of the operations not only of the individual unconscious but also of collective fantasy as well, that is, of ideology and its power over us. As simple as this seems, it is still important to be precise about just what form of ideology we mean here, because this will determine Emerson's rhetorical strategies, including his silence, in the course of the essay. Slavoj Žižek's definition of the law as it shapes ideological belief is useful at this point. Like Emerson and following Kant, Žižek suggests that our only obedience is to internal dictates, which we fail to recognize as such:

> We find reasons attesting our belief because we already believe . . . "External" obedience to the Law is thus not submission to external pressure, to so-called non-ideological "brute force," but obedience to the Command in so far as it is "incomprehensible" . . . what is "repressed" then, is not some obscure origin of the Law but the very fact that the Law is not to be accepted as true, only as necessary—the fact that its authority is without truth.[16]

If the law's authority is without truth, then it is as we have seen because the law provides the necessary structuration of belief and not some a priori justification. In "Fate" the best example of ideology thus construed occurs with Emerson's lengthy discussion of evolutionary determinism and our capitulation to it. The very nature of this determinism is its insistence on the inescapable effects of brute force in our supposedly human constitutions: "The menagerie, or forms and powers of the spine, is a book of fate: the bill of the bird, the skull of the snake, determines tyranically its limits. . . . People seem sheathed in their tough organization."[17] Physical determinism as "brute force" is one of Emerson's primary examples of fate, but he concludes its discussion with the comment, "This limitation is impassable by any insight of man" (953). Had Emerson read Darwin when first composing the essay, one might read this more loosely as a capitulation to the random, rather than the determined. But given the likely influence of Robert Chambers, what remains impassable to the insight of man is precisely an obscure *divine plan*, that is, the law itself.[18] As Žižek notes, fate here achieves its status as law not because it is an arbitrary force of nature, but precisely insofar as it remains opaque to thought or understanding.

For Žižek, such an understanding of the law, as that which we unknowingly project and obey as external, links the study of ideology with Lacanian psychoanalysis. In this model there is no overcoming of ideology. Ideology, or the law, like the workings of the unconscious, is not some transcendent, unavailable truth; rather it is an illusion, or error, already inscribed in the way we see things. This is the error of the "transference" itself, a necessary error governing the entire structure of the Emersonian self. It is a knowledge that we must attribute to the Other in order to get started thinking at all. The "truth," whether of the unconscious or of ideology, can only become true as mediated through this illusion. In this respect, the power of any ideology is simply a measure of our collective transference to it. Because of this paradoxical structure—in which truth arises only from misrecognition—the best one can do is understand ideology as a necessary structural illusion, much like the symptom in Lacan's later phases of thought, and accept it.[19]

This construction of ideology differs considerably from more traditional Marxist notions in which a critical-ideological procedure could free us from our illusions. But it differs as well from the more complex understanding of ideology that governs the analyses of the new Americanists. Bercovitch provides a recent example, when he writes, "Ideology, we have seen, arises out of historical circumstances, and then re-presents these, rhetorically and conceptually, as though they were natural, universal, inevitable, and right; as though the ideals promulgated by a certain group or class . . . were not the product of history but the expression of self-evident truth."[20] Unlike a straightforward Marxist, Bercovitch claims there is no escape from ideology, but nonetheless, ideology remains for him only a partial field that colors all social relations and can therefore be exposed for what it is. Since ideology is said to arise out of historical circumstances, a Nietzschean genealogy, for example, could bring to light the original circumstances by which a particular piece of conceptual rhetoric became the law, and could thus begin to unravel a belief empty of any natural authority. The idea is not that we can break free of ideology altogether, since we are always embedded in "historical circumstance," but that ideologies can be reinterpreted to be made explicit: this is the essential project of Bercovitch's *The Rites of Assent*. In this respect, Bercovitch shares with Žižek, or with any psychoanalytically oriented critic, a belief that opposes interpretation to ideology. At the same time, Bercovitch insists that interpretation itself, at least in the American version, always returns finally to and as ideological closure.

By contrast, Žižek would argue that ideology, far from being an historically contingent construct, partakes more of the timelessness and uncontainability of unconscious thought, for it is a set of beliefs that provides the very structuration and possibility of our thought and behavior. It would be misleading to think that such beliefs could become conscious and thereby lose their force, for like the Lacanian symptom or transference, ideology conceals nothing. It retains its force just insofar as it remains incomprehensible: it constitutes itself first and always as an essential lack and contingency in the believing subject and, therefore, never as closure, or else as a closure concealing a radical and vertiginous gap in belief itself. Coleridge, with his geometrical postulate and self-evidence, provides another example. As I suggested earlier, this allusion to foundational truths on Emerson's part indicates not so much an insistence on a bedrock of fact, as a sense of the contingency of America itself, a recognition that Americans are grounded in no more than the speech they use and the ways in which they behave. America is not there waiting to be discovered, but rather constructed as a concept appearing to have an autonomous authority. Bercovitch would doubtless agree up to this point. Emerson, too, knows very well that we believe first and then find justification for those beliefs. Instead of assuming that one might return to "historical circumstance" as if it might reveal the reasoning behind a particular belief, Emerson's construction of belief in "Fate" suggests there is nothing whatsoever behind belief. Far from being based on law, or the truth, or even on historical circumstance, belief marks an unspecifiable gap within the concept of America itself; this gap makes "America" possible in the first place. In this sense, an Emersonian construction of ideology and belief is not false consciousness per se; rather it is woven into the very structure of who we are.

Such a construction calls into question the entire epistemology of most contemporary ideological criticism, at least as it is practiced in American Studies. If ideology were no more than false consciousness, then the traditional demystifying critique of ideology would work. But it is not simply a matter of exposing illusions. As Emerson's opening paragraph suggests, what we fail to recognize is not the reality of what we are doing, but rather the illusion that structures our reality. None of Emerson's readers would have denied the fact of slavery; indeed, many would have supported it. The illusion is that, despite the fact of slavery, America amounts to all it claims to be in its foundational documents, indeed, that slavery provides evidence of those claims. Put another way, we might say that the readers Emerson most hopes to influence with this essay may know that their notion of their constitutional liberties masks a particular form of exploitation, but they continue to believe that they are upholding the ideals of the constitution nonetheless. This is what Emerson means by calling the Declaration no more than a paper preamble or "windy conceit." Perhaps it is also what prompts him to begin his discussion of fate proper with the statement: "But let us honestly state the facts. Our America has a bad name for superficialness. Great men, great nations, have not been boasters and buffoons, but perceivers of the terror of life."[21] Ostensibly Emerson refers to something like American optimism in general, but within the more specific context of the antagonism between freedom and limitation, Emerson is surely suggesting that our belief in freedom is so superficial as to be a form of buffoonery.

To unmask the ideology that makes such beliefs possible, by, for example, arguing directly against slavery, would therefore have no effect because it would simply be co-opted to prove the very point it seeks to contradict. Moreover, direct argument would, of course, duplicate the ideological closure it attempts to thwart. As Richard Rorty has pointed out:

> Any argument to the effect that our familiar use of a familiar term is incoherent, or empty, or confused or vague, or "merely metaphorical" is bound to be inconclusive and question-begging. For such use is, after all, the paradigm of coherent, meaningful, literal speech. . . . Interesting philosophy is rarely an examination of the pros and cons of a thesis. Usually it is, implicitly or explicitly, a contest between an entrenched vocabulary which has become a nuisance and a half-formed new vocabulary.[22]

Emerson seems to understand this when he writes, "But Fate against Fate is only parrying and defence."[23] The goal is, instead, to reorient the language of the entire argument such that the original terms no longer mean anything. This is not so easy. Rorty claims further that new vocabularies achieve currency in a typically Jamesian fashion: they will fit with some of our old truths but will also explain more things than the vocabulary they replace, and so on. One trouble with this view, and it pervades most forms of pragmatism, is that it tends to repress just how difficult change is to achieve. Ideology, in fact, of whatever sort, operates precisely by making any deviation from its dictates unthinkable. As Emerson writes midway through the essay, "Once we thought, positive power was all. Now we learn, that negative power, or circumstance, is half" (949). I suppose one could supply the elided quotation marks here to read Emerson as saying that at one time we thought we had power, but now we have learned that our power is checked. But Emerson may also be asking us to consider things without quotation marks, which is to say, not as dictation, but more open-endedly. As if to say, "*when* we thought, we were powerful. But now that we act on received belief, that negative power, i.e., what we have learned, is half" (949). All we have learned and accept as given is exactly a measure of our lack of thought, for ideology forecloses thought by masquerading as unalterable law. Construed in terms of the tropes with which Emerson opens the essay, ideological belief ends the conversation by dictating to us the final script.

Emerson, I think, knows all of this. In what can only be a self-referential remark, he reminds us late in the essay, "I know not what the word *sublime* means, if it be not the intimations in this infant of a terrific force. A text of heroism, a name and anecdote of courage, are not arguments, but sallies of freedom" (957). The passage recalls the resistance to representation everywhere present in Emersonian rhetoric. Remember, too, that "infant" literally means one without speech, one like Emerson who cannot or will not name the subject that he addresses. Yet in this silence *is* a terrific force, precisely because by not speaking, by refusing to enter the ideological argument in any direct sense, Emerson takes a first step toward freedom from it, and we with him. His method will be to move us from the unconscious dream of ideology, not to something that might be construed as freedom from it, but at least to a mode of thinking that is less susceptible to the attempts at closure toward which ideology of any sort is always pushing us. The sublimity of Emerson's text would inspire such thinking, or rather thinking once again as reading. If Emerson's text can achieve the sublimity implied by his own self-description, then it is because, as in the writing of "Whim," the text both embodies and instigates a process beyond the closure implied by representation. The seductions of Emerson's silence, our transference to it, cannot be named, only performed. Such performance would, in its unrepresentable nature, subvert any closure—ideological or otherwise. In turn, it would be just such open-endedness that contains the very promise of a democracy able to acknowledge its own contingency.

Rhetoric and Responsibility

The ways in which Emerson achieves this in "Fate" are many. Evading direct argument, Emerson turns his attention to subtle retropings, which occur on a wholly rhetorical level and, perhaps for just this reason, attain a kind of persuasiveness always absent from direct argument. The first explicit instance of such retroping occurs in the third paragraph of the essay. Having lamented our inability to reconcile the oppositions that riddle the age, he announces with uncharacteristic clarity, "What to do? By obeying each thought frankly, by harping, or if you will, pounding on each string, we learn at last its power.... If one would study his own time, it must be by this method of taking up in turn each of the leading topics which belong to our scheme of human life" (943). On both a literal and a structural level, Emerson will do just this, first as he considers topics such as biological determinism, phrenology, and racial difference, and then by dividing the entire essay into alternating considerations of fate and power. But this passage also picks up on the concerns implicit in the opening paragraph of the essay and sketches the means to a possible solution.

Here, Coleridge's primary construction, the cyclical line, has become a string upon which one might play many musical notes. The inescapable nature of the self-evident evidently can be retroped with a type of mimetic rhetoric that both enacts and states its purpose. Emerson neither says that his subject is the status of our foundational truths nor does he argue against the ways in which we have acted on them. Instead of a discursive statement/counterstatement, he begins with a trope that invites open-ended interpretation and then proceeds quietly to supply an example with his own refiguration. This type of retroping characterizes the entire essay. Even within the ostensibly philosophical concerns that generate its structure, the physical terms in the essay's first section are not negated by the metaphysical; they are transumed on their own ground. The image of biological determinism, for example, which in the first half of the essay appears as "some ruling quality in each son or daughter of the house" (946), becomes in the second half: "When the boy grows to be a man, and is master of the house, he pulls down that wall and builds a new and a bigger" (957). So, too, the unhappy statement that bodily weight determines the elections (948), is turned to our favor when will is said to be, "pound to balance pound" (956). There are other instances of this rhetorical turning, such as when the ineffectual eye beams of the drowning men at the close of the first half of the essay (952), become the glance of the hero whose "eye has the force of sunbeams" (957). None of these examples works by discursive argument, but each shows at a rhetorical level that what we took as law, say the workings of biological determinism, is no more than an effect of our language and, therefore, available to reinterpretation and change.

In this respect, the rhetoric of the essay exemplifies the type of thinking with which Emerson wishes to replace ideological belief. The meaning of this thinking and the obstructions to it are perhaps best explored by way of Emerson's quotation of what appears to be an aphorism by Schelling: "'There is in every man a certain feeling, that he has been what he is from all eternity, and by no means became such in time.' To say it less sublimely,—in the history of the individual is always an account of his condition, and he knows himself to be a party to his present estate" (948). The passage is tricky both because of its immediate context in the essay, and because of the Schellingian context that Emerson has elided. In the first place, Emerson adduces the quote in the midst of a discussion of determinism as our inescapable fate, as if Schelling were describing the merely mechanical. Surely this is one of the essay's many ironic moments, for even as the passage appears amidst Emerson's resigned diatribe about the power of fate, it also serves to remind us that the second half of the essay will turn fate into character. Later, in fact, the last sentences of the passage are retroped to read, "The soul contains the event that shall befall it, for the event is only the actualization of its thought . . . each creature puts forth from itself its own condition and sphere" (963). This type of retroping does not inhere in the words themselves, but rather in an interpretation of tone, supported by context. In a gesture that should by now be familiar, the refiguration that occurs in the second half of the essay does not discover a meaning that was there all along; instead, it creates meaning retroactively, a strategy that itself duplicates the working of ideology. Once this possibility has been made available, the earlier section on the finality of biological determinism can only be taken as a kind of pragmatic irony with which Emerson thoroughly discredits the very position he purports to take.[24]

This rereading does not end quite so simply. The Schelling quotation is, in fact, no aphorism. It is taken from *The Treatise on Human Freedom* at the very point at which Schelling is attempting to distinguish consciousness from freedom in order to explain evil. Here are the sentences immediately following the passage that Emerson quotes:

> Irrespective of the undeniable necessity of all acts and in spite of the fact that every person, observing himself, must admit that he is not

> good or evil by chance or by his free will, the evil-doer does not feel himself forced in his acts, but accomplishes them *with* his will. . . . he who says, as if to exculpate himself for an unjust deed: I was made like that, is for all that conscious of the fact the he is like that by his own fault, although he is also justified to say that it was not possible for him to act in any other way.[25]

If the evil-doer accomplishes his acts with his will, and yet also under compulsion, then according to Schelling's reasoning, it is because of an unconscious choice for evil that took place before conscious choice. Because evil results as if from an almost transcendental, atemporal choice, it appears fated or dictated when it was in fact freely made, just like ideology itself. Moreover, we might say that the elided context of the Schelling quotation itself operates like unconscious thought. Once the context has been supplied, it changes our sense of the meaning of the part of the quotation that Emerson actually uses and allows us a less elliptical understanding that, quite to the contrary of what the quote seems to say, includes our responsibility in who we are. In this respect, the passage exemplifies one solution to the problem with which the essay starts, that of having abandoned our words. Quite literally, Schelling's words are not Emerson's; doubly so, because taken out of context they signify their opposite. By contrast, if we locate the proper context for the quotation, in essence we are making the words our own and taking responsibility for their meaning.

Emerson's rhetorical strategy thus invites us to enact the passage from unconscious thought to consciousness that the quotation describes. More to the point, this passage is shown to have a specific moral dimension. Just what is it that Emerson wishes to come to light so that we might take responsibility for it? Schelling, after all, is specifically discussing the origin of evil as a choice we have made which nonetheless seems fated. Emerson, in turn, uses this passage as an apparent justification for biological determinism. This particular form of determinism shows up in "Fate" as an example of a limitation we cannot overcome. This entire section of the essay is Emerson's ironic capitulation to fate; it is also the closest he comes to linking our acceptance of fate with an acceptance of slavery. Notably, just before the Schelling quotation, Emerson refers to physical determinism of all sorts as "this despotism of race"—finally, race seems to be his subject here. Although Emerson seems to be talking about cows and sheep, he takes a different turn: "You have just dined, and, however scrupulously the slaughter-house is concealed in the graceful distance of miles, there is complicity,—expensive races,—race living at the expense of race."[26] And a little later, "How shall a man escape from his ancestors, or draw off from his veins the black drop which he drew from his father's or his mother's life?" (946). Read straightforwardly, these examples suggest that physical determinism is final and, because of its finality, can be used to justify our belief, for example, in a hierarchy of races. Indeed, Cornell West has read in Emerson more generally a tendency to try to justify racial inequality with quasi-Darwinian principles.[27] It is true that without saying so, Emerson reminds us of one the chief arguments used to justify slavery in America, but contrary to West's reading, Emerson's use of the Schelling quotation has the effect of quietly devastating this argument. It is as if Emerson were saying that our belief in racial inequality is just one of those unconscious choices for evil about which Schelling speaks. It appears to be eternally true, that is, not something we know we have chosen, but something given or dictated, before any choices were made. We then use physical determinism to justify this choice as a compulsion. In fact, it is precisely this always-already character of determinism and racial inequality that makes them such powerful arguments for slavery. According to this logic, far from something that we authorize through an unconscious choice, slavery becomes no more than the inescapable corollary to an already given "fact."

As the Schelling quotation should make clear, however, determinism, like everything else, is a construct designed to justify our choices. Emerson notes in the midst of his apparent acceptance of this determinism, "Read the description in medical books of the four temperaments, and you will think you are reading your own thoughts which you had not yet told."[28] Slavery, then, is neither natural nor given. If it seems so, then it is because our own thought and creation remain alienated from us, not so much as unconscious, but as proceeding from the Other. It is exactly this alienation, this unconsciousness, that Schelling, and Emerson with him, designate as evil.

In terms of the operation of ideology, the Schelling passage illustrates why ideology as such cannot be overcome and, hence, why direct argument is pointless. In the first place, the Schelling quotation says that what appears as compulsion is nonetheless a choice; in no respect does it suggest that we could return to a time before the choice was made. It can only be reconstructed after the fact, as it were, as an effect of interpretation. But without this opacity, the thinking subject could not get underway at all. In short, we have another instance of the way in which ideology is an illusion written into the very structure of the believing subject. Emerson's reinterpretation of the Schelling passage suggests all that is left is a form of acknowledgment in which we take cognizance of a particular belief as our own, as something we have only made, even though we are compelled to believe in it as law. This is not to say that the responsibility of interpretation is merely a veiled form of one's powerlessness within an unchangeable situation, but rather that interpretation is a consequence of choice and decision, even if unconscious, which become available precisely because of certain opacities in the structure of belief. It is our way of taking up the scripts we are given and changing them merely by the fact of actively addressing them with our own words. As exemplified by Emerson's treatment of the quotation, then, belief and the words with which we express it are at once instruments of closure and the means of personal expression. This difference, however, can only be discerned through actual linguistic engagement, through a willingness to place our own words in relation to those of an Other in an attempt to continue the conversation. Emerson's avoidance of direct opposition becomes the rhetorical equivalent of the very behavior with which we could avoid the type of confrontation that leads to war or secession.

In 1836, at the behest of certain southern members, the House of Representatives voted the first of what were called "gag resolutions." These declared that all petitions or papers relating in any way to slavery and its abolition be "laid on the table." Having failed to persuade their antagonists of the value of slavery, this contingent resorted to the outright suppression of all those voices opposed to their own. The chief spokesperson against this resolution was John Quincy Adams, himself no abolitionist, but instead a staunch defender of freedom of speech, of the press, and of petition. Despite many attempts to silence Adams, the northern representatives were finally brought to support him, and in 1844, the gag rule was repealed.

In one sense, this peculiar and rather shocking episode in American history might cast Emerson's silence in "Fate" as being more ironic than even his sharpest critics have yet discerned. It would be as if Emerson, himself a very vocal abolitionist elsewhere, were belatedly and bitterly enforcing his own gag rule on a contested topic that by 1851 could only have seemed hopelessly insoluble. I bring this piece of legislation up, however, not so much as further evidence of Emerson's irony, but because in conclusion, I wish to revise something suggested at the beginning of this chapter. We may indeed wonder why in "Fate" Emerson fails to mention slavery and focuses instead on the abstract issue of freedom and fate. We may further take this silence as evidence of Emerson's refusal to participate in the public issues of his day. In fact, as is well known, Emerson, despite his deeply conservative streak, was a fierce abolitionist who lectured often and eloquently against slavery. Just after penning "Fate," he came up with the only constructive proposal to solve the difficulties generated by the Kansas-Nebraska Act. While John Brown was planning his massacre, and William Lloyd Garrison was burning the Constitution as "an agreement with Hell," Emerson publicly argued that slavery be abolished by granting full compensation to slaveholders.[29] Nobody took up the proposal.

How are we to take up Emerson's proposal in "Fate"? I have been suggesting that his refusal of direct reference or argument is itself a means of persuading us to rally against slavery, but perhaps Emerson's stance on slavery, in his life or his writing, is finally beside the point. The title of essay, after all, is "Fate"—that which is spoken—and its subject indeed may be more our ways of speaking, along with both our freedom and responsibility to do so, than any particular issue that our speech might address. The essay does not argue for or against slavery or succession, but in the rhetorical strategies that replace such argument, Emerson's words exemplify, and teach us to exemplify, the behavior necessary for the liberal democracy that he supports. Throughout my discussion of Emersonian reading I have been speaking about transferences we form to the text that enable us to transform ourselves. Such transferences can only be rhetorical, and whether they take shape in response to unstated rhetorical pressures that a text brings to bear on us, or as the uncanny possibility of being receptive to our own receptivity, they are not responses to arguments anymore than transformation is the result of force or violence. Emerson's text is everywhere at work drawing us into such transferences. If in our reading of Emerson we are busy transforming ourselves, then it will also be true that we are engaged in the very activity that defines us as citizens of a liberal democracy in the first place.

If ideological argument represents an attempt at closure, Emerson's rhetoric, by contrast, shows us how, in Rorty's terminology, to keep the conversation going. And, as Rorty has persuasively suggested, when we speak to each other,

> We would only have a real and practical standoff, as opposed to an artificial and theoretical one, if certain topics and certain language games were taboo— . . . . That would be just the sort of society which liberals are trying to avoid—one in which "logic" ruled and rhetoric was outlawed. It is central to the idea of a liberal society that, in respect to words as opposed to deeds, persuasion as opposed to force, anything goes. This openmindedness should not be fostered because, as Scripture teaches, Truth is great and will prevail, nor because, as Milton suggests, Truth will always win in a free and open encounter. It should be fostered for its own sake. *A liberal society is one which is content to call "true" whatever the upshot of such encounters turns out to be.*[30]

If logic is opposed to liberal democracy, it would be in the sense that it precludes the possibility of response from the other. Everything would already be accounted for so that we would have no need to become anything other than what we already were, and we could always be certain of knowing just what that was. Again, it is the question of futurity, here of democracy itself. It is the task of Emerson's text to lead us into an encounter with futurity, to teach us how to participate in such encounters, and to value them for themselves alone, by learning to take responsibility for the words we do use. This responsibility, like that implied at the close of "Experience," is nothing other than the willingness to expose ourselves to encounter, not as a polemical project, but rather by presenting ourselves with the full awareness that our words may or may not be taken up, and that in any case, we cannot determine the particular ways in which they will be taken up or rejected. Logic might afford us such a guarantee, but in doing so, it would eliminate our participation as truly political beings. Far from indifference, the stance implied in Rorty's formulation marks our acknowledgment that our words are fully our own, even when we ourselves cannot possibly know all they can mean. Similarly, whether we are for or against slavery, our position has no more justification than the fact that we take it up, but that position nonetheless remains ours. I suppose we could think of such acknowledgments as the perfection of a personal geometry, but these acknowledgments would also supply the outline of a nation borne in and by the ongoing practices of its citizens. Such, precisely, would be the contours of the therapeutic intent of Emersonian letters.

Reference Matter

Notes

Acknowledgments

1. Emerson, "Experience," *Emerson: Essays and Lectures*, 491. (All further references to Emerson's works, unless otherwise noted, are to this Library of America edition. I have used this edition wherever possible because for many of the readings that follow, it is helpful to have a text readily available, and although *The Complete Works of Ralph Waldo Emerson* is the definitive text, most readers are unlikely to have it handy. The work is hereafter referred to as *EEL*.)

Introduction

1. De Tocqueville, II:16.   2. Ibid., II:3.
3. Cavell, *Senses*, 33.   4. Plato, sec. 595a–608b.
5. Emerson, "Plato; or the Philosopher," *Representative Men*, 28, 29–30.
6. Whitman, 414, 425.   7. Thoreau, 93–94.
8. Here is Nietzsche in "On Truth and Falsity . . . ": "What, then, is truth? A mobile army of metaphors, metonyms, and anthropomor-

phisms—in short, a sum of human relations, which have been enhanced, transposed, and embellished poetically and rhetorically, and which after long use seem firm, canonical, and obligatory to a people: truths are illusions about which one has forgotten that this is what they are; metaphors which are worn out" (46–47). In the most reductive sense, one might say that Derrida's entire work has been a running commentary on this passage.

9. For Cavell, this has been an ongoing project since *In Quest of the Ordinary.*

10. Milton, 167.

11. Kierkegaard, I:31.

12. Schlegel, Athenaeum frag. 252.

13. Lacoue-Labarthe and Nancy, 29.

14. Wittgenstein, *Culture and Value,* 24.

15. Rorty, *Contingency,* 3–22.

16. Emerson, "Plato," *Representative Men,* 38.

17. Hollander's "The Philosopher's Cat" constitutes the best discussion of this distinction that I know of. Hollander's analysis is particularly interesting in that, without being in the least deconstructive, it effectively insists upon the fictive nature of philosophical constructs.

18. Plato, 597A–602C.

19. Bentham, II:253–54.

20. Emerson, "The Poet," *EEL,* 445.

21. Emerson, "Poetry and Imagination," *The Complete Works of Ralph Waldo Emerson,* 8:19.

22. Emerson, "The Poet," *EEL,* 450.

23. Emerson, "Plato," *Representative Men,* 38.

24. Emerson, "The Poet," *EEL,* 457.

25. See, for example, Bercovitch, *The Puritan Origins of the American Self* and *The American Jeremiad* for accounts of the trajectory of secularization in America. For a more general discussion of the dynamics of secularization, see Homans.

26. Emerson, "History," *EEL,* 240.

27. Cavell has elegantly contextualized this function of Emerson's writing within a philosophical tradition of skepticism and moral perfectionism that extends from Plato through Kant to Wittgenstein. Particularly, Cavell has focused on what he calls "aversive thinking," or that gesture whereby the self turns away from itself toward what Emerson calls in "History," "our unattained but attainable self." It is Cavell's concern here to assimilate Emerson to a philosophical tradition. More than any other commentator, Cavell has indeed taught us that, as he puts it, Emerson's thought is up to

the pitch of anything we might wish to call philosophy at all. Primarily because of Cavell's work, we can now see how America's apparently non-philosophical philosopher-poets actively engage the same epistemological and moral questions taken up by the great skeptics of the European tradition extending from Montaigne through Descartes, Kant, Feuerbach, and Nietzsche. The points at which I diverge from Cavell have to do with the ways in which Emerson's text acts on a reader and the nature of the subjectivity that reading produces. In Chapter 2 I take up this matter in detail.

28. One of the most curious aspects of Cavell's work on Emerson is that his discussion of self-creation seems fully dependent on a sophisticated understanding of the dynamics that govern the psychoanalytic process. Yet Cavell himself seems hesitant to draw this parallel.

It is Freud who first understood that readers of texts are not the analysts they often suppose themselves to be, but are instead quite the opposite. In *The Interpretation of Dreams*, Freud remarks that the text of *Oedipus Rex* unfolds like the process of analysis. He is not speaking here of the ways in which Oedipal themes emerge in the play, but rather of the rhetorical turns and disclosures that alter the audience as it views the play. Following an Aristotelian model, Freud implies that the audience transfers its self-pity and fear onto the characters of the play and so achieves a kind of catharsis (294–98). When introducing the Oedipus complex as a universal developmental reality, Freud reoriented his emphasis toward the thematic, in a way that anticipates the majority of psychoanalytic literary criticism. But his original observation about how the play prefigures the workings of the psychoanalytic process (rather than the contents it uncovers), more closely anticipates the ways in which I propose to look at the works of Emerson. What Freud suggests implicitly is that it is the play itself that fills the role of analyst as it acts upon the audience. I will argue that Emerson's essays quite self-consciously assume this position for their readers. It is not the text that forms a transference to the analyst/reader, but the reader who forms a transference to the text. By this, I mean that the text, like the analyst, creates the rhetorical conditions through which the reader can re-present his or her self and so gain certain forms of self-understanding that would not otherwise have been available.

29. Ricoeur, 344–418; and Lear, 148–52. A number of readers have suggested that the auto-creation of the subject through literary production lies at the center of what we call Romanticism. I will emphasize how this process occurs in the American Romanticism of Emerson, while at the same time, sketching out the ways in which a philosophical problem anticipates the tasks of psychoanalysis (which is, I suppose, to suggest that Freud

and his inheritors are part of a Romantic tradition). This is to say that America inherited philosophy as an implicit form of personal and cultural therapeutic analysis, although the distinction between philosophy and psychoanalysis is by no means as absolute as it may seem. A great deal of scholarship has been devoted to the continuities between philosophy and psychoanalysis, and rightly so. It was Socrates who called the philosopher the physician of the soul and insisted that philosophy teach us how to live. The pragmatic goal of philosophy has persisted in the Western tradition, culminating in Wittgenstein's idea in *Philosophical Investigations* that "philosophies are forms of therapy" (#129). Philosophy can teach us how to live healthily, but at the same time, it often differs from psychoanalysis in its ideas about what constitutes health and how to bring it about. Socrates, for example, subjects his interlocutors to the rigors of the dialectic, but only so they can emerge into the world of perfect forms that transcend the vicissitudes of appearance, change, and the dialectic itself. By contrast, most sorts of psychoanalysis would show us that these vicissitudes are precisely our identity, and the best we can hope for are greater degrees of freedom from their determination. Perhaps in the most general sense, the difference between philosophy and psychoanalysis is the difference between truth and freedom.

30. Chase and Poirier are perhaps the two most distinguished representatives of the first generation of Americanist critics to view our literature as divorced from "social reality." More recently, and for other reasons, a new group of Americanists has insisted on the same evasion. For a more complete discussion of this history, see Chapter 6, "Measures of Silence," in this volume.

31. Barfield, 11.

32. Cavell, *Philosophical Passages*, 29.

Chapter 1

1. Richardson, 6.

2. Emerson, "The American Scholar," *EEL*, 53, 57, 70.

3. Given the essay's topic of America's cultural belatedness, it is interesting that even the essay itself was belated, delivered not at commencement, but the day after. See Richardson, 262.

4. Cavell, *Conditions*, 33–46, is the notable exception. Cavell reads the essay as recognizing that we have not yet started thinking and, therefore, not yet quite started existing both as individuals and as a nation.

5. Richardson, 263.

6. Emerson, "The American Scholar," *EEL*, 53.

7. Rorty, *Philosophy*, 132.
8. Emerson, "The American Scholar," *EEL*, 67.
9. This is what Cavell suggests in *Conditions*, 42; namely, that we must transform instinct into thought according to what might be considered a psychoanalytic paradigm. I would agree that we must become conscious of what we already know without thinking, but not necessarily in the usual sense of reappropriating the Other of the unconscious. In "The American Scholar" Emerson figures this turn as what he calls reading, but the full implications of this process do not become clear until *Essays: First Series*, a topic I take up in the next chapter.
10. Emerson, "The American Scholar," *EEL*, 70.
11. As Richardson observes, "What is being liberated here is not America—not American literature or the American intelligentsia—but the single person" (265).
12. This structure is what Derrida calls "teleiopoesis" in *The Politics of Friendship*. "The sentence speaks of itself, it gets carried away, precipitates and precedes itself, as if its end arrived before the end . . . the race is finished in advance, and this is future-producing" (31). We might think of the messianic structure of teleiopoesis as a double-double bind and, therefore, as an unbinding. To get started, the speaker must suppose the coming of those whom he envisions, and yet, they do not exist until he has called them.
13. Cavell, *Conditions*, 42–43.
14. Here, in "The American Scholar," receptivity still appears to presuppose an other to whom we are receptive. But as I indicate later, in "Self-Reliance," receptivity comes to partake of the teleiopoetic structure that characterizes Emerson's address here. Receptivity, in the later Emerson, is a name for that which cannot be named, for a logically impossible act of auto-foundation.
15. Van Leer, 8. As Van Leer knows, Emerson was, of course, familiar with the work of Kant, Schelling, Schlegel, and Fichte, as well as with the French, British, and American interpretations of their individual works. But this familiarity should be read in light of the statement in "The American Scholar, "There is then creative reading as well as creative writing" (59). Emersonian receptivity takes this further to imply that creative reading is creative writing, or at least that without creative reading there can be no creative writing.
16. Hollander, 206.
17. Carlyle, "Characteristics," 1.
18. Schlegel notes at the end of "On the Essence of Criticism," that the character sketch "in philosophy is . . . by far the most difficult, either

because its *Darstellung* is as yet less complete than that of poets, or because of the very essence of the genre," but in either case, the character sketch of the philosopher becomes the location at which philosophy will be poeticized through the function of criticism. The character sketch in fact becomes the very place in which poetry and philosophy become one, for the poet, insofar as he forms the character of philosophy, is now a critic, and the philosopher has been poeticized (Schlegel qtd. in Lacoue-Labarthe and Nancy, 109).

19. Lacoue-Labarthe and Nancy, 29.
20. Kant, *Critique of Pure Reason*, 123.
21. Ibid., 19.
22. Kant, *Critique of Judgment*, 10–12.
23. Ibid., 198.
24. Ibid.
25. Lacoue-Labarthe and Nancy, 48.
26. Hegel, 131–45.
27. See Lacoue-Labarthe and Nancy. The solutions envisioned by the Jena Romantics appear to take place wholly on the ground of genre. By developing different genres and then redefining them, they create the ground for auto-production. First, in the fragment which is the very "genre of germination" (48), in its constitutive and positive incompletion; second, in what they call the "Idea," which consists in the mixing of genres characteristic of the essay itself, a mixing that brings into play the exemplary function of the artist who teaches us how to complete ourselves (72–78); third, in a literature of literature whereby a novel, for example, would become also a theory of the novel (86–95); and finally in a *poesis* of philosophy or that form of criticism that seeks to present, with the object, its conditions of possibility (106–11).

Needless to say, Emerson does not envision a classification of genre as the solution to the problem that he sketches, but literature will nonetheless remain the privileged place of expression for auto-production. As he writes in "Circles," "Literature is a point outside of our hodiernal circle, through which a new one may be described. The use of literature is to afford us a platform whence we may command a view of our present life, a purchase whence we may move it" (408). What does this sentence describe if not the way in which literature underwrites auto-production?

28. Carlyle, "Characteristics," 38.
29. Emerson, "The American Scholar," *EEL*, 67. The fact that this sentence figures so largely in Cavell's interpretation of the essay indicates just how similar are the ideas of moral perfectionism and *Bildung*.

30. Lacoue-Labarthe and Nancy, 87.

31. It is nonetheless worth pondering this particular transatlantic link that has received virtually no attention since Wellek's early essay on the influence of German philosophy on Emerson, an essay in which Wellek notably underestimates the importance of Kant. Is it germane that, as Carlyle remarks in "Characteristics," Saxon is our mother-tongue? And that it is mother England's English as well as American English? As if England now were not a parent from whom we had broken, but a brother?

32. This dynamic would, then, help to explain why the essay repeatedly is read as a call for literary nationalism and nothing more. Even those who wish to defend Emerson's philosophicality tend to pass over this essay.

33. Emerson, "The American Scholar," *EEL*, 53–54.

34. This of course is a major theme throughout Fichte's work, a question that takes flight from his insistence that consciousness cannot be understood in the same way as the object world. Fichte's ideas on this subject are particularly important to Carlyle and the question of mechanism, for it is precisely mechanism that cannot come to reflect on itself.

35. Emerson, "The American Scholar," *EEL*, 53.

36. Here, one must wonder if Emerson did not know that the pole-star of Harp, that is, the constellation Lyra, is named Vega, meaning "great plain." As if poetry is itself to become that great plain of America.

37. Emerson, "The American Scholar," *EEL*, 54, 63.

38. Cavell, *Conditions*, 39. The title of the book alone suggests how much emphasis Cavell puts on this figure. I find it interesting that he pins this interpretation specifically to the etymology of "conceptualize," that is, to *capere*, which is "to take" and "to hold to oneself." This kind of taking might well imply what Emerson calls "reception." The real etymological villain here is that of "comprehend," because of its implication of totality.

39. Emerson, "The American Scholar," *EEL*, 56.

40. Coleridge, *Biographia Literaria*, 185–86.

41. Richardson notes that during the period at which Emerson was thinking through this essay, his enthusiasm for "the new German thought" was balanced by an equal aversion. As he noted in his journal, "On the whole what have these German Weimarish art-friends done? They have rejected all the traditions and connections, have sought to come thereby one step nearer to absolute truth. But still they are not nearer than others" (Emerson qtd. in Richardson, 264).

42. Emerson, "The American Scholar," *EEL*, 62, 65, 68, 60, 71.

43. We might note a similar play on "labor" and "conceive," a play generating a new type of thinking. In the Myth of the One Man, it is through

one's labors that one achieves one's ends—that is, fulfills one's humanity. Later in the essay, Emerson writes, "Labor is everywhere welcome; always we are invited to work." To conceive, to think, to labor—these verbs weave a subtext into the essay, the task of which is to subtly transform our sense of their meaning. To conceive is to think, but it is also to give birth to; likewise labor is work as well as the act of giving birth. It is as if Emerson wished to remind us why we think and why we work, and how we should do so. Neither act should be mechanical or detached from us, but rather part of bringing ourselves into being.

44. Emerson, "Spiritual Laws," *EEL*, 305.

45. For a helpful overview of the concept of *Witz*, see Lacoue-Labarthe and Nancy, 52–53.

46. Emerson, "The American Scholar," *EEL*, 56.

47. For the different senses of the Kantian maxim, see particularly *Critique of Pure Reason*, 243–44; and *Groundwork of the Metaphysic of Morals*, 399–421.

48. Emerson, "The American Scholar," *EEL*, 58.

49. One can hear as well in this section the influence of Emerson's contemporary, Sampson Reed. In *Observations on the Growth of the Mind*, Reed had come very close to Schlegel's sense of the function of criticism: the function of the reader or critic is "to approximate to that intellectual and moral condition in which the work originated," and to "call forth the power of poetry in himself" (Reed qtd. in Richardson, 71).

50. As in the section on nature, and despite his apparent diatribe against the bibliomaniacs, Emerson again stresses that reading is not something we achieve, but rather the principle according to which we act all the time. "Books are for the scholar's idle times," but as Cavell has noted, since the derivation of "scholar" is the Greek *scholia*, or leisure, books are for the scholar all the time, in *Conditions*, 126.

51. Schelling's influence is notable here. Consider these sentences: "There is no consciousness without something which is both excluded and attracted. That which is conscious of itself excludes what it is conscious of as not itself and yet must also attract it as, precisely, that of which it is conscious, thus as itself, only in another form" (Schelling qtd. in Bowie, 23). Significantly, Schelling goes on to speak of "the misfortune of all being," that is, its perpetual alienation in the Other that attracts it. It is, as I suggest in later chapters, just this alienation that Emerson learns to avoid by dissolving self and Other as essences. This dissolution is already implicit in Schelling, yet not sufficiently so to suggest a means of overcoming the alienation in the Other.

52. Emerson, "The American Scholar," *EEL*, 61.

53. Ibid., 60. Given that Carlyle uses "manufacture" to indicate the sick sort of thought and creation, Emerson's retroping here of manufacture as part of an organic process suggests a kind of cure of Carlyle.

54. Carlyle, "Characteristics," 42–43.

55. Throughout I have used "Other" in uppercase, whenever the word refers to a concept. My usage is not intended to reflect Lacanian usage.

Chapter 2

1. Brewer, 524.
2. Emerson, "Self-Reliance," *EEL*, 271.
3. Emerson, "Intellect," *EEL*, 417.
4. Ibid., 426. Already here we can see that the effects of eloquence, literally our hearing, and therefore passive reception, of the Other's words, removes limits of the self. Once this is the case, the listener would, of course, neither be able to represent himself to himself nor to thematize the source of his reception.
5. *Genesis*, 32:17–30.
6. Zornberg, 230.
7. Ibid., 234–35.
8. *Genesis* 32:28–29.
9. Given the passivity that emerges as central to Emersonian receptivity, it is interesting that Zornberg accentuates both Jacob's concern with control over his experience and the way in which he must eventually learn to relinquish such control (217–30).
10. De Tocqueville, II:3.
11. Emerson, "Intellect," *EEL*, 427.
12. *Corinthians I* 13:1–2.
13. Emerson, "Friendship," *EEL*, 341.
14. Emerson, "History," *EEL*, 247.
15. Emerson, "Intellect," *EEL*, 427.
16. Emerson, "History," *EEL*, 237.
17. In "History," the One Mind still appears to have the mythical status of an origin that the One Man has in "The American Scholar." As I suggest later, however, the theory of reading sketched in "Self-Reliance" demythologizes the One Mind by doing away with origins altogether. If there is One Mind, then it would only be in the sense that we can no longer tell where our ideas, and, indeed, our very subjectivity, originate at all.
18. Emerson, "History," *EEL*, 250.
19. In James's and in Rorty's works, the importance of rhetoric and belief carry the weight of what Emerson calls reading; in both cases, they are the means through which we create and recreate ourselves. In Peirce, this connection is perhaps less clear, but as Walter Benn Michaels has shown, Peirce, too, declares the subject/object problem false and replaces it with the idea that the self is an interpretation and performs interpretations;

put otherwise, reading is constitutive of the self, and readers are therefore constituted (Michaels, 185–200).

20. Cavell, *Conditions*, 31–32. In terms of the passage from "History" on which Cavell's interpretation depends, moral perfectionism does seem to ground Emerson's project. The concept of receptivity, however, as developed in "Self-Reliance" is the very undoing of moral perfectionism if such perfectionism is seen to require a particular Other as a guide. The whole point of receptivity, as I suggest in the next sections, is to undo any thematizable source of reception.

21. Danto, 79.

22. In "The Politics of Interpretation," an essay that predates the Emerson material in *Conditions*, Cavell intriguingly suggests in passing that reading in general is nothing other than our transference to the text (52–54). Provocative as this idea is, Cavell never specifies what he means by transference, although overall, he seems to assimilate it to an idea of seduction as instruction. In *Conditions*, the idea of transference to the text is implicit throughout, a link that underscores the instructional nature of the transference as Cavell formulates it earlier. I would say, however, that seduction is probably the more important dimension in Emerson, and since we are dealing with texts, its seductions can only occur rhetorically, an idea that Cavell does not develop. In the following sections, I take up this question of how the text might seduce us, and why it does so by formulating transference in a quite specific way, a way that precludes instruction in any straightforward sense. This is perhaps only to suggest that therapy need not be instructive in the usual sense of the word.

23. Emerson, "Self-Reliance," *EEL*, 259.

24. "Vocation" is, of course, literally, a calling, that which singles me out as most precisely myself. This sense of vocation as calling will become particularly important in "Experience" as that which institutes my responsibility. But it is equally the case in "Self-Reliance" that "vocation," a call of which neither the origin nor the destination can be specified, remains a highly charged word.

25. So far we would be well within the classical phenomenological reduction for which the cogito provides the initial model. If this provides the starting point, however, then Emerson will diverge wholly from this model as rhetoric comes to replace any possibility of representation.

26. Here is Descartes in the second Meditation: "I am, I exist, is necessarily true every time that I pronounce it or conceive it in my mind" (24). This makes quite clear the link between thought and representation.

27. "I would not doubt in any way what the light of nature made me see

to be true, just as it made me see, a little while ago, that from the fact that I doubted I could conclude that I existed" (Descartes, 37).

28. Van Leer, 128–31.

29. Emerson, "Self-Reliance," *EEL*, 265–66.

30. "Freud's method is Cartesian—in the sense that he sets out from the basis of the subject of certainty" (Lacan, *Four Fundamental Concepts*, 35).

31. For Freud, this opposition is really nonoppositional, since everything finally must be reduced to the light of representational consciousness or consigned to oblivion. Take, for example, the relation between the drives and their representatives: "Even in the unconscious, moreover, an instinct cannot be represented otherwise than by an idea. If the instinct did not attach itself to an idea or manifest itself as an affective state, we could know nothing about it" ("The Unconscious," *Standard Edition*, 14:122). (Hereafter the *Standard Edition* is referred to as *SE*.)

32. Emerson, "Self-Reliance," *EEL*, 259.

33. In a curious way, Emerson anticipates the Freudian notion of primary repression, an act that technically occurs before there is anything to be repressed.

34. Emerson, "Self-Reliance," *EEL*, 241.

35. Cavell notes this feature of Emersonian reading as well and adds, "to think otherwise, to attribute the origin of my thoughts simply to the other, thoughts which are then, as it were, implanted in me—some would say caused—by let us say some Emerson, is idolatry" (*Conditions*, 57). This may be the case, but at the same time, as I suggest in the next chapter, because the source of the thoughts cannot be thematized, there is a necessary moment in the reading process in which thoughts do indeed seem to be implanted in us.

36. Emerson, "History," *EEL*, 255.

37. Emerson, "Self-Reliance," *EEL*, 259.

Chapter 3

1. Freud, "An Autobiographical Study," *SE*, 20:21.

2. Freud, *Therapy and Technique*, 168, 105, 176. (I use this edition, hereafter referred to as *TT*, whenever possible because it is more readily available to the reader than the *Standard Edition*.)

3. For an excellent summary of the various levels at which thematic psychoanalytic criticism usually takes place, see Skura.

4. Felman qtd. in Gallop, 28.

5. Lacan, "The Direction of the Treatment," *Écrits*, 231–36. If this is the

case, then it is because Lacan thinks of countertransference as a kind of imaginary identification. To move beyond that identification into the relation in which both transference and countertransference are manifestations of desire itself undoes any notion of subjectivity that would require distinguishing between text and reader, analyst and analysand, and so between transference and countertransference.

6. This question is too complex to tackle in any detail here, but for a general overview of the extremity of the dispute, I would refer the reader to *Essential Papers on Transference*, edited by Aaron Esman.

7. Gallop, 30.

8. Freud, *The Interpretation of Dreams*, 601–3, for example.

9. Freud, "Further Recommendations in the Technique of Psychoanalysis: Recollection, Repetition and Working Through," *TT*, 160.

10. The double nature of the transference is treated most fully in "The Dynamics of the Transference," *TT*, 105–15.

11. Freud, "The Psychoanalytic Method of Treatment," *TT*, 124.

12. Rieff, 21.

13. Freud, "The Dynamics of the Transference," *TT*, 112.

14. Emerson, "The American Scholar," *EEL*, 54.

15. Emerson, "Self-Reliance," *EEL*, 263.

16. Freud, "The Dynamics of the Transference," *TT*, 106.

17. Consider Freud's statement in the 1912 paper, "Recommendations for Physicians on the Psychoanalytic Method of Treatment": "Expressed in a formula, he [the physician] must bend his own unconscious like a receptive organ towards the emerging unconscious of the patient, be as the receiver of the telephone disc. As the receiver transmutes the electric vibrations introduced by the sound-waves back again into sound waves, so is the physician's mind able to reconstruct the patient's unconscious, which has directed his associations, from the communications derived from it" (*TT*, 122). Such a description anticipates the current emphasis on countertransference as a central analytic tool, an emphasis, however, which Freud himself consistently evaded. That evasion is doubly marked here by the oddity of Freud's figure. We would hardly think of the relation between a receiver and sound waves as intersubjective, and indeed, the whole point of the passage is to remove the analyst as any actual person—with feelings, thoughts, in short, all manifestations of countertransference—from the analytic exchange.

18. It can perhaps now, with the work of scholars such as Edmundson and Homans, go without saying that this objectivizing perspective was central to Freud's attempt to establish his fledgling discipline as a science.

19. In Winnicott and in Lacan, the emphasis on the lived experience of the transference, not so much as a repetition but as something created in the present, is quite clear. It is perhaps least clear in the work of American ego psychologists because they see this moment of the transference as dangerously regressive.

20. Indeed, as Masud Kahn has suggested, the relationship of the transference is precisely Freud's most enduring clinical legacy. His definitive contribution will be "the creation of this unique human situation where a person can explore the meaning and experiential realities of life, through a relationship with another, and yet, not be intruded upon or manipulated in any way that is not true to his own self or values" (Kahn qtd. in Rudynytsky, 3–4).

21. Freud, "The Dynamics of the Transference," *TT*, 114–15.

22. Emerson, "Self-Reliance," *EEL*, 112.

23. Indeed, the appeal of the Lacanian model in trying to understand just what Emerson might be up to has to do particularly with Lacan's emphasis on process, transition, and dialogue. At the same time, the Hegelianism of Lacan's thought tends at times to obscure the priority of all that belongs to the register of the real. It is for this reason that I have brought up Freud first because it is, I believe, in his version that the unspoken, and literally unspeakable, experiential moment of the transference—the real itself—appears most clearly, even if only to be superseded. Without Freud we might well miss the importance of this moment in Lacan altogether, especially because so much commentary on Lacan takes its departure specifically from the dialecticizing, Hegelian phase of Lacanian thought.

24. André Green has suggested thinking about this kind of repetition compulsion as the beating of a heart. The emphasis is not on repetition in the sense that no content is being repeated. Instead, compulsion becomes the dominant point (unpublished lecture, Oct. 20, 1997, delivered at New York University).

25. A difficulty that needs to be stated at the outset is that Lacan's treatment of rhetoric itself would seem thoroughly at odds with all that we have been saying about the direction in which Emerson is moving. The assimilation of the unconscious in Lacan to the figures of rhetoric, let us say the structural dimension of his thought, has the effect as Borch-Jacobsen points out, of restricting "the operations of the unconscious to a rhetoric that is itself restricted, . . . rhetoric restricted to the figures of speaking well" (*The Emotional Tie*, 64). Rhetoric as the figurality of language is, of course, only half of the story, especially in terms of Emerson, where the

emphasis falls again and again on the importance of persuasion (albeit not persuasion as conceived by Lacan).

26. Lacan, *Seminar, Book III*, 251; and *Seminar, Book II*, 228–29.

27. Žižek, 109. Žižek's formulation of symbolic desire helps to underscore how similar this process is to the Levinasian concept of substitution that is so central to Emersonian responsibility.

28. The volume entitled *Playing and Reality* develops all of these aspects of transitional phenomena, that is, as a developmental concept and as a metapsychological proposition.

29. Perhaps the other most significant example here would be narrative psychoanalysis, which, despite its occasionally positivist rhetoric, does give rise to a subject created in the present through the stories it tells to an Other and so finally to a kind of nonsubject, which is endlessly displaced in narrative constructions that cannot be said clearly to originate with the patient or with the analyst. See, for example, Schafer.

30. See, for example, Lacan, *Four Fundamental Concepts*, 263–76.

31. Žižek, 118.

32. Emerson, "Self-Reliance," *EEL*, 263.

33. Cavell, *This New Yet Unapproachable America*, 82–83, for example, but this is a persistent theme in Cavell's thinking.

34. Nietzsche qtd. in Borch-Jacobsen, *The Emotional Tie*, 65–66.

35. Emerson, "Self-Reliance," *EEL*, 271.

36. Emerson, "Fate," *EEL*, 263. See also Cavell, *Conditions*, 80.

37. Fink, 27.

38. Lacan, *Four Fundamental Concepts*, 187–202, 230–43, for example.

39. Emerson, "Self-Reliance," *EEL*, 262.

40. Emerson, "Spiritual Laws," *EEL*, 311.

41. See, particularly, "Compensation," "Character," and "Fate."

42. Borch-Jacobsen, *Emotional Tie*, 89.

43. We could also understand such an ethic by backtracking through an unlikely chronology from Lacan to Montaigne. As is well known, Emerson was a careful reader of Montaigne, and we find everything we have been examining already there in typically aphoristic form. In the essay "De l'experience," in nothing other than a discussion of reading, Montaigne writes:

> We take the opinions and knowledge of others into our keeping and that is all. We must make them our own. We are just like a man who needing fire, should go and fetch some at his neighbour's house, and having found a fine big fire there, should stop there and warm himself, forgetting to carry any back home. (qtd. in Sulieman, 270)

If Montaigne chooses as his example fire, it is perhaps because he, like Emerson, is thinking specifically of what we should take from the reading process—not the thought of the Other, but rather the inspiration or spark itself. At the same time, on another level, we could quite literally die of the cold when we arrived home without the fire we went to seek. The passage reminds us that the alternative to taking the fire with us is a kind of death, a failure to become ourselves in the most authentic sense. I want to say that Emerson has this passage in mind when he writes in "Self-Reliance," "nor is his [man's] genius admonished to stay at home, to put itself in communication with the internal ocean, but it goes abroad to beg a cup of water from the urns of other men." Who would admonish us, except Emerson himself, or any writer thinking of reading as a process of self-creation? We may need to go to the Other, certainly not to beg a cup of anything, but rather to learn how to communicate with that vast internal ocean that is ourselves. Any text that allows us to do less—to feed on its opinions, to presume it to know—simply shirks its responsibility to the reader who has yet to achieve the unattained but attainable self.

In the simplest sense, the provocation of the text instigates the reader to do something for him- or herself, an instigation, then, that is ethical.

44. Emerson, "Culture," *EEL*, 1029.

Chapter 4

1. Packer, "The Curse of Kehama" in *Emerson's Fall*; Cameron, "Representing Grief," and Cavell, "Finding as Founding" in *This New Yet Unapproachable America*. In mentioning each of these interpretations as I do here, I necessarily compress and skew the complexity of three of the finest interpretations of this essay. Especially in the cases of Cameron and Cavell, it is not entirely fair to say that each privileges one of the essay's emphases over the other. The kind of preservative repression with which Cameron deals, for example, is not without philosophical implications anymore than Cavell's interpretation of skepticism as the mourning of the passing of the world is without psychoanalytic implications. It would perhaps simply be a matter, in each case, of drawing out these implications more thoroughly. In any event, the works of Packer, Cameron, and Cavell on this particular essay mark one of the biggest shifts in the larger understanding of Emerson's overall project.

2. All of these particular figures of counting should be read against Derrida's exposition in *The Politics of Friendship* of the general importance of counting and economy in the philosophical history of friendship. This fig-

ure is, as he demonstrates via the Aristotelian sentence, "Oh friends, there is no friend," the very question of friendship and community itself.

3. Emerson, "Experience," *EEL*, 471.

4. In the essay entitled "Substitution," Levinas calls this exchange an "anteriority . . . older than the a priori . . . something irreversibly past, prior to all memory and all recall" (94). If this is the case, then it is because, as he explains, "the subject is affected without the source of the affection becoming a theme of representation" (90). The relation between Lacanian transference and Levinasian substitution is here revealed to be extremely similar. If this connection is obscured, especially by Lacan himself, then it is perhaps because substitution, as a structurally necessary moment that cannot be escaped, would prove analysis to be a redundancy.

5. Emerson, "Experience," *EEL*, 472.

6. Freud, "On Mourning and Melancholia," *General Psychological Theory*. The distinction between mourning and melancholia underlies the distinction made by Abraham and Torok between introjection and incorporation so important in Cameron's argument. Both distinctions suppose, however, that some form of identification is at work. I would argue instead that the very community Emerson tries to envision would escape, if such a thing is possible, the very logic of identification itself.

7. Emerson, "Experience," *EEL*, 472.

8. The idea that death is the institution of absolute singularity and, therefore, of a new kind of community is a topos traceable, albeit with different emphases, from Heidegger through Bataille, Levinas, Blanchot, Nancy, and Derrida. It is, I would add, implicit in Lacan, but without the necessary stress on death as community.

9. Freud, *The Ego and the Id*, 24.

10. For a full analysis of this particular problematic in Freudian identification, see Borch-Jacobsen, *The Freudian Subject*, 113–26; and *The Emotional Tie*, 58–61.

11. Emerson, "Experience," *EEL*, 473–74.

12. The relation of the particular Other to alterity itself is indeed vexed. As Derrida asks in *The Politics of Friendship*, "If, through 'the call to die in common through separation', this friendship is borne beyond being-in-common, beyond being-common or sharing, beyond all common appurtenance (familial, neighbourhood, national, political, linguistic and finally generic appurtenance), beyond the social bond itself—if that is possible—then why elect, if only passively, this Other with whom I have no relation of this type rather than some other with whom I have none of the sort either? . . . Why am I not the friend of just anyone? Am I not, moreover,

just that, in subscribing to such a strong and at the same time disarming and disarmed proposition? There could never be any appeasing response to this question, of course" (297–99). There is an answer; it is what philosophy calls "finitude," but Derrida is right to remark that this is hardly appeasing.

13. Emerson, "Experience," *EEL*, 482.
14. Levinas, "Time and the Other," *Levinas Reader*, 44.
15. Emerson, "Experience," *EEL*, 484.
16. This dynamic is what Lacan would refer to as "the two deaths." There is first the natural death, say that of Waldo at the opening, which is part of the natural cycle of birth and death in a continual transformation, and absolute death, that is, the destruction of the cycle itself which in turn frees nature from its own laws and opens the future to the absolutely new, without foundation or ground. The difference between these two deaths is that between biological death and its symbolization we have the eradication of the symbolic itself, that is, the real. See *Écrits*, 28–29, 101–6.
17. Emerson, "Experience," *EEL*, 485.
18. Levinas, "Substitution," *Levinas Reader*, 90.
19. Emerson, "Experience," *EEL*, 487–88.
20. It would not be a question here of recognizing myself in the death of the Other, but rather of thereby coming to experience my own irreversible alterity, itself nonspecularizable.
21. Emerson, "Experience," *EEL*, 473.
22. Despite all of the apparent incompatibilities between this view and those of Rorty on the relation between the private and the public domains, it is worth pondering the close of *Contingency, Irony and Solidarity* here: "I want to distinguish human solidarity as the identification with 'humanity as such' and as the self-doubt which has gradually, over the last few centuries, been inculcated into inhabitants of the democratic states.... The identification seems to me impossible—a philosopher's invention, an awkward attempt to secularize the idea of becoming one with God" (198). I understand Rorty here to be questioning the very possibility of an immanent community, but I find this somewhat obscured by the implicit assumption that the private individual as ironist somehow retains a substantial being. If this were the case, then we would have to say that the private and public realms are incommensurable, rather than one and the same.
23. Emerson, "Experience," *EEL*, 490–91.
24. Obviously this construction of responsibility owes a great deal to responsibility as developed by Levinas in *Otherwise than Being*. We can think of it as a kind of structural responsibility that cannot be evaded. The difference between Emerson and Levinas, it seems to me, hinges on the

question of whether or not such a structural possibility can be marked in any way, or, put otherwise, whether or not we can be responsible for our responsibility. Levinas, I think, leaves this question open and perhaps even unaddressed. By contrast, in Emerson, the negative limit of this responsibility is always being marked—this is his writing itself.

25. Emerson, "Experience," *EEL*, 490.

Chapter 5

1. Emerson, "Experience," *EEL*, 491–92.
2. Emerson, "Representative Men," *The Collected Works of Ralph Waldo Emerson*, IV:51.
3. The confluence of Emerson's publishing projects at this time argues for continuity between the ideas in *Representative Men* and ostensibly earlier works. In the wake of *Essays: Second Series* in which "Experience" appears, Emerson undertook two other major projects. In 1841 he toiled laboriously, correcting proofs of the first edition of *Essays: First Series*. When that edition sold out in 1845, he began an extensive revision for the reprinting in 1847. At roughly the same time, he set to work on the series of essays entitled *Representative Men* that, perhaps because he worked on them at the same time, appear to continue revising the ideas developed in the first two series of essays.
4. Emerson, "Plato," *Representative Men*, 27. (All further references to *Representative Men* are indicated *RM*.)
5. Emerson, "Plato," *RM*, 29–30.
6. Emerson, "Self-Reliance," *EEL*, 117.
7. Emerson's acquaintance with Montaigne was indeed long-standing. He had first come across a translation of Montaigne in his father's library in the early 1820s, while teaching at his school for girls in Roxbury. Of Montaigne's essays he noted in an 1873 journal entry, "No book before or since was ever so much to me as that," and since Whicher's *Freedom and Fate*, it has become a commonplace that the essay on Montaigne is a self-portrait.
8. Emerson, "Uses of Great Men," *RM*, 7.
9. Kant, *Critique of Judgment*, 162.
10. Emerson, "Uses of Great Men," *RM*, 5.
11. Kant, *Critique of Pure Reason*, 13. I would like to thank Elizabeth Duquette both for pointing out this particular instance to me and for the benefit of her overall expertise on the nature of the example, as she explores it in her dissertation, "Exemplifying Philosophy: the Rhetoric of Exemplarity in Nineteenth Century Literature and Philosophy" (Dept. of English, New York University, 1998).

12. Descartes, 113.
13. Hollander discusses this exemplary example in useful terms in *Melodious Guile*, particularly in terms of the way in which the allusiveness of the example tends to dissolve its exemplary function (217–21).
14. Kant indeed classes his omitted examples with "aids to clearness," *Critique of Pure Reason*, 13.
15. Hawthorne, 29.
16. Emerson, "Uses," *RM*, 20.
17. This constitutive incompletion is precisely the center of what Nancy calls the "inoperative community."
18. Emerson, "Montaigne; or the Skeptic," *RM*, 114.
19. Emerson, "Goethe; or the Thinker," *RM*, 193.

Chapter 6

1. I do not mean to suggest here that the Enlightenment subject escapes a social dimension. One might say, instead, that for the Enlightenment subject, autonomous reason and social responsibility are kept apart, thus freeing the subject to a certain extent. Descartes, for example, balances the freedom of the cogito with a "provisional morality" designed to keep him afloat amidst total doubt. Similarly, Kant says we must reason autonomously—this would be the subject of reflection—but we must also obey in the world of practical reason. The difference in the Emersonian subject is that the private and the public, the reflective and the social, far from being kept apart, are one and the same.
2. See, for example, Cavell, *This New Yet Unapproachable America*, 86–89; Van Leer, 177–87; Packer; and Whicher, 114.
3. Sacvan Bercovitch is perhaps the most articulate and influential of such readers, particularly in *The Office of the Scarlet Letter* and *The Rites of Assent*, but we can include with him critics such as Myra Jehlen in *American Incarnation*; Donald Pease in *Visionary Compacts*; Jane Tompkins in *Sensational Designs*; and Michael Gilmore in *The Middle Way*.
4. Tanner, 322; and Bercovitch, *Office*, 126.
5. Emerson, "Experience," *EEL*, 490.
6. Emerson, "Self-Reliance," *EEL*, 262. This passage, as might be imagined, has caused a good deal of consternation among Emerson's critics. For some, such as Harold Bloom, who otherwise entirely approves of Emerson, it identifies Emerson with all that is wrong with America: "Self-Reliance translated out of the inner life and into the marketplace is difficult to distinguish from our current religion of selfishness" (9). By contrast, Cavell has commented on this passage that it cannot possibly mean what it seems

to. He attempts to rescue Emerson here by suggesting that Emerson "does not exactly mean that he will further harden his heart but that by and by he will live in a society that has achieved manhood, that one day human kind will not require the dole from one another" (*Conditions*, 135). Perhaps, but it may also be that Emerson means just what he says here, while, at the same time, rejecting all forms of cultural hegemony. However distasteful it may be, Emerson may well be suggesting that these popular causes are not his causes. To acknowledge this disavowal would constitute something very like the rejection of ideology that I see Emerson pursuing in "Fate."

7. As far as I am aware, Cavell is the only reader of Emerson to take up this silence in a sustained way (*Philosophical Passages*, 12–41). Cavell wants to suggest that "Fate" is Emerson's way of saying that argument and polemic are evasions of philosophy, and that philosophy cannot in any event abolish slavery. If, as Cavell then suggests, this is one more attempt on Emerson's part to inherit philosophy for America, then why would he want to inherit it in this way? I suppose that what I find odd about this reading is that Cavell effectively ignores the specific content of Emerson's silence by equating slavery with a failure of thought in a very general way. In doing so, he would seem to repeat the very gesture against which his commentary ostensibly takes shape.

8. Banta, 8.
9. See, particularly, Packer; and Whicher.
10. Emerson, "Fate," *EEL*, 943.
11. Coleridge, *Biographia Literaria*, 240.
12. Emerson, "Fate," *EEL*, 953–54.
13. This consideration of Emerson's stake in our consent to the system we have created owes a great deal to Cavell. See, particularly, *Conditions*, xxxvii, 18, 25–26, 28.
14. Such consent is not inconsistent with the unconscious decision developed in "Experience." We could say that here, Emersonian responsibility comes into play. I may not be able to justify my consent in this sense of grounding it on producible reasons, but I can witness such consent by saying, "Yes, this is my decision."
15. Emerson, "Fate," *EEL*, 949–50.
16. Žižek, 38.
17. Emerson, "Fate," *EEL*, 946.
18. I would like to thank Barbara Packer for pointing out to me this crucial difference between Darwin's and Chamber's brands of determinism.
19. Žižek, 28–33.
20. Bercovitch, *Rites of Assent*, 356.
21. Emerson, "Fate," *EEL*, 944.
22. Rorty, *Contingency*, 8–9.

23. Emerson, "Fate," *EEL*, 954.
24. Emerson's procedure here is very similar to what Žižek, following Peter Sloterdijk, calls "kynicism": "the classical kynical procedure is to confront the pathetic phrases of the ruling official ideology—its solemn, grave tonality—with everyday banality and to hold them up to ridicule, thus exposing behind the sublime noblesse of the ideological phrases the egotistical interests, the violence, the brutal claims to power. This procedure, then is more pragmatic than argumentative; it subverts the official proposition by confronting it with the situation of its enunciation" (Sloterdijk qtd. in Žižek, 29).
25. Schelling, *Treatise on Human Freedom*, 78–79.
26. Emerson, "Fate," *EEL*, 945.
27. West, 29–35.
28. Emerson, "Fate," *EEL*, 946.
29. Morrison, 360–61.
30. Rorty, *Contingency*, 51–52.

Works Cited

Banta, Martha. "Gymnasts of Faith, Fate, and Hazard." *American Transcendental Quarterly* 21 (1979): 6–20.
Barfield, Owen. *Saving the Appearances: A Study in Idolatry.* London: Faber and Faber, 1957.
Barthes, Roland. *S/Z.* Trans. Richard Miller. New York: Hill and Wang, 1974.
Bentham, Jeremy. "The Rationale of Rewards." *The Works of Jeremy Bentham.* 11 vols. London: n.p., 1843.
Bercovitch, Sacvan. *The American Jeremiad.* Madison: University of Wisconsin Press, 1978.
———. *The Office of the Scarlet Letter.* Baltimore: Johns Hopkins University Press, 1991.
———. *The Puritan Origins of the American Self.* New Haven, Conn.: Yale University Press, 1975.
———. *The Rites of Assent: Transformations in the Symbolic Construction of America.* New York: Routledge, 1993.
The Bible: King James Version. New York: New American Library, 1971.

Blanchot, Maurice. *The Writing of the Disaster*. Lincoln: University of Nebraska Press, 1995.
Bloom, Harold, ed. Introduction to *Ralph Waldo Emerson*. Philadelphia: Chelsea House Press, 1985.
Borch-Jacobsen, Mikkel. *The Emotional Tie: Psychoanalysis, Mimesis, and Affect*. Stanford: Stanford University Press, 1993.
———. *The Freudian Subject*. Stanford: Stanford University Press, 1988.
Bowie, Andrew, trans. Introduction to *On the History of Modern Philosophy*, by Friedrich Wilhelm Joseph von Schelling. Cambridge: Cambridge University Press, 1994.
Brewer, Ebeneezer Cobham. *Brewer's Dictionary of Faith and Fable*. Ed. Ivor H. Evans. Centenary Edition. London: Cassell, 1970.
Cameron, Sharon. "Representing Grief: Emerson's 'Experience.'" *Representations* 15 (summer 1986): 15–41.
Carlyle, Thomas. "Characteristics." Vol. 3 of *Critical and Miscellaneous Essays*. 5 vols. New York: AMS Press, 1980.
———. "Signs of the Times." Vol. 1 of *Critical and Miscellaneous Essays*. 5 vols. New York: AMS Press, 1980.
Cavell, Stanley. *Conditions Handsome and Unhandsome: The Constitution of Emersonian Perfection*. Chicago: University of Chicago Press, 1990.
———. "The Politics of Interpretation: Politics As Opposed to What?" In *Themes out of School: Effects and Causes*, by S. Cavell, 27–60. Chicago: University of Chicago Press, 1984.
———. *In Quest of the Ordinary: Lines of Skepticism and Romanticism*. Chicago: University of Chicago Press, 1988.
———. *Philosophical Passages: Wittgenstein, Emerson, Austin, Derrida*. Oxford: Blackwell, 1995.
———. *The Senses of Walden*. Chicago: University of Chicago Press, 1981.
———. *This New Yet Unapproachable America: Lectures After Emerson and Wittgenstein*. Albuquerque, N. Mex.: Living Batch Press, 1989.
Chase, Richard V. *The American Novel and Its Tradition*. Garden City, N.J.: Doubleday, 1957.
Coleridge, Samuel Taylor. *The Biographia Literaria*. In *Selected Poetry and Prose of Samuel Taylor Coleridge*, ed. Donald Stauffer, 109–428. New York: Random House, 1951.
Danto, Arthur. "Literature as/and/of Philosophy." In *Post-Analytic Philosophy*, ed. John Rajchman and Cornel West, 63–83. New York: Columbia University Press, 1985.
De Tocqueville, Alexis. *Democracy in America*. Trans. Henry Reeve. 2 vols. New York: Vintage, 1945.

Derrida, Jacques. *The Politics of Friendship.* Trans. George Collins. London: Verso, 1997.

Descartes, René. *Meditations on First Philosophy.* Trans. Laurence J. Lafleur. Indianapolis, Ind.: Bobbs-Merrill, 1960.

Duquette, Elizabeth. "Exemplifying Philosophy: The Rhetoric of Exemplarity in Nineteenth Century Literature and Philosophy." Diss., Dept. of English, New York University, 1998.

Edmundson, Mark. *Towards Reading Freud: Self-creation in Milton, Wordsworth, Emerson, and Sigmund Freud.* Princeton, N.J.: Princeton University Press, 1990.

Emerson, Ralph Waldo. *The Collected Works of Ralph Waldo Emerson.* Eds. Wallace E. Williams and Douglas E. Wilson. 4 vols. Cambridge: Harvard University Press, 1987.

———. *Emerson: Essays and Lectures.* Ed. Joel Porte. New York: Vintage-Library of America, 1983.

———. "Poetry and Imagination." In *The Complete Works of Ralph Waldo Emerson,* ed. E. W. Emerson, 7:7–75. 12 vols. Boston: Houghton Mifflin, 1903.

———. *Representative Men.* Ed. Pamela Schirmeister. New York: Marsilio, 1996.

Esman, Aaron H., ed. *Essential Papers on Transference.* New York: New York University Press, 1990.

Felman, Shoshana. "Introduction." *Yale French Studies* 55–56 (1977): 5–10.

Fichte, Hubert. *Werke.* Berlin: n.p., 1971.

Fink, Bruce. *The Lacanian Subject: Between Language and Jouissance.* Princeton, N.J.: Princeton University Press, 1995.

Freud, Sigmund. *The Ego and the Id.* Ed. James Strachey; trans. Joan Riviere. New York: W. W. Norton, 1980.

———. *Freud: General Psychological Theory: Papers on Metapsychology.* Ed. Philip Rieff. New York: Collier, 1963.

———. *Freud: Therapy and Technique.* New York: Collier, 1963.

———. *The Interpretation of Dreams.* Ed. and trans. James Strachey. 1955. Reprint, New York: Avon Books, 1965.

———. *The Standard Edition of the Complete Psychological Works.* Ed. James Strachey, Anna Freud, Alix Strachey, and Alan Tyson; trans. James Strachey. 23 vols. London: Hogarth, 1966.

Gallop, Jane. *Reading Lacan.* Ithaca, N.Y.: Cornell University Press, 1985.

Gilmore, Michael. *The Middle Way: Puritanism and Ideology in American Romantic Fiction.* New Brunswick, N.J.: Rutgers University Press, 1977.

Hawthorne, Nathaniel. *The Scarlet Letter.* In *Hawthorne: Novels,* ed. Millicent Bell, 115–345. New York: Vintage-Library of America, 1983.

Hegel, Georg Wilhelm Friedrich. *The Phenomenology of Mind.* Trans. J. B. Baillie. London: Macmillan, 1931.

Hollander, John. "The Philosopher's Cat." In *Melodious Guile: Fictive Patterns in Poetic Language*, 207–32. New Haven, Conn.: Yale University Press, 1988.

Homans, Peter. *The Ability to Mourn: Disillusion and the Social Origins of Psychoanalysis.* Chicago: University of Chicago Press, 1989.

James, William. *Essays in Radical Empiricism.* Lincoln: University of Nebraska Press, 1996.

———. *Pragmatism.* Cambridge: Harvard University Press, 1976.

Jehlen, Myra. *American Incarnation: The Individual, the Nation, and the Continent.* Cambridge: Harvard University Press, 1986.

Kant, Immanuel. *Critique of Judgment.* Trans. J. H. Bernard. New York: Hafner, 1951.

———. *Critique of Practical Reason.* Ed. and trans. Lewis White Beck. 3d ed. New York: Macmillan, 1993.

———. *Critique of Pure Reason.* Trans. J. M. D. Meiklejohn. London: Colonial Press, 1900.

———. *Prolegomena to Any Future Metaphysics.* Ed. Lewis White Beck. New York: Liberal Arts Press, 1950.

Kierkegaard, Sören. *Either/Or.* Trans. Swenson, David F., and Lillian Marvin Swenson. 2 vols. Princeton, N.J.: Princeton University Press, 1971.

Lacan, Jacques. *Écrits: A Selection.* Trans. Alan Sheridan. New York: W. W. Norton, 1977.

———. *The Four Fundamental Concepts of Psycho-analysis.* Ed. Jacques-Alain Miller; trans. Alan Sheridan. New York: W. W. Norton, 1978.

———. *Seminar, Book II: The Ego in Freud's Theory and in the Technique of Psychoanalysis, 1954–1955.* Ed. John Forrester; trans. Sylvanna Tomaselli. New York: W. W. Norton, 1988.

———. *Seminar, Book III: The Psychoses.* Trans. Russell Grigg. New York: W. W. Norton, 1993.

Lacoue-Labarthe, Phillippe, and Jean-Luc Nancy. *The Literary Absolute: The Theory of Literature in German Romanticism.* Trans. Philip Barnard and Cheryl Lester. Albany: State University of New York Press, 1988.

Lear, Jonathan. *Love and Its Place in Nature: A Philosophical Interpretation of Freudian Psychoanalysis.* New York: Farrar, Straus, Giroux, 1990.

Levinas, Emmanuel. *Otherwise than Being.* Trans. A. Lingis. The Hague: Martinis Nijhoff, 1981.

———. "Substitution." In *The Levinas Reader*, ed. Seán Hand, 88–127. Oxford: Blackwell, 1989.

———. "Time and the Other." In *The Levinas Reader*, ed. Seán Hand, 37–59. Oxford: Blackwell, 1989.

Michaels, Walter Benn. "The Interpreter's Self: Peirce on the Cartesian Subject." In *Reader-Response Criticism: From Formalism to Post-Structuralism*, ed. Jane Tompkins, 185–200. Baltimore: Johns Hopkins University Press, 1980.

Milton, John. "The Areopagitica." In *The Portable Milton*, ed. Douglas Bush, 151–205. New York: Penguin, 1983.

Morrison, Samuel Eliot, ed. *The Oxford History of the American People*. Vol. 2. New York: New American Library, 1972.

Nancy, Jean-Luc. *The Inoperative Community*. Trans. Peter Connor, Lisa Garbus, Michael Holland, and Simona Sawhney. Minneapolis: University of Minnesota Press, 1991.

Nietzsche, Friedrich. *Beyond Good and Evil*. Trans. Walter Kaufman. New York: Vintage, 1966.

———. *Course on Rhetoric*. In *Subject of Philosophy*, by Phillippe Lacoue-Labarthe; trans. Douglas Brick. Albany: State University of New York Press, 1986.

———. "On Truth and Falsity." In *The Portable Nietzsche*, ed. Walter Kaufman, 42–47. New York: Penguin, 1954.

Packer, Barbara. *Emerson's Fall: A New Interpretation of the Major Essays*. New York: Continuum, 1982.

Pease, Donald. *Visionary Compacts: American Renaissance Writing in Cultural Context*. Madison: University of Wisconsin Press, 1987.

Plato. *The Republic*. Ed. James Adam. Cambridge: Cambridge University Press, 1963.

Poirier, Richard. *A World Elsewhere: The Place of Style in American Literature*. New York: Oxford University Press, 1966.

Reed, Sampson. *Observations on the Growth of the Mind*. Boston: Cummings, Hilliard, 1826.

Richardson, Robert. *Emerson: The Mind on Fire*. Berkeley and Los Angeles: University of California Press, 1995.

Ricouer, Paul. *Freud and Philosophy: An Essay on Interpretation*. Trans. Denis Savage. New Haven, Conn.: Yale University Press, 1970.

Rieff, Philip, ed. Introduction to *Freud: Therapy and Technique*. New York: Collier, 1963.

Rorty, Richard. *Contingency, Irony, and Solidarity*. Cambridge: Cambridge University Press, 1989.

---. *Philosophy and the Mirror of Nature*. Princeton, N.J.: Princeton University Press, 1979.

Rudynytsky, Peter. *The Psychoanalytic Vocation: Rank, Winnicott, and the Legacy of Freud*. New Haven, Conn.: Yale University Press, 1991.

Schafer, Roy. "Narration in the Psychoanalytic Dialogue." *Critical Inquiry* 7, no. 1 (autumn 1980): 29–54.

Schelling, Friedrich Wilhelm Joseph von. *On the History of Modern Philosophy*. Trans. Andrew Bowie. Cambridge: Cambridge University Press, 1994.

---. *Treatise on Human Freedom*. Frankfurt: Manfred Frank, 1978.

Schlegel, Friedrich. *"Lucinde" & The Fragments*. Trans. Peter Firchow. Minneapolis: University of Minnesota Press, 1971.

Skura, Meredith Anne. *The Literary Use of the Psychoanalytic Process*. New Haven, Conn.: Yale University Press, 1981.

Tanner, Tony. *The Reign of Wonder: Naiveté and Reality in American Literature*. Cambridge: Cambridge University Press, 1965.

Thoreau, Henry David. *Walden*. Ed. William Howarth. New York: Modern Library, 1981.

Tompkins, Jane. *Sensational Designs: The Cultural Work of American Fiction, 1790–1860*. New York: Oxford University Press, 1985.

Van Leer, David. *Emerson's Epistemology: The Argument of the Essays*. Cambridge: Cambridge University Press, 1986.

Wellek, René. "On Emerson and German Philosophy." In *Confrontations: Studies in the Intellectual and Literary Relations between Germany, England and the United States during the Nineteenth Century*, by R. Wellek, 411–27. Princeton, N.J.: Princeton University Press, 1965.

West, Cornel. *The American Evasion of Philosophy: A Genealogy of Pragmatism*. Madison: University of Wisconsin Press, 1989.

Whicher, Stephen. *Freedom and Fate: An Inner Life of Ralph Waldo Emerson*. Philadelphia: University of Pennsylvania Press, 1953.

Whitman, Walt. Preface to *Leaves of Grass*, by Walt Whitman; ed. J. H. Miller. Boston: Houghton Mifflin, 1959.

Winnicott, Donald. *Playing and Reality*. London: Routledge, 1982.

Wittgenstein, Ludwig. *Culture and Value*. Trans. Peter Winch. Chicago: University of Chicago Press, 1980.

---. *Philosophical Investigations*. Trans. G. E. M. Anscombe. Oxford: Blackwell, 1953.

Žižek, Slavoj. *The Sublime Object of Ideology*. London: Verso, 1989.

Zornberg, Avivah. *Genesis: The Beginning of Desire*. Philadelphia: Jewish Publication Society, 1995.

Index

In this index an "f" after a number indicates a separate reference on the next page, and an "ff" indicates separate references on the next two pages. A continuous discussion over two or more pages is indicated by a span of page numbers, e.g., "57–59." *Passim* is used for a cluster of references in close but not consecutive sequence.

Adams, John Quincy, 186
Affect, 67, 84–94 *passim*,
"Alienated majesty," 16, 79–85, 91, 95, 99, 106, 173f
Aristotle (*Rhetoric*), 71

Banta, Martha, 167
Barfield, Owen, (*Saving the Appearances*), 19
Barthes, Roland (*S/Z*), 74
Bataille, Georges, 138
Bentham, Jeremy, 6
Bercovitch, Sacvan, 192n25, 209n3; *The Rites of Assent*, 176–77

Bible, 62
Bildung, 34, 40f, 53, 62, 196n29
Blanchot, Maurice, 138
Bloom, Harold, 209n6
Borch-Jacobsen, Mikkel, 113, 203n25
Brown, John, 186

Cadava, Eduardo, 32
Cameron, Sharon, 119–20, 205n1
Carlyle, Thomas, 13, 40–43 *passim*, 48, 53, 151; "Characteristics," 34–36, 40, 50; "On Heroes and Hero Worship," 152; "Signs of the Times," 40–41
Cavell, Stanley, 2, 20, 32, 45, 93, 105,

108, 192n9, 194n4, 195n9, 197n38, 200n22, 201n35, 209–10n6, 210n7; on "Experience," 120, 205n1; and moral perfectionism, 32, 73–75, 192n27, 196n29, 200n20
Chambers, Robert, 176
Chase, Richard, 166, 194n30
Coleridge, Samuel Taylor, 13, 41, 46, 177, 181; *Biographia Literaria*, 46, 169, 172
Community, 126–49 *passim*; 161–64
Corinthians, 66

Daguerre, Louis, 152–54
Danto, Arthur, ("Philosophy As/And/Of Literature"), 74
Darwin, Charles, 176
David, 44
Democracy, 126, 145–50 *passim*, 162; relation between private and public in, 169–72, 180, 187–88
Derrida, Jacques, 3, 138, 192n8, 195n12, 205–6n2; (*The Politics of Friendship*)206–7n12
Descartes, Rene, 77–78, 79, 156, 209n1; the cogito, 37, 67, 77, 79f, 94–98 *passim*, 200n25, 00n26; *The Meditations*, 156–57
Dickens, Charles, 2
Deuteronomy, 114
Duquette, Elizabeth, 208n11

Edmundson, Mark, 202n18
Emerson, Edward, 149
Emerson, R. W., 18–19, 21, 25, 33, 53, 113–15, 171, 187–88; "The American Scholar," 12–13, 17, 25–55 *passim*, 59–62 *passim*, 67, 72, 80, 122, 149, 153, 162, 165, 175, 195n15, 199n17; "Character," 34; "Circles," 196n27; *The Conduct of Life*, 167; *Essays; First Series*, 61, 67f, 208n3; *Essays; Second Series*, 208n3; "Experience," 18–19, 68, 119–46, 161, 171, 188, 200n24, 210n14; "Fate," 18–19f, 108, 167–87; "Friendship," 67; "History," 15, 68–73, 81–82, 88, 91, 98, 104; "Intellect," 61–68, 84; "The Poet," 7–11, "Poetry and Imagination," 8 —*Representative Men*, 2, 9, 18–19, 34, 50, 149–56, 160–65, 208n3; "Plato; Or, the Philosopher," 2f, 6, 9, 150–51, 161f; "Swedenborg; Or, the Mystic," 162; "Montaigne; Or, the Skeptic," 151, 162f; "Shakespeare," 151, 152–54, 162; "Napoleon; Or, the Man of the World," 151, 162; "Goethe; Or, the Writer," 163–64; "Self-Reliance," 50, 60, 69–85 *passim*, 91–99, 103–12 *passim*, 134, 147, 166, 172, 174f, 199n17, 200n24, 205n43
Emerson, Waldo, 123f, 137, 142, 144–46, 207n16

Felman, Shoshana, 87, 91
Fichte, Hubert, 38–46 *passim*, 195n15, 197n34
Fink, Bruce, 109
Freud, Sigmund, 17f, 98–99, 193n28, 193–94n29, 201n30; on transference, 86–96 *passim*, 105, 113, 202n17, 203n23; on mourning, 18, 124–25
Futurity, 129–36 *passim*, 142–46 *passim*, 188

Gag resolutions, 185–86
Gallop, Jane, 88
Garrison, William Lloyd, 186
Genealogical method, 69, 177
Gilmore, Michael, 209n3
Goethe, 40
Green, Andre, 203n24

Hawthorne, Nathaniel, 149, 156–59 *passim*, *The Scarlet Letter*, 158–61
Hegel, G. W. F., 38f, 132
Heidegger, Martin, 15
Hollander, John, 34, 192n17; *Melodious Guile*, 209n13
Homans, Peter, 192n25, 202n18

Identification, 100–110 *passim*, 124–25, 140, 155

Ideology, 166, 175–87 *passim*
Individualism, 12, 17, 80, 133, 139–46 *passim*, 166–67

Jacob, 63–66, 199n9
James, Henry, 17
James, William, 73, 199n19
Jehlen, Myra, 209n3
Jena Romantics, 4–5, 36–40 *passim*, 53

Kahn, Masud, 203n20
Kansas-Nebraska Act, 186
Kant, Immanuel, 13f, 49, 59, 73, 145, 156, 173, 175, 195n15, 197n31; and romanticism, 36–39, 50; influence on Emerson, 42–46 *passim*, 209n1; *Critique of Judgement*, 37–38f, 154
Kierkegaard, Soren, 4–5

Lacan, Jacques, 17, 75, 79, 91, 96, 111, 138, 176, 203n23, 204n43, 206n8; on transference, 87, 98–103, 113, 202n5, 203n19, 206n4; the real in, 99, 108f, 201n30, 207n16
Lacoue-Labarthe, Phillippe, 5, 36, 41, 196n27 (*The Literary Absolute*), 36, 39
Lear, Jonathan, 16
Letters, 7, 45–46, 55, 59–60; American context of, 13, 17, 54, 163; as Futurity, 29–31, 54–55; as passage from private to public, 12, 17–18, 44, 54, 147, 149, 167, 188; pragmatic nature of, 7, 12f, 167, 188; as therapeutic, 11ff, 27, 36, 44f, 188; as transformation, 27, 30, 48, 75. See also Reading
Levinas, 133, 138, 206n4, (*Otherwise than Being*), 207n24

Melville, Herman, 13, 166 (Moby Dick), 2
Michaels, Walter Benn, 199n19
Milton, John, "The Areopagitica," 4; *Paradise Lost*, 9
Montaigne, Michel de, 204–5n43, 208n6

Mourning, 119–20, 124–29 *passim*, 133, 140–41

Nancy, Jean-Luc, 5, 36, 41, 138, 196n27, 209n17; (*Literary Absolute*), 36, 39
Nationalism, 2, 12, 26–33, 45, 52–53
Nietzsche, Friedrich, 3, 15, 32, 77, 79, 138; "On Truth and Falsity in an Ultra-moral Sense," 3, 191–92n8; "Course on Rhetoric," 105

Oedipus Rex, 193n28

Packer, Barbara, 119, 205n1, 210n18
Pease, Donald, 209n3
Philosophy, 4–6f, 10, 14, 16, 210n7; American, 10, 158, 170f, 194n29; literature as, 2–15 *passim*, 36–42 *passim*, 53; quarrel between literature and, 1–21, *passim*, 75, 150; traditional project of, 1f, 14ff, 28, 59, 62, 80, 148, 150, 187ff
Peirce, C. S., 2, 73
Plato, 9, 150; "The Republic," 3, 6
Plutarch, 151
Poe, Edgar Allen, 7
Poirier, Richard, 194n30
Politics, Emersonian, 148, 151, 158, 166–67
Pragmatism, 2, 179

Reading: and representation, 75, 107–8, 135–139 *passim*, 153; as historicity, 70–73 *passim*, 98; identification and, 70–71, 81–85 *passim*, 91, 104, 106; as performativity, 15–16, 84–85, 99, 113, 122; as self-creation, 15–16, 50, 70–75 *passim*, 81, 107, 113, 165, 205n43; as transference, 86–88, 113, 122, 147; in "The American Scholar," 48–55 *passim*; relation between private and public in, 109–115, 201n35. See also Letters
Receptivity, 18, 111f, 200n20; dynamic of, 84–85, 105–6, 108, 122, 125, 157–58, 187, 195n14, 199n9; as trauma, 52–55, 108, 122–23; in "The

American Scholar," 33, 48–49, 51–52, 60–68 *passim*; in "Experience," 122–25, 143–45
Reed, Sampson, 13; *Observations on the Growth of the Mind*, 198n49
Representativeness, 19, 72, 115, 138, 149, 151–56, 157–62 *passim*; relation between private and public in, 154–55, 159–61; and exemplarity, 156–58
Richardson, Robert, 195n11, 197n41
Ricoeur, Paul, 16
Rieff, Philip, 90–91
Rorty, Richard, 5, 28, 73, 179, 187, 199n19; *Contingency, Irony and Solidarity*, 207n22

Schelling, F. W. J. von, 41, 195n15, 195n18, 198n51; *Treatise on Human Freedom*, 182–85
Schlegel, Friedrich, 5, 36, 41, 195n15, 198n49
Self-creation (auto-production), 39–42 *passim*, 49–53 *passim*, 67, 167, 174. *See also* Reading, Letters
Shelley, P. B., (*Defence of Poetry*), 3
Slavery, 167f, 171, 178, 183f, 186ff, 210n7
Sloterdijk, Peter, 211n24

Socrates, 194n29
Stowe, Harriet Beecher, 13

Tanner, Tony, 166
Thoreau, Henry David, 2f, 7, 13, 149
Tocqueville, Alexis de, 1f, 9, 14, 64
Tompkins, Jane, 209n3
Transference, 16–18, 86–113, 125, 187; as error, 101–2, 176–80 *passim*; as mimesis or enactment, 90–97 *passim*; as repetition, 89–94 *passim*, 99, 101

Van Leer, David, 33, 78, 195n15

Walpole, Horace, 2
Wellek, Rene, 197n31
Whicher, Stephen, 208n6
Whitman, Walt, (*Leaves of Grass*), 3, 149
Winnicott, D.W., 96, 102, 203n19
Wittgenstein, 5, 15; *Philosophical Investigations*, 194n30
Witz, 48–49, 153

Zeno, 60
Žižek, Slavoj, 101, 175–77, 204n27, 211n24
Zornberg, Avivah, 63, 199n9

Library of Congress Cataloging-in-Publication Data

Schirmeister, Pamela, 1958–
  Less legible meanings : between poetry and philosophy in the work of Emerson / Pamela Shirmeister.
    p.   cm.
  Includes bibliographical references and index.
  ISBN 0-8047-3015-6 (alk. paper)
  1. Emerson, Ralph Waldo, 1803–1882—Criticism and interpretation.
2. Philosophy, American—19th century. 3. Philosophy in literature.
I. Title.
PS1638.S26 1999
814'.3—dc21   99-39450

∞ This book is printed on acid-free, archival-quality paper.

Original printing 1999

Last figure below indicates year of this printing:
08   07   06   05   04   03   02   01   00   99

Typeset by Robert C. Ehle in 10.5/13 Minion, with Rococo ornaments

OHIO UNIVERSITY LIBRARY

Please return this book as soon as you have finished with it. In order to avoid a fine it must be returned by the latest date stamped below. All books are subject to recall after two weeks or immediately if needed for reserve.

CF